Acclaim for **WENDY KAMINER**'s

SLEEPING WITH EXTRA-TERRESTRIALS

"An immensely enjoyable, thought-provoking book that is likely to be widely condemned."
—*The San Diego Union-Tribune*

"Entertaining." —*Harper's Bazaar*

"Kaminer has the comic timing of Jack Benny; she registers incredulity at the ripest moments. . . . *Sleeping with Extra-Terrestrials* is Wendy being insightful and witty about irrationalism. That is why people—I hope thousands of them—will buy this book."
—Jack Beatty, author of *The Rascal King: The Life and Times of James Michael Curley*

"A bracing, thought-provoking book."
—*Entertainment Weekly*

WENDY KAMINER

SLEEPING WITH EXTRA-TERRESTRIALS

—

Wendy Kaminer is the author of five previous books, including *I'm Dysfunctional, You're Dysfunctional*. Her articles and reviews have appeared in *The New York Times*, *Newsweek*, *The Nation*, and *The New Republic*. She is a columnist at *The Atlantic Monthly* and a fellow at the Radcliffe Institute for Advanced Studies.

SLEEPING WITH

EXTRA-TERRESTRIALS

‑

THE RISE OF

IRRATIONALISM

AND PERILS

OF PIETY

‑

WENDY KAMINER

VINTAGE BOOKS

A DIVISION OF RANDOM HOUSE, INC.

NEW YORK

TO WOODY

The Library of Congress has cataloged the Pantheon edition as follows:
Kaminer, Wendy.
Sleeping with extra-terrestrials: the rise of irrationalism and perils of piety /
Wendy Kaminer.
p. cm.
Includes bibliographical references.
ISBN 0-679-44243-X
1. Belief and doubt. 2. Credulity. 3. Irrationalism (Philosophy).
4. Skepticism. I. Title.
BF773.K35 1999
306'.0973—dc21   99-21468

Vintage ISBN: 0-679-75886-0

Book design by Barbara M. Bachman

www.vintagebooks.com

Printed in the United States of America

BVG 01

CONTENTS

—

INTRODUCTION 3

1. PIOUS BIASES 18

2. THE SECTARIAN PUBLIC SQUARE 56

3. POP SPIRITUALITY BOOKS AND
   THE GOSPEL OF GOOD NEWS 98

4. GURUS AND THE SPIRITUALITY BAZAAR 130

5. JUNK SCIENCE 162

6. THE THERAPEUTIC ASSAULT ON
   REASON AND RIGHTS 189

7. CYBERSPACY 219

8. THE STRENUOUS LIFE 244

NOTES 257

ACKNOWLEDGMENTS 279

SLEEPING WITH

EXTRA-TERRESTRIALS

INTRODUCTION

—

Before I begin my critique of irrationalism, I have a confession to make: I go to a homeopath. Homeopathy may have about as much scientific credibility as reports of alien abductions and ESP; but I suspend disbelief and weather my embarrassment, because, somehow, homeopathy has helped me. When I first met with my homeopath she asked me to describe my greatest fears. Aside from being old and sick and infirm, I said, my greatest fear was that someone would find out I'd consulted a homeopath.

I mention this partly in the spirit of disclosure, partly to illustrate the power of any belief system that can make people feel better, and partly to explore our concept of irrationalism. When I go to my homeopath maybe I'm following one of the precepts of the recovery movement that I've always derided: I'm thinking with my heart and not my head. Or maybe I'm acting rationally after all. Believing in homeopathy may be irrational, but not using homeopathy if it works would be even more irrational. I care only if medicine works, not why. (I have the vaguest understanding of antibiotics.)

So I don't listen to scientists eager to tell me why homeopathic remedies can't possibly work, because they violate the laws of chemistry. Assuming that the scientists are right, and the remedies I've taken are mere placebos, why would I want to start doubting—and diminishing—their effectiveness? Why not be susceptible to placebos?

It would be irrational, however, for anyone to take my account of homeopathy's effectiveness at face value. Maybe I'm lying, or maybe I'm imagining that homeopathy has helped me. Maybe I'm confusing correlation with causation: perhaps I began feeling better coincidentally, for some unknown reason, at about the time I turned to homeopathy. If you're intrigued by my report, you should ask me to substantiate it, with some objective evidence. You should try to duplicate my experience.

The contrary willingness to accept untested personal testimony as public truth is at the heart of the irrationalism that confronts us today. Ours is an evangelical culture. So many people convinced that they've been saved by Jesus, abused by Satanists, cured by homeopathy or the laying on of hands, abducted by aliens, or protected by angels seek public acknowledgment that their convictions are true. Imbued with messianic fervor, or simply seeking "validation," they are not content to hoard the truth; they are compelled to share it and convert the unenlightened, relying on the force of their own intense emotions. Generally, the only proof offered for a fantastic belief is the passion it inspires in believers.

It is usually futile to ask for more. Once, I found myself engaged in a "debate" with a caller on a radio show who claimed that she and her family had been abducted and molested by aliens. I suggested that it was, perhaps, unrealistic of her to expect strangers to believe her story merely on the basis of her testimony. So she offered as evidence of her encounters "bodily markings," "bodily memories," and (in a stab at empiricism) "metallurgically flattened shrubbery" outside her house. I told her I was sorry for her trouble. Sometimes I think I'm sleeping with an extra-terrestrial too.

While only a minority of listeners may have found this story of an alien encounter credible, many would probably have believed a more familiar supernatural tale—the report of a visit from a guardian angel or a conversation with Jesus. In presuming that her feelings constituted evidence of historic fact, the caller had religion on her side, in addition to both high and low culture, which also promote belief in revealed truths. Popular psychologies assume the authenticity of subjective experience. Academic fashions locate truth in individual narratives, and falsehood in the quest for objectivity.

The celebration of subjectivity discourages demands for corroboration. Let someone testify with great vehemence to an after-death experience, a foray into past lives, or an abusive sexual encounter in childhood, only recently recalled, and courtesy compels us to listen deferentially. A lingering cult of victimhood lends credibility to tales of abuse, and the etiquette of a confessional society deters cross-examination. Equally vehement expressions of doubt or disbelief may even be considered abusive. The mores of personal development are naturally relativistic: Everyone has his or her reality. A fact is simply what is true for you.

Subjective perceptions are touchstones as well for religious traditions that celebrate direct, individual relationships with God, from mysticism to methodism—although religion posits universal truths, not disparate individual realities. The therapeutic culture borrows from religion's focus on sensation when it conflates feelings and facts. The truth lies in what you feel, not in what you know "in your head," much less in what you can prove, personal development experts say. In this culture, feelings of abuse become evidence of abuse, as if rape or sexual harassment were ineffable realities, like the mystic's sense of oneness with God.

Like fiction writers whose imaginings aim to reveal emotional truths, recovery movement gurus, experts on angels, and other aficionados of New Age, as well as adherents of mainstream religions, traffic in "feeling realities." They exhort us ultimately to rely on our hearts, not our heads, to heed the voice of our own experience, as well as the alleged experiences of others who testify before us, to ignore the naysaying of science or reason—except that, unlike fiction writers, the experts on God, spirituality, and personal development claim to be dispensing actual facts—about incest, reincarnation, or celestial civilizations, the utopian future of humankind, the coming of the Messiah, or the divinity of Jesus Christ.

There is some irony in this relationship between popular therapy, established religion, and New Age spiritualism. (I consider the latter a form of religion.) Popular therapy generally focuses on individual health or fulfillment and promotes belief in relative, individual realities, assuming that diametrically opposed perceptions of the same people or events may be equally true: generally, it resists choosing between conflicting accounts of siblings who experience and describe their families differently (although believers in the ubiquity of child abuse will choose the claims of accusers over the doubts and denials of other family members). Organized religion and diffuse spirituality movements represent the contrary quest for absolutes: individual experience is exalted when it leads us to a presumptively universal truth—like the existence of an omniscient, transcendent being, or inevitability of reincarnation.

In other words, to the extent that therapy focuses on self-actualization, it tends to imbue the subjective with normative value: it uncovers the self. For religion, the value of subjective perception tends to be primarily instrumental: it leads us to God.

Yet the relativism of therapy has become the handmaiden of religious or spiritual absolutism. The therapeutic culture teaches us to believe or at least take seriously impassioned reports of personal experiences, from the mundane to the miraculous. And, thanks partly to the recovery movement, the practice of therapy itself has become spiritualized, focusing on "care of the soul" as well as the psyche.

The marriage of psychology and religion is hardly new. William James presided over it, quite brilliantly, one hundred years ago. The coupling was inevitable. Images of God and various "spiritual entities" are inextricably bound with our own self-images, and as James observed, religions begin with "the feelings, acts, and experiences of individual men in their solitude . . ."[1] This does not reduce the religious experience to mere psychological or physiological reflex. James greatly respected individual intimations of the Divine, and resisted attributing them to "organic dispositions."[2] But he consistently emphasized the links between temperament, belief, and ideology: "[T]he whole man within us is at work when we form our philosophical opinions. Intellect, will, taste, and passion co-operate . . ."[3]

The personal development tradition has always demonstrated the relationship between attitude and doctrine. Positive thinking, rooted in the nineteenth-century mind-cure movement (one of James's subjects), has always included magical thinking and has always qualified as a "religion of healthy-mindedness."[4] It's not surprising that America's premier, mass-market pop psychologist—Norman Vincent Peale—was a positive thinker and a clergyman.

As an amateur therapist, Peale was anomalous only in the degree of his success. Less entreprenurial members of the clergy have long engaged in counseling members of their congregations. They have had to balance relativism and compassion for troubled individuals with the moral tenets of their faiths. Now, the relationship between religion and therapy is in reverse: therapists are exhorted to join the clergy in the quest for absolutes. Popular nostrums warn us not to separate the search for self from the search for God, even as neurology provides physiological answers to existential questions. (The spiritualization of pop therapies has not been deterred by an increased reliance on Prozac and other psychotropic drugs.) It's not surprising that while some practitioners respond by paying more attention to the patient's spiritual yearning, others presume to satisfy it. Therapists who claim psychic powers or help their patients recover memories of past lives, as well as memories of abuse in this life, dispense supposedly universal truths—about life after death, ESP, and other metaphysical questions.[5]

But whether it offers to help us find a Higher Power or simply forge a better understanding of our parents, therapy has long been a quasi-religious endeavor, as well as a quasi-scientific one. The elevation of individual testimony or sensation over logic and verifiable fact—in other words, faith—has always linked popular psychology to spirituality and religion. Western religious faith—or supernaturalism—is the primary subject of this book. I was graced with relatively little of it and have sometimes regretted my resistance to believing in a supreme being and various visions of immortality. I'm not oblivious to the comfort that supernaturalism may provide or unimpressed by the powerful human impulse to believe; nor am I utterly secure in my disbelief. Skepticism is attitude, not dogma.

Writing about spirituality and religion, I've found it necessary to clarify my own beliefs or lack of them, as well as my intentions (which is why this introduction is itself a bit confessional). Not quite brave enough for atheism, or absolutely sure of my judgment, I fall back on agnosticism—either a cowardly or judicious alternative to religious belief. I'm not an evangelist and don't aim to dissuade anyone from believing in transcendent realities and supernatural occurrences. I express opinions mainly because I find them so hard to suppress.

For my lack of missionary zeal, I have been castigated by a few militant atheists, who are irritated by my disinclination to try persuading people to abandon their faith that God exists (while some religious people regard me as a militant atheist intent on promoting worship of unspecified "secular idols"). But even if I harbored a desire to impose my faithlessness in God on others, why embark on such a futile exercise? It would require megalomaniacal belief in my own powers of persuasion to anticipate even modest success. The human need for divinities seems fundamental.

I don't mean to denigrate this need and the impulse to believe, which seems inseparable from the impulse to create. Creative insights can come to the most atheistic artists and scientists with the force of revelation. Romantic poets sought truth in imagination, and so, in a way, did the pragmatic, secularist John Dewey. He regarded the formulation of social ideals as a collaborative, creative process, involving the interaction of imagination with experience.[6] From this perspective, if you don't consider the Bible a history of the sacred, you may read it for what it reveals about the human imagination and ideals of justice and compassion. To a nonbeliever, art doesn't celebrate the gods; it creates them.

Religion is art, as well as politics; it comprises the personal, individual experience of divinity, or the supernatural, and the theologies, social institutions, and bureacracies that follow. I focus alternately on both the personal and the political (and I include in my definition of religion established denominations and New Age). I don't envision this book as an attack upon organized religion, individual religious beliefs, or nonsectarian spirituality movements, although I am quite impatient with public piety. I do hope to interrogate conventional wisdom about the virtues of religious belief and institutions with a discussion of their vices.

I don't deny that organized religions offer people psychic comfort and community, as well as important social services, but I fiercely oppose their periodic assaults on secular government. I don't deny the benevolence of faith in God, when it nurtures courage, compassion, confidence, or simply the capacity to endure, any more than I can overlook the malevolence that erupts in religious wars. I would not wish to eradicate faith—the capacity to entertain ideals in spite of harsh realities. "We cannot live or think without some degree of faith," William James remarked. Sometimes "the part of wisdom clearly is to believe what one desires."[7]

I don't disagree, although for me, the operative word in the latter sentence is "sometimes." I don't disparage temperament, emotionalism, or intuition, whatever intuition may comprise. (In one view, it is simply the rational mind processing information very quickly.) I do not dispute the value of personal testimony in establishing personal truths, or even collaborating with reason in our choice of universal values. I'm not suggesting that any of us could or should erect an impenetrable wall between reason and emotion. I know that my own convictions reflect my temperament. I rely on emotions and intuitions not just in my private life but in my work and consider them a kind of intelligence—but not a reliable, independent source of supposedly universal truths.

The assertion that knowledge requires reason as well as sensation is hardly controversial. Not many people would suggest that we should dispense with science education and expect students to intuit the laws of physics (although one best-selling New Age bible, *The Celestine Prophecy,* by James Redfield, comes close, expressing such contempt for science and reason that they seem not just superfluous but misleading).

The notion that behavior benefits from the exercise of reason would meet with general approval as well. Violence prevention programs focus on teaching at-risk individuals to understand and control their emotions. (People who commit crimes often exhibit poor impulse control.) People counseled by bad therapists may value any expression of emotion, but others who have received good therapy, or no therapy at all, recognize that emotionalism is not always productive or appropriate. Grown-ups know not to throw tantrums at work or to vent their rage at ex-spouses in public. That emotional impulses should sometimes be suppressed and that reason is a valuable suppressant are hardly controversial assertions.

Still, whenever I've criticized the devaluation of reason implicit in the mandate to "think with our hearts," I've been accused by some of utterly devaluing emotion. In the vacuous world of pop spirituality, in particular, emotionalism and reason are not considered differing perceptual modes to be held in careful balance; they are competitors in a zero-sum game.

This view of reason as the enemy of knowledge—the supposedly deeper, more authentic knowledge of our emotions—is the threat of unmitigated religious faith. Of course, not everyone who worships God or seeks transcendence disdains science or reason (any more than believers in the kingdom of heaven develop no attachments to secular states). Some even try to reason their way to God, and one alleged trend of the late 1990s was a revival of spirituality among scientists. ("Science Finds God," a *Newsweek* cover story declared on July 20, 1998.) But for many true believers, reason is ultimately irrelevant to the search for God. Faith reveals what reason can't discern.

Mystery, after all, is central to religious belief. A comprehendable God would be no God at all but an idealized human being. Worship would merely be an exercise in egotism. Pure rationalism can be anathema to religion. Reasoning your way to God, you're likely to find only yourself.

Acknowledging the limitations of rationalism need not translate into an unmitigated attack on it; if freethinkers and other heretics, like Galileo, have been persecuted by their churches, religions have also inspired and supported scholarship, argument, and intellectual inquiry. In his 1998 encyclical "Fides et Ratio," Pope John Paul II stressed the mutual interdependence of faith and reason, pointing out the weaknesses of each when not tempered by the other: "Deprived of what Revelation offers, reason has taken side tracks which expose it to the danger of losing sight of its final goal" (discovering truth). "Deprived of reason, faith has stressed feeling and experience, and so runs the risk of no longer being a universal proposition." The pope based his defense of reason partly on faith that right reasoning will always lead us to God (he seems to have assumed his conclusion). But as the papal encyclical demonstrates, established Western religions have complicated, conflicted relationships to reason, which are beyond the scope of this book. My concern is not the operation of reason within religious traditions but the operation of faith in the secular world.

Blind antipathy to reason is central to many best-selling pop spirituality and personal development books and much New Age rhetoric. It permeates our culture, influencing members of mainstream churches as well as adherents of New Age. It is a trend worth critiquing. People inclined to take the most fantastic claims at face value—that Shirley MacLaine communes with spirits, that millions of people have repressed memories of satanic ritual abuse, or that guardian angels watch over them—may also believe that the FBI blew up the Alfred P. Murrah federal building in Oklahoma City, despite an absence of evidence; or they may believe that the Holocaust never happened, despite a ghastly plethora of proof.

Belief in God need not lead to belief in the Easter Bunny (although an atheist would find no difference between the two). But religions may engender habits of belief that affect the way people function politically. It's worth noting that the loonier conspiracy theories that circulated in the 1990s combined mistrust of government with belief in the supernatural. Consider accusations that the government has been covering up evidence of extra-terrestrial visitations. Watch *The X-Files*, the TV show with a cultlike following based on the premise that the government is covering up a broad range of weird supernatural phenomenon.

Few of us are free of superstitions or a fascination with Twilight Zones. I am surely not, and I'd hate to lose the pleasure of suspending disbelief—so long as I suspend it knowingly. Besides, we can't always distinguish the supernatural from natural phenomenon we don't yet understand. (Fax machines, like radio waves, seem magical to me.) But we should, at least, seek relatively mundane explanations for miraculous phenomena, like reported landings of UFOs or weeping statues of saints, before assuming that the most fantastic explanations are true.

Why is superstition problematic? One premise of this

book is that religious faith is not always compartmentalized. Some people are able to separate beliefs that can only be taken on faith—like a belief in Christ's divinity—from assertions that ought to be subject to empirical testing—like the claim that prohibitions on mandatory school prayer have increased the crime rate or that welfare benefits cause teenage pregnancies. But many of our public policy debates are conducted quite irrationally. Religion also helps inculcate some absurd political beliefs—like the contention of late Nation of Islam leader Elijah Muhammad that white people were created in a laboratory by a mad scientist. Prejudice (another form of faith), not reason, often holds sway.

The media is often blamed for the debasement of public discourse, with some justification: the *Crossfire* model of debate has probably made us stupider. Where did we ever get the idea that there are only two sides to every argument? But religions make a more subtle, indirect, and unnoticed contribution to our increasing irrationalism. I suspect that many people develop habits of faith, or unreason, that discourage them from thinking critically about empirical realities. The effect of religious faith on reason is one of the unexamined perils of piety.

In general, secularist concern about religion focuses on the adoption of sectarian beliefs by the state, and the opening chapters of this book are devoted to critiquing church–state alliances and the political excesses of religious institutions. I found myself unable or unwilling to separate an exploration of irrationalism from a critique of public piety, and, in any case, both seemed overdue. As an agnostic, nominal member of a minority faith, I have always been sensitive to the majoritarianism of assaults on secular government, which are, in effect, assaults on the individual religious experiences of minorities. The rights and interests of individual believers clash with religious institutions when the institutions seek the sponsorship of the state. Crusades to breach the boundaries between church and state constitute a much greater threat to religious tolerance than any number of evangelical atheists. Theocracies throughout history have made that clear.

When I talk about public piety, I'm not simply talking about celebrations of established mainstream faiths. I include among the pious the adherents of New Age, which, like the therapeutic culture, has surely contributed to rationalism's decline. But New Age beliefs are not institutionalized; there are virtually no New Age churches that threaten the separation of church and state. Generally, in my discussion of politics and policy, I've focused on established faiths; in critiquing cultural trends and the denigration of rationalism, I've focused on New Age and popular therapies.

New Age has always relied on pseudoscience, which thrives in our high-tech culture, in this supposedly scientific age. So I've included a discussion of junk science, which is often the bridge between good faith and bad policy. Junk science ranges from fanciful notions of quantum physics to the misuse or misunderstanding of scientific research (hard and soft) to naïveté about social science, which is reflected in pop psychologies and their assumptions about human behavior. A related disregard for reasoning and objectivity helped shape the therapeutic culture and has infected popular feminism (to my dismay). I could not or did not want to ignore the excesses of that culture, notably its impact on the justice system and our notions of individual rights (dramatized most clearly in the recently discredited child abuse cases involving claims of recovered memories; they illustrate vividly the dangers posed by faith to public policy). Nor could I ignore popular feminist celebration of irrationalism, which is, for me, a recurrent theme. Finally, in considering rationalism and its future, I found myself thinking about the nascent digital culture, which offers its own form of piety and evangelism.

My underlying concern about the cognitive effects of individual religious belief is quite speculative, and some may consider the hypothesis that habits of faith sometimes break habits of reasoning presumptuous. I have offered a few examples of grossly irrational public policies—like the war on drugs, which seems shaped by religious fervor (a view of drug use as sinful) much more than by rational discussions of crime control or public health. Different people will offer different lists of irrational laws and policies, and each list might fill an encyclopedia. I'm not interested in writing a political or legal treatise, much less an encyclopedia, and I cannot say for sure that public discourse would be more rational if we were more willing to confine religious faith to the realm of religious doctrine. But I entertain the possibility. The potential effect of religious faith on reasoning and the formulation of public policy transforms private beliefs into public issues. For me, that justifies this inquiry.

If some people feel comforted by believing in angels or the wisdom of *The Celestine Prophecy,* or a vision of God in His heaven, as I feel helped by homeopathy, what's the harm? There is no harm in irrationalism so long as it remains within realms that don't require reason. If my experience with homeopathy doesn't make me susceptible to every snake oil salesman in the market and doesn't lead me to persuade others to abandon traditional medical approaches that promise to help them for unproven alternative cures, it doesn't harm me or anyone else and isn't worthy of public comment. Other people's personal religious beliefs and reading habits are none of my business (and surely don't require my approval). But the possible public consequence of their inclination to believe is everyone's business and merits everyone's concern.

I raise the question about the relationship between faith in the religious or spiritual realm and irrationalism in the realms of policy and public life without knowing the answer. I have only suspicions and speculations, inferred partly from facts, which is why I am a social critic and not a social scientist. This is, at heart, a work of opinion. Freed from the burden of proof, I do have some affinity for preachers, after all.

CHAPTER 1

■

PIOUS BIASES

It was King Kong who put the fear of God in me, when I was eight or nine years old. Blessed with irreligious parents and excused from attending Sunday school or weekly services, I had relatively little contact with imaginary, omnipotent authority figures until Million Dollar Movie brought *King Kong* to our living room TV. Tyrannical and omnipotent (I never found his capture and enslavement believable), he awakened my superstitions. Watching Kong terrorize the locals, I imagined being prey to an irrational, supernatural brute whom I could never outrun or outsmart. Since I could not argue with him, my only hope was to grovel and propitiate him with sacrifices. Looking nothing like Fay Wray, I took no comfort from the possibility of charming him; besides, his love was as arbitrary and unpredictable as his wrath.

For the next several years, like the natives in the movie, I clung to rituals aimed at keeping him at bay. (I can only analyze my rituals in hindsight; at the time, I was immersed in them unthinkingly.) Instead of human sacrifices, I offered him neatness, a perfectly ordered room. Every night before going to bed,

I straightened all the articles on my desk and bureau, arranged my stuffed animals in rectangular tableaus, and made sure all doors and drawers were tightly shut. I started at one end of the room and worked my way around, counterclockwise; when I finished, I started all over again, checking and rechecking my work, three, four, or five times. I can't remember how many rounds I forced myself to make.

Going to bed became an ordeal. I hated my rituals; they were tedious and time-consuming and very embarrassing. I knew they were stupid and always kept them secret until, eventually, I grew out of them. I still harbor superstitions, of course, but with much less sense of shame and much more humor; I find them considerably less compelling.

If I were to mock religious belief as childish, if I were to suggest that worshiping a supernatural deity, convinced that it cares about your welfare, is like worrying about monsters in the closet who find you tasty enough to eat, if I were to describe God as our creation, likening Him to a mechanical gorilla, I'd violate the norms of civility and religious correctness. I'd be excoriated as an example of the cynical, liberal elite responsible for America's moral decline. I'd be pitied for my spiritual blindness; some people would try to enlighten and convert me. And I'd receive hate mail. Whenever I've publicly questioned the value of religiosity or suggested that atheism is not incompatible with morality, I've received vicious responses from people who claim to love God. Once, when I told my mother that I was writing a defense of atheism for a national magazine, she warned me not to say that I was Jewish. "Pretend that you're a Lutheran," she suggested.

Yet despite the opprobrium heaped upon atheists and agnostics (who constitute a very small minority), conventional wisdom holds that we suffer from an excess of secularism. "The great malady of the twentieth century" is " 'loss of soul,' " best-selling author Thomas Moore has declared, complaining that "we don't believe in the soul."[1] Of course, if that were true, there'd be no buyers for his books. Meanwhile, with varying degrees of success, virtuecrats from Hillary Rodham Clinton and William Bennett to Gary Bauer have tried to capitalize politically on a sense of moral decay reflecting a much-lamented decline of religion and consequent rise in cynicism. Considering the ubiquity of religious belief, their complaints reflect a cognitive dissonance matched by the popularity of pornography in a society that deplores it.

According to polls taken in the 1990s, almost all Americans (95 percent) profess belief in God. Only 4 percent identify themselves as atheists or agnostics. Fifty-nine percent say that religion is very important in their lives; 29 percent rate it fairly important. Seventy-six percent imagine God as a heavenly father who actually pays attention to their prayers. Forty-six percent believe in the biblical account of Creation. Nearly one-half (46 percent) of all Americans describe themselves as born-again. A majority of Americans (68 percent) belong to a church or synagogue, and 60 percent say they attend services regularly. An even larger majority apparently expect their piety to pay off: three-quarters of Americans rate their chances of going to heaven as excellent or good; only 4 percent expect to go to hell.[2]

Adherence to mainstream religions is supplemented by experimentation with an eclectic collection of New Age beliefs and practices. As religion scholar Robert Wuthnow has observed, "one kind of belief in supernatural phenomena reinforces another." Roughly half of all Catholics and Protestants surveyed by Gallup in 1990 believed in ESP; nearly as many believed in psychic healing. Fifty-three percent of Catholics and

40 percent of Protestants professed belief in UFOs, and about one-quarter put their faith in astrology. A 1996 *Newsweek* poll found that 41 percent of people surveyed believed in astrology, and 66 percent believed in ESP. Forty-nine percent believed that the government is concealing information confirming that UFOs are real or that aliens have visited the earth. Over 25 percent of people surveyed by Gallup in 1994 professed belief in reincarnation and the possibility of communicating with the dead. Twenty-five percent of people surveyed by *Newsweek* in 1996 said they believed in channeling.[3] Once I heard Shirley MacLaine explain the principles of reincarnation on the Phil Donahue show. "Can you come back as a bird?" one woman asked. "No," MacLaine replied, secure in her convictions, "you only come back as a higher life form." No one asked her how she knew.

In this climate of faith in the most ridiculous propositions—with belief in guardian angels commonplace—mocking religion is like burning a flag in an American Legion hall. But by admitting that they're fighting a winning battle, advocates of religiosity would lose the benefits of appearing besieged: like liberal rights organizations that attract more money when conservative authoritarians are in power, religious groups inspire more believers when secularism is said to hold sway.

The more desperate a cause is made to appear, the more passionate a defense it elicits. By the mid-1990s when America was clearly in the midst of yet another Great Awakening, editors at the *Wall Street Journal* were still protesting an "ardent hostility toward religion," which made religious people "suspect."[4] According to William Bennett, "much of society ridicules and disdains [religion], and mocks those who are serious about their faith."[5] When they were forced by facts to acknowledge that God enjoys unshakable, nonpartisan, majoritarian support, champions of religion or spirituality charged that liberal intellectual elites are secularists who disdain belief in God and have denied it a respected, public role. Newt Gingrich attacked the "secular, anti-religious view of the left."[6] *Wall Street Journal* editorialists wondered at the "prejudice against religion by much of our judicial and media elites."[7] Robert Bork cited the "intellectual classes" as the "major obstacle to a religious renewal."[8]

The critique of liberal secularism issued from liberals as well as conservatives. Maryland lieutenant governor Kathleen Kennedy Townsend chastised "liberal democrats" for failing to recognize that the "repairing of American moral fabric" required a spiritual renewal. The left "cut itself off from religion," considering religious fervor "gauche," Townsend charged.[9] Yale law professor Stephen Carter confirmed that educated professionals tend to be embarrassed by belief. In *The Culture of Disbelief,* his best-selling complaint about the fabled denigration of religion in public life, Carter acknowledged that belief was widespread but argued that it had been trivialized by the rationalist biases of elites and their insistence on keeping religion out of the public sphere.[10] Echoing conventional wisdom, left and right, a 1995 cover story in the *Washington Monthly* charged liberals with "opting for moral relativism" and alienating "those who believe in morality. . . . The left, or what remains of it, seems to have forgotten how powerful a force religion is."[11]

Assumptions about liberal irreligiosity were rarely challenged, yet virtually none were substantiated. No faithless liberals were named; no influential periodicals or articles were cited, perhaps because they were chimeras. Robert Bork has accused the "intellectual classes" of dismissing religion as "primitive superstition" and perpetuating the belief that "science has left atheism as the only respectable intellectual stance";[12] but I try in vain to identify even one class of such intolerant, atheistic intellectuals. Having resided in Cambridge for over ten years, surrounded by the liberal intelligentsia, I can name no one (myself included) so contemptuous of religious belief.

What is Bork talking about? Review the list of prominent, left-of-center opinion makers and public intellectuals. Who among them mocks religion? In the 1990s, several gained or increased their prominence partly through their embrace of religious belief. Harvard professor Cornel West is part preacher. Rabbi Michael Lerner (founder of the communitarian journal *Tikkun*) came into public view briefly as Hillary Clinton's politics of meaning guru. Gloria Steinem greatly expanded her mainstream appeal by writing about spirituality. Bill Moyers has paid regular homage to traditional and alternative faiths in a series of television specials; he introduced New Age holy men Joseph Campbell and Robert Bly to the American public and televised conversations on the Book of Genesis. *New Yorker* columnist Joe Klein promoted "faith based" social service programs. Social activist Marian Wright Edelman, of the Children's Defense Fund, invoked biblical authorities to support her opposition to welfare reform. Liberal political theorists, preoccupied with civic virtue, promoted religiosity.

Evidence of renewed interest in religion and "spiritual renewal" permeated the culture. How could liberals resist paying homage to it? Both traditional and New Age religions even found their way into the workplace: in the 1990s, increasing numbers of companies hired ministers and priests to counsel employees.[13] Prayer groups and Bible study groups appeared in the office, on the heels of New Age management consultants, who had already insinuated themselves into the corporate world. In the

1980s, the drive to increase productivity created lucrative new markets for enterpreneurs from the human potential movement, like est leader Werner Erhard, who had previously profited from the hunger for individual fulfillment. Erhard's Transformational Technologies (TransTech) included among its clients Boeing, RCA, and Scott Paper Company.[14]

New Age training programs, which involved the usual array of visualization and positive thinking techniques, meditations, and self-hypnosis, generated complaints from some workers concerned about their privacy and religious freedom. The belief that we are in total control of our destiny, popularized by New Agers like Erhard, is anathema to some who believe that we are ultimately governed by God's will, not our own. But the introduction of established religion into the workplace has been devisive as well. Between 1991 and 1997, religious discrimination cases at the Equal Employment Opportunity Commission increased 43 percent.[15] Employees typically claimed that workplace rules, like restrictions on wearing religious clothing, violated their right to practice religion, or they complained that proselytizing by fellow employees or bosses constituted harassment.

Whether the introduction of religion into the workplace generated more or less strife than virtue, in the 1990s religiosity was clearly in vogue. Even Hollywood, our own Gomorrah, found God. By the mid-1990s, sympathetic treatments of religious belief were becoming fashionable on network TV.

Encouraged by the success of CBS's *Touched by an Angel* and cognizant no doubt of the public's increasing religiosity, the major networks introduced a spate of new shows about ministers, priests, and the rank-and-file faithful. They included *Soul Man, Good News, 7th Heaven, Nothing Sacred,* and *Promised Land* (a spin-off of *Touched by an Angel*). Some of the new shows starring religion came and went quickly (like a great many irreligious shows), but they were sufficiently numerous to resemble a trend. A 1997 study by the conservative Media Research Center found a fivefold increase in depictions of religion on prime-time television since 1993 and a tendency to portray religion positively.[16] A preoccupation with faith was reflected in prime-time dramas as well as shows designed for religious audiences. Frank Pembleton, a lead character in the critically acclaimed *Homicide,* pondered God's apparent tolerance of evil. On *NYPD Blue,* Andy Sipowicz blamed God for the murder of one son but had his faith restored by the birth of another (and the insistent religiosity of his wife). "As a nation, we're basically looking for strong, religious values," president of CBS entertainment Leslie Moonves explained. "I think it's a great trend in both entertainment and the country." [17]

The trendy deference toward religion also affected the supposedly liberal, mainstream press. It began offering unprecedented coverage of religion, taking care not to offend the faithful. A 1996 op-ed piece that I was invited to write for the *New York Times* on Hillary Clinton's "conversations" with Eleanor Roosevelt was cleansed of any irreverence toward established religion (although I was expected to mock New Age). I was not allowed to observe that while Mrs. Clinton was criticized for talking to Eleanor Roosevelt, millions of Americans regularly talk to Jesus, long deceased, and that many people believe that God talks to them, unbidden. (At least Mrs. Clinton didn't imagine that Mrs. Roosevelt answered back.) I was not permitted to point out that to an atheist, the sacraments are as silly as a seance. The simple truth of these observations was no defense. They were excised because they were deemed "offensive." ("It's gratuitously offensive," my editor said repeatedly, as we wrangled over each remark. "It's not gratuitous," I responded in vain.)

The uncritical and essentially uninteresting press coverage

enjoyed by established religions did not necessarily protect individual members of the clergy who fell from grace. Sinners like Jimmy Swaggart, and Jim Bakker and his ex-wife, Tammy Faye, were subject to ridicule. Catholic priests found to have molested children in their care were appropriately villified (and prosecuted), and at times, the press even questioned the Church's vigilance in policing child abuse cases internally, while courts were asked to hold it to account. As claims of child abuse surfaced, the Church found a formidable opponent in the therapeutic culture. But while the sins of religious leaders and, on occasion, religious institutions were exposed, religious rituals and belief systems were shielded from critical review.

Religious belief is an exceedingly powerful social and political force, yet it remains largely unexamined—except when it gives rise to "cults" and other outré minority sects. The Reverend Sun Myung Moon is always fair game, but not the pope. Followers of charismatic New Age channelers, like J. C. Knight or Elizabeth Clare Prophet (a.k.a. Gura Ma), who predicted Armageddon in 1990, are apt to be ridiculed or pitied; but the press is respectful of people who believe that they have seen the Virgin Mary or that statues of her weep. When a mute, paralyzed fourteen-year-old girl in Massachusetts attracted thousands of followers because she is rumored to be "co-suffering with Christ and in possession of miraculous healing powers," the *Boston Globe* reported the story sympathetically, without questioning belief in miracles or wondering about the hysteria below the surface of it.[18]

There are, in fact, some important organizational distinctions between traditional churches and cults, which justify concern about the latter. Cults (as I define them) generally revolve around central, supreme authority figures, who demand worship and absolute obedience; and they form homogenous, totalistic communities that isolate people from the world, depriving them of alternative perspectives and relationships, as well as information. Some people may benefit from cult membership, but others are bound to be victimized by insane or unscrupulous cult leaders, or fellow followers.[19]

But traditional religions can pose dangers to fanatical believers as well, and religious fanatics sometimes pose dangers to society. It is a combination of cowardice and prejudice that discourages us from critically examining established religions, as we examine cults. I suspect that media elites offer virtually no analysis of the religious impulse or majoritarian religious beliefs mainly because they fear appearing impious or giving offense. Less reverent than timid, the press flatters adherents of mainstream faiths instead of challenging them.

What's striking about journalists and intellectuals today, liberal and conservative alike, is not their mythic Voltairian skepticism but their deference to belief and utter failure to criticize, much less satirize, America's romance with God. With very few exceptions (like the incisive Katha Pollitt) social critics have abandoned the tradition of caustic secularism that once provided refuge for the faithless: People "are all insane," Mark Twain remarked in *Letters from the Earth.* "Man is a marvelous curiosity . . . he thinks he is the Creator's pet. He believes the Creator is proud of him; he even believes the Creator loves him; has a passion for him; sits up nights to admire him; yes and watch over him and keep him out of trouble. He prays to him and thinks He listens. Isn't it a quaint idea." No prominent liberal thinker writes like that anymore.[20]

Religion is "so absurd that it comes close to imbecility," H. L. Mencken declared in *Treatise on the Gods,* which included a scathing attack on the clergy for which any commentator would be forced to apologize today. "The priest, realistically considered, is the most immoral of men, for he is always willing to sacrifice every other sort of good to the one good of his arcanum—the vague body of mysteries that he calls the truth." [21] Mencken had no more respect for theologians: "The average theologian is a hearty, red-faced, well-fed fellow . . . He disseminates his blather, not innocently, like a philosopher, but maliciously, like a politician." [22]

Mencken was equally scornful of the established church: "Since the early days, [it] has thrown itself violently against every effort to liberate the body and mind of man. It has been, at all times and everywhere, the habitual and incorrigible defender of bad governments, bad laws, bad social theories, bad institutions. It was for centuries, an apologist for slavery, as it was an apologist for the divine right of kings." [23] Mencken was not entirely unsympathetic to the wishful thinking behind virtually all religion—the belief that we needn't die, that the universe isn't arbitrary and indifferent to our plight, that we are governed by a supernatural being whom we might induce to favor us. Still, while a staunch defender of the right to say or think virtually anything, no matter how stupid, he singled out as "the most curious social convention of the great age in which we live" the notion that religious opinions themselves (not just the right to utter them) "should be respected . . . theologians continued their assault upon sense without much resistance, and the enlightenment is unpleasantly delayed . . . No, there is nothing notably dignified about religious ideas. They run, rather, to a peculiarly puerile and tedious kind of nonsense." [24] Name one widely published intellectual today who dares to write like that. Name one mainstream journal that would publish Mencken's assault on religion today.

If it is sincere, the view of intellectuals as hostile to belief is, at best, anachronistic, reflecting intellectual fashions of the early twentieth century. It was nearly a hundred years ago, in

1903, that Bertrand Russell declared that the absence of God and an afterlife was a virtual certainty. "Man is the product of causes which had no prevision of the end they were achieving . . . his origin, his growth, his hopes, his fears, his loves and beliefs, are but the outcome of accidental collocations of atoms . . . [Nothing] can preserve an individual life beyond the grave." That there are no divinities, no Master Planners, no hope of anything but eventual extinction for humans and the universe itself were facts of life for Russell: "[A]ll these things, if not quite beyond dispute, are yet so nearly certain, that no philosophy which rejects them can hope to stand," he concluded.[25] But it is Bertrand Russell's philosophy that stands mainly as historical artifact today.

Russell would be surprised and Mencken nauseated by public discourse in late-twentieth-century America. Since the early 1990s, public policy discussions, left and right, have been suffused with piety. Virtue talk among conservatives routinely invokes "Judaeo-Christian" ideals (excluding the nation's Moslems and members of other minority sects from the moral landscape). Among liberals, the search for a transcendent source of virtue has given rise to communitarianism, which regards secular as well as religious affiliations as unique, essential wellsprings of morality. In this view, goodness, or our better selves, derive from membership in community; communal claims, therefore, take precedence over conflicting assertions of individual rights, which are associated with selfishness, alienation, and anomie. The community standing against the individual is like virtue standing against vice.

Communitarian ideas gained considerable visibility when they were embraced or adapted by the Clintons. Hillary Clinton's call for a "politics of meaning" partly reflected the influence of communitarian Michael Lerner (who coined the phrase), but, as she stressed, it was an expression of her own long-standing religious beliefs. Declaring that America was suffering from a "sleeping sickness of the soul," lamenting our "spiritual vacuum," and stressing the need to "sense that our lives are part of some greater effort," Mrs. Clinton demonstrated the affinities between communitarianism and established religion.[26] Both imagine the immersion of individuals in a "greater effort"; both require individual submission to a presumably virtuous Higher Power, either divine or communal (although many religious traditions do value individual intimations of God). Both preach the existence of transcendent, immaterial realities.

Communitarianism and other liberal appeals to civic virtue are not always overtly religious, but they do tend to rely on vague, spiritualized notions of the body politic. Walter Lippmann observed, seventy years ago, that the democratic ideal of popular sovereignty itself is political mysticism: democrats spiritualize public opinion, regarding it "as men in other societies looked upon uncanny forces." Abandoning belief in the divinity of kings and natural superiority of the aristocracy, democrats imagine an "oversoul" organizing and guiding the public will, Lippmann observed. They reason that "since out of drift and incoherence settled aims do appear, there must be a mysterious contrivance at work somewhere over and above the inhabitants of a nation. They invoke a collective soul, a national mind, a spirit of the age which imposes order upon random opinion."[27] In this view, punditry itself, either liberal or conservative, is often an act of faith, an exercise in inchoate supernaturalism.

When elites piously protest the secularist biases of elites, you have to wonder: Do the protesters see themselves, with their appeals to values and standards and incessant obeisance to God, as atypical of their class? Do the pundits imagine that by lamenting the proverbial demise of religious belief they are demonstrating disrespect for religion within their own profession? Observations about the irreligiosity of other, unnamed elites are undermined by their own banality.

In fact, the rise of virtue talk—which often takes the form of communitarianism on the left and nostalgia for Victorianism on the right—has resulted in a striking re-moralization of public policy debates. Today, it's rare to hear a nonnormative analysis of social problems, one that doesn't focus on failings of individual character or collective virtue: Discussions of structural unemployment have given way to jeremiads about the work ethic; increasingly punitive approaches to juvenile crime focus on the amorality of youthful offenders, portraying it as an irremedial character flaw, not a reaction to the harsh deprivation that shaped them.

Character itself is often seen as a function of religiosity. Although genetic determinism offers alternative explanations for bad characters, it frustrates efforts to fix responsibility and blame for bad behavior. Once the discussion turns to questions of individual responsibility, it is apt to focus on the individual's relationship with God. The effort to build character has resulted partly in a crusade to save souls. Among academic and media elites as well as politicians and pop spirituality gurus, there is, by now, considerable agreement that social pathologies such as crime, drug abuse, teenage pregnancy, and chronic welfare dependency are, at least in part, symptomatic of spiritual malaise—loss of faith in God or a more generalized anomie. Some blame TV—but it has also bowed to public piety.

Because virtue is commonly presumed to derive exclusively from religious teachings or, at least, spiritual sensitivities, virtue talk quickly evolved into God talk. Because public life is supposed to be nonsectarian, spirituality, as opposed to denominational religion, has ecumenical appeal. Proposing a mandatory moment of silence in public schools, one legislator remarked to me that silent meditations would not violate constitutional strictures against establishing religion, because they would introduce spirituality, not religion, into the classroom. Readers of popular literature on personal and spiritual development will recognize his distinction: Religion implies adherence to a particular belief system, the experts tell us; spirituality is simply a general embrace of belief.

Spirituality is an alluring product in a pluralistic marketplace: It's so inclusive. It embraces traditional religious and New Age practices, as well as forays into pop psychology and a devotion to capitalism. Exercises in self-esteem and recovery from various addictions have been presented as spiritual endeavors by codependency experts like John Bradshaw. The generation of wealth has been spiritualized by such best-selling personal development gurus as Deepak Chopra, author of *The Seven Spiritual Laws of Success*, which offers "the ability to create unlimited wealth with effortless ease."[28] (Some sixty years ago, Napoleon Hill's best-selling *Think and Grow Rich* made readers a similar promise.) Cults have become increasingly materialistic; you can chant for a new condo or car, along with a little enlightenment. According to Cynthia Kisser, director of the Cult Awareness Network, "Cults offer business training, commercial and social opportunities, computer training, and spiritual opportunities. Cults are developing some niche marketing." The late Frederick Lenz, known as Zen master Rama, or the "yuppie guru" (and the self-proclaimed reincarnation of a Hindu deity), exhorted his acolytes to study computer programming and meditation. According to one twenty-eight-year-old follower: "Rama said we were on the fast track to Buddhism, that we weren't going to wear robes or shave our heads because that doesn't work in America. We were going to wear tuxedos and make money and be Buddhists. I thought, 'Hey, this is exactly what I want.' "[29]

Spirituality discourages you from passing judgment on any of these endeavors, no matter how shallow or silly they seem. It is egalitarian, ranking no one religion over another, and it doesn't require people to choose between faiths. You can claim to be a spiritual person without professing loyalty to a particular dogma or even understanding the one you claim to embrace. Spirituality makes no intellectual demands on you; all it requires is a general belief in immaterialism (which can be used to increase your material possessions).

But the conviction that we have souls or spirits unbounded by the material world gives rise to religion. To an atheist who does not believe in any transcendent force or being, the popular distinction between spirituality and religion is merely semantic. Whatever their doctrinal differences, Western religions share a core belief in the soul and the supernatural. Religion is simply spirituality institutionalized.

It is, however, the historic, institutional status of denominational religion that protects it from irreverence. While New Age attitudes and ideas are quite popular, among members of mainstream faiths as well as seekers of alternative spiritual truths, they are also vulnerable to attack. New Age dates back to the nineteenth century, at least, and represents a changeable, heterogeneous assortment of beliefs, drawn from Eastern religions, Western spiritualism, occultism, and the human potential movement. (It is sometimes difficult to distinguish from New Thought, a nineteenth-century religious movement focusing on alternative healing and positive thinking.) New Age has always presented itself as an alternative to established Western religions. As J. Gordon Melton has observed, it "arose not so much as a new religion but as a new revivalist religious impulse," that emphasized mystical experiences and Eastern religious traditions.[30]

Partly because it challenges institutionalized faiths and because its hodgepodge of beliefs has never given rise to an institutionalized theology of its own, New Age is not immune from mockery. While the mainstream media salaams before established religion, it regularly questions or satirizes ideas about the supernatural that are classified as New Age. It's easy to imagine a TV sitcom making fun of a character who visits psychics and astrologers and channels Sarah Bernhardt but virtually impossible to imagine it laughing at anyone who takes the Bible literally and believes that someone named Jonah once lived in a whale.

Conservative advocates of religion, preoccupied with civic virtue, would be among the first to join in the derision of New Age beliefs. Some would happily and haughtily dismiss adherents of New Age as airheads, or potheads—casualties of the '60s. Not that conservatives have been entirely unaffected by New Age, or the personal development tradition. Newt Gingrich partook of America's optimistic, positive thinking, personal development tradition. A fan of pop futurists Alvin and Heidi Toffler and consultee (along with Bill Clinton) of management guru Stephen Covey, Gingrich produced his own self-help manual for the nation, *To Renew America*. Gingrich was allied politically with ersatz intellectual Arianna Huffington, who has combined right-wing republicanism with pop spirituality, publishing *The Fourth Instinct: The Call of the Soul* in 1994. (People are genetically encoded to find God, I've heard her declare, without explanation or a stab at substantiation.)

Nancy Reagan had her astrologer. But when conservatives, and centrists, talk about inviting religion into the public schools, they're not suggesting that we teach the collected works of Shirley MacLaine.

The deference paid to mainstream religion, compared to the derision with which we're encouraged to regard New Age and pop spirituality, is intellectually indefensible. Protestants, Catholics, Moslems, and Jews are no less superstitious than people who believe in shamans, witches, and astrologers (as many Protestants, Catholics, Moslems, and Jews do). "Superstition" is simply a derogative term for a belief about the supernatural that you don't share.

Why should it be socially acceptable to make fun of psychics and not priests? What's the difference between crossing yourself or hanging a mezuzah outside your door and avoiding black cats? Believing that you've been abducted by aliens or that Elvis is alive is, on its face, no sillier than believing that Christ rose from the dead or that God parted the Red Sea so that Moses and his followers might traverse it. People who believe that God heeds their prayers have probably waived the right to mock people who talk to trees and guardian angels or claim to channel the spirits of Native Americans.

The differences between organized religion and the disorganized collection of beliefs that constitutes New Age are primarily . . . well . . . organizational. The established churches perform social and political as well as spiritual functions; they are social institutions that administer schools and public welfare programs. Not just communities of worship, they are bureaucracies—and bases for political organizing. They exert considerable political power, demonstrated thirty years ago by the civil rights movement and by the Christian Coalition today. On a smaller scale, New Age movements do fulfill some social functions—through the alternative adult educational programs, retreats, or support groups they engender. They may yet exert electoral influence. (Best-selling New Age author Marianne Williamson is trying to politicize her followers.) And at least one rigid, hierarchical church, the Church of Scientology, may be classified under the expansive rubric of New Age, along with the occasional cult; but these are intrinsically insular, totalitarian systems that exert relatively little influence in the mainstream or on New Age culture. New Agers tend to be unaffiliated, or labile in their allegiances.

It's not surprising to find considerable crossover between organized religion and popular spiritualism—demonstrated by the Reverend Louis Farrakhan's forays into numerology or Bill and Hillary Clinton's consultations with pop gurus Marianne Williamson and Stephen Covey or the pope's interest in miracles. That people combine adherence to established theologies with belief in occult and paranormal phenomenon is hardly surprising. Adherents of established religion and the most marginalized New Age ideas have a common penchant for suspending disbelief.

They may scoff at each other's particular convictions, but cult followers, New Agers, and members of mainstream sects share a capacity for faith in supernatural occurrences, which, in the popular view, means they share a capacity for virtue. It divides them from atheists and agnostics, whom virtuecrats are apt to consider only a little more virtuous than many prison inmates. In fact, condemned prisoners who find God, as many do, may elicit more sympathy or understanding from fellow believers than law-abiding citizens who disdain even the impulse to worship Him. In one view, all atheists are potential criminals, anyway. Godlessness is often associated with crime, and religiosity with deterrence. "Kids who do God are less likely to do drugs or turn to crime," according to editorial writers at the *Wall Street Journal*. (They forget that thirty years ago kids did drugs to find God, on some magical mystery tour.) [31]

The popular association of atheism with amorality was dramatized by the case of Michael Carneal, the fourteen-year-old boy who opened fire on a prayer meeting at his high school, in Kentucky, in December 1997. He was an atheist, according to initial reports. Or, he had associated with atheists who mocked prayer. The story seemed to confirm the virtuecrats' worst fears about godlessness, although it was impossible to know precisely what the charge of atheism implied. The term "atheist" is used loosely to include people considered insufficiently reverent or devout and people who oppose attempts to inject Christian practices and beliefs into public life. Still, the day after Carneal shot and killed three of his classmates and wounded five others, the *New York Times* saw fit to report vague rumors about his irreligiosity.

It's unlikely that the *Times* would have repeated suspicions that Carneal had been hanging out with Methodists or Presbyterians. The paper did report that his family minister held a press conference to say that Carneal had been confirmed, but that was in response to the rumors about his atheism. In our increasingly pious culture, the word "atheist" is an epithet. Carneal's family and church made sure the charge was immediately refuted.

Of course reports of Carneal's atheism had arguable relevance (if only they had been substantiated). He did shoot up a prayer meeting. Efforts to make sense of this senseless shooting naturally focused on Carneal's feelings about religious practice. But describing him as an atheist was treated as the end of a discussion about his motive when it could only have been the beginning. Atheism may simply reflect the indifference of an utter lack of faith in God, not any active hostility toward religion, and no propensity to kill.

There's no reason to believe that more religion would have saved Carneal or his classmates. He was apparently raised by a devout family in a devout community. What caused Carneal's crime? Perhaps psychosis. In 1998, he pled guilty, but mentally ill, and received a twenty-five-year sentence without the possibility of parole. But shortly after the murders, after the explanation of atheism was discredited, the press circulated vague reports that Carneal was influenced by a violent movie. Over one year later, in April 1999, the parents of three murdered students filed a federal lawsuit against a collection of computer companies and media firms, claiming that Carneal was influenced by video games, erotic Websites, and a Leonardo DiCaprio film. Like irreligiosity, the entertainment media is a favorite scapegoat for bad behavior. Conservatives complain about a decline in personal responsibility, but in the service of censorship or old-time religion they are likely to declare that the devil, or a movie, made him do it.

Atheists might counter that sometimes religion causes crime. In a little-noticed 1998 case, a woman admitted that she suffocated her seventeen-year-old daughter during an exorcism ritual: the girl was possessed by a demon, her mother explained, pleading not guilty to murder. Her attorney suggested that the killing was predictable: "All you have to do is turn on the television on Sunday and you hear one preacher after another talking about sin and the devil and about driving out one's demons. What she did should not come as a surprise to anyone who has heard those preachers."[32]

I don't quite agree with this statement. The murder of a seventeen-year-old girl by her own mother will always come as a surprise to me, or so I hope. I would not blame religion for this

murder, and absolve the murderer, any more than I'd blame
pornography for rape and absolve the rapist, any more than I'd
blame violence in the media for juvenile crime. I don't want to
scapegoat religion the way true believers scapegoat the lack of it.
I am simply pointing out the folly and unfairness of regarding
religious belief as an unadulterated good, and atheism as evil.

Atheists are generally demonized much more than sinners
who embrace belief (and only get high on God or the emotionalism of revival meetings). If you regard faith as a gift, not a
choice or an achievement, the vilification of nonbelievers seems
grossly unfair; but atheists are often condemned by people who
believe that God has clearly revealed his Truth, and only moral
perversity prevents some from acknowledging it. Scripture
teaches that "what can be known about God is plain to them,
for God has shown it to them."[33] Pop theologies suggest that
repentant sinners on their way to heaven will look down upon
ethical atheists bound for hell. Popular spirituality authors, who
tend to deny the existence of hell, and evil, suggest that atheists
and other skeptics are doomed to spiritual stasis (the worst fate
they can imagine). *Embraced by the Light,* a best-selling book
about after-death experiences, describes atheists as "virtual
prisoners on this earth," comparing them to people "bonded to
the world through greed, bodily appetites, or other commitments." They will not progress until "they learn to accept the
greater power around them . . ."[34] You might pity such faithless
souls, but you wouldn't trust them.

Have I overstated popular hostility toward atheism? Considering survey evidence, Robert Wuthnow sees a dramatic rise in
tolerance for atheists during the past fifty years. According to
one 1994 survey, 74 percent of Americans agree that someone
who does not believe in God "can be a good or ethical person."[35] But many people are loath to admit their prejudices to

pollsters, even prejudices that are widely held. Disagreement with the statement that "an atheist can be a good person" implies intolerance, and many people are no more likely to acknowledge intolerance than a taste for sex and violence in the media. General hypothetical questions about the potential morality of atheists are also unlikely to tease out a strong preference for religious belief or indicate if respect for nonbelievers is merely hypothetical.

According to surveys conducted in the early 1980s, before millennial fever and religious revivalism took hold, nearly 70 percent of all Americans agreed with the general principle that the freedom to worship "applies to all religious groups, regardless of how extreme their beliefs are." But, only 26 percent agreed that the "freedom of atheists to make fun of God and religion" in public places "should be legally protected no matter who might be offended." Seventy-one percent held that atheists "who preach against God and religion" should not be permitted to use civic auditoriums. Almost the same number (69 percent) agreed that civic auditoriums should be open to Protestant revival meetings. It's worth noting that intolerance for atheism was stronger even than intolerance of homosexuality. A smaller majority (59 percent) agreed that gay liberation groups should not be allowed to use public halls to organize for gay rights.[36]

Pressure to declare your spirituality and at least confirm your openness to God is strong in our supposedly secular culture. As Wuthnow observes, "Most Americans—at least five out of six—have been raised in some religious tradition, and these traditions have generally been closely linked to their sense of ethnic, racial, national, or regional identity."[37] I'd add that their religious traditions provide them with a moral identity as well, and people demand professions of religious faith from elected officials, in order to be assured of their fitness to lead. When politicians proclaim their belief in God, regardless of their religion, they are signaling their trustworthiness and adherence to traditional moral codes of behavior, as well as their humility. The confidence required to run for office, the arrogance that assumption of high office breeds, may be mitigated by religion. Even the president must worship a higher power in the hope of gaining its mercy and support.

The political uses of religiosity were dramatized by the pious apology delivered by President Clinton at the annual prayer breakfast in September 1998, shortly after he acknowledged having engaged in an "inappropriate relationship" with Monica Lewinsky. Having been excoriated by the press and members of both parties for the angry, unrepentant tone of his initial four-minute confession to the nation, Clinton badly needed to demonstrate or simulate humility in the face of his sins and a self-abasing eagerness to atone.

To skeptics, like me, Clinton was Elmer Gantry, Sinclair Lewis's priapic preacher whose power derived from his ability to believe what he preached, when he preached it, while ignoring it in practice. Tearfully, Clinton practically thanked Ken Starr for providing him with a chance to atone. The scandal that tormented the public, paralyzed Congress, and crippled any chance of enacting the Democratic agenda to which Clinton was supposedly committed was, after all, "a blessing," the president suggested, because it forced him to confront his sins. Apparently, it did not occur to Clinton that some who cared deeply about the state of the nation couldn't care less about the state of his soul. It was hard to take seriously the professed humility of someone who remained utterly self-centered, elevating his private interest in atonement over the public interest in governance. People who opposed the Starr investigation and impeachment proceedings because they considered the Lewinsky affair a private matter were apt to relegate Clinton's repentance to the private sphere as well.

Religions, however, often encourage public displays of piety and prayers for salvation. As Harvey Cox has observed, the Baptist revivalist tradition from which Bill Clinton emerged celebrates public confessions and denouncements of sin. At revivals, "the penitent is the star of the show."[38] Baptists are hardly alone in their fascination with the drama of sin and redemption, which is a staple of the therapeutic culture as well as religion. In 12-step groups, the salvation story was dramatized in the "journey" from addiction to recovery. So, it's not surprising that there was relatively little discussion of the propriety of the president's performance. Debate focused on its sincerity.

Religious leaders were divided over the virtue of Clinton's contrition and its relevance to the question of public forgiveness or punishment. On the right, Pat Robertson called for impeachment, reminding an audience of Christian Coalition members that "the God of Abraham, Isaac, and Jacob is a God of law and justice."[39] Other members of the clergy, including some who regularly invoked the God of Abraham, Isaac, and Jacob, instead of Jesus, were more charitable. Rabbi Allan Cohen, who attended the September 12th prayer breakfast, reported back to his congregation that the president was sincerely repentant and worthy of forgiveness. Cohen spoke with the president after his apology and was impressed by his demeanor: "He looked me straight in the eye. I'm willing to give someone the benefit of the doubt when they look me in the eye," the rabbi remarked[40] (apparently oblivious to Clinton's reputation for looking people in the eye and lying to them).

Meanwhile, the president assembled an official panel of spiritual advisers, described as his personal "accountability group." It consisted of three ministers: Tony Campolo, described as an evangelical Baptist; J. Philip Wogamen, pastor of the Methodist church that the Clintons attended; and Gordon MacDonald, recovering adulterer and self-help author (whose fans reportedly included Hillary Clinton). We were told that every week one of these men would visit Clinton, read Scripture with him, and provide spiritual counseling. To retain his political power and regain some moral authority, the man regularly exalted as leader of the free world had to reveal himself as another lowly sinner and servant of the Lord.

As Clinton's passion play made clear, belief in God levels human hierarchies while offering infallible systems of right and wrong. Freudianism has a similar leveling effect: neurosis attaches to humans like original sin. But Freud laid down no equivalent moral code, dictated by a Deity, to replace the religious precepts he disdained (although he did assume his own godlike omniscience). His legacy was not a familiar set of objective moral truths but a process for discovering supposed truths about yourself. This did not rid us of sanctimony. In a culture that defines self-knowledge as a virtue, the analysand can lay claim to moral superiority; but that superiority confers limited rights to sit in judgment on others. The only moral imperative that one bathed in self-knowledge can issue is "know thyself," preferably with the aid of a therapist, support group, or at least a good book.

This is precisely the sort of relativism decried by virtuecrats, particularly conservatives, and often blamed nonsensically on the 1960s. Anyone who lived through that decade and witnessed the civil rights movement, antiwar protests, the counterculture, or the renaissance of feminism knows that it was a much more self-righteous than relativistic period. Antiwar activists were quite dogmatic about the evils of the Vietnam War and the military–industrial complex; civil rights activists and feminists pointed out the immoralities of sexist and racist institutions. Even the notorious "permissiveness" of the '60s reflected prevailing dogmas about psychological and cultural health. Chastity was bad (it represented repression). Promiscuity was good. Cocktails were regressive; marijuana was hip.

The counterculture didn't eschew moral codes; instead it rejected particular notions of moral behavior associated with the 1950s and replaced them with alternative moralities. American triumphalism that prevailed on the right was displaced on the left by expiationism—the politics of atonement. (Liberals were the "blame America first" crowd, former U.S. ambassador to the UN Jeanne Kirkpatrick famously proclaimed.) As Richard Rorty suggested in his 1998 book, *Achieving Our Country,* the left adopted a rather religious view of America as a sinful nation, more in need of redemption than reform.[41]

We're often reminded that God was declared dead in the '60s, but, in fact, as Garry Wills has noted, "religious profession and observance generally held steady."[42] And for those members of the counterculture inclined to eschew traditional religious practice, the ethos of the time offered some of the moral certainty of religion. It was hardly a decade of compromise. Protesters were not relativists who based their fight to revolutionize American society on mere personal preferences. They were absolutists, convinced that the revolution they proposed was an objective moral good.

The relativism of which conservatives complain is more a product of the therapeutic culture that emerged in the 1980s, when the political center shifted to the right and introspection became more fashionable than activism. In the '90s, liberals, too, lamented the retreat from public to private concerns, while some feminists and social issue conservatives, pursuing very different agendas, sought to transform private concerns (notably sexual relationships) into matters of public interest, subject to regulation.

Feminist puritanism was aimed at controlling sexual violence and exploitation and advancing equality (at the expense of speech and privacy rights). Social issue conservatives supported sexual inequality (or the reinstatement of traditional gender roles) and the enforcement of sectarian moral codes that criminalized abortion, imposed civil if not criminal penalties on homosexuality, and favored the one-income, male-headed nuclear family idealized in the 1950s. As Senate Majority Leader Trent Lott remarked in 1998, reminiscing about his youth in Mississippi, the decade of the '50s was a "good time for America."[43]

Giving him the benefit of the doubt, the best you can say of Lott is that in describing the 1950s as a "good time," he simply forgot about the bad times for African-Americans, especially in Mississippi: In 1955 Emmet Till, a black teenager, was lynched for whistling at a white woman; in 1956 the state established the Mississippi Sovereignty Commission, which spied on and harassed citizens who violated virtual bans on interacial sex or worked for racial equality. Lott also ignored or forgot the injustices visited upon victims of McCarthyism. His sunny view of the 1950s is characteristic of the religious right, which (without embracing racism) seeks to revive the moral code that dissidents in the 1960s fought to replace. At the end of the century, conservative activists have this in common with the 1960s radicals and left-wing champions of political correctness—unshakable, unaccommodating belief in their own righteousness.

The protests of the '60s demonstrated the power of political belief systems, which sometimes rival the religious. But absolutism about the virtues or vices of free markets, private property, or civil rights lacks the tenacity and universal appeal of absolutist beliefs about God. By declaring your faith in a popular deity, you imply that an omnipotent, omniscient (and benign) force is the source of your values and ideas. You appropriate the rightness of divinity. By rejecting religious belief, you acknowledge that there are no unimpeachable authorities to guide you. You have only your own instincts and ability to reason. Disbelief diminishes moral credibility. In the popular view, we cannot be good without gods.

It's not surprising that belief makes so many people sanctimonious. Whether or not it makes them good is impossible to know. "[T]here is no such thing as religion in the singular. There is only a multitude of religions," John Dewey pointed out[44] (and when I use the term "religion" to denote a universal phenomenon, I'm using the term as shorthand for religious belief). As Dewey stressed, the differences among religions are "so great and shocking" that they preclude generalizations about religion's virtues and vices. From this perspective, conventional paeans to religion are nonsensical—as nonsensical as conventional tributes to voluntarism. America's voluntary associations include hate groups and violence-prone private militias, as well as the PTA, the League of Women Voters, and the Sierra Club. America's religions, both traditional and New Age, are equally diverse, ranging from the totalistic Church of Scientology to the Society of Friends.

Considering their histories, you can safely call organized religions mixed blessings, at best. Apart from their obvious atrocities—the Crusades, the Inquisition, the Salem witch trials, endorsement of slavery in nineteenth-century America, terrorism in the Middle East today—religions have been a font of quotidian oppressions, from my liberal point of view, at least.

Branding homosexuality and family planning as sinful, some religions have encouraged gross discrimination against lesbians and gays and heterosexual women, denying them equal rights, much less the social freedom to bear children or enter into the personal relationships they choose. Condemning racial integration and labeling miscegenation a sin, they have sanctified race discrimination.[45] Fearful of science, sex, and untrammeled human creativity, some religions have been enemies of knowledge, demanding censorship of erotic or merely offensive art, and information about sexuality or evolution, along with challenges to their authority. You question more extreme fundamentalist forms of religion at your peril, as Salman Rushdie discovered.

Fearful of offending anyone's religious beliefs, we often ignore the obvious: religions sanctify bad behavior, along with the good, and they are often quite divisive. In public life, religions naturally breed sectarianism, a particularly vicious form of identity politics. The superiority and sense of belonging some find in their racial or ethnic identities is whetted by the conviction that their side has been chosen by God. Shortly after reportedly atheistic schoolboy Michael Carneal shot his classmates, People for the American Way, an organization that fights religious intolerance (and the Christian Coalition), received a surge of religiously motivated hate mail. Sometimes religion makes hatred seem holy.

Yet religions have been forces of liberation, as well. The civil rights movement demonstrated Christianity's power to inspire and maintain a struggle against injustice. Some would argue that the Nation of Islam continues that struggle today. In the last century, abolitionists, as well as slave owners were backed by religious authority. Some nineteenth-century women's rights activists derived strength from faith in God, despite clerical

opposition that condemned feminism and sanctified the relega-
tion of women to the home. Today, churches provide moral
leadership in the fight to maintain social welfare programs and
eradicate abortions. (Even if you oppose the denial of abortion
rights, as I do, you have to acknowledge that the anti-abortion
movement is driven at least partly by moral ideals.) In recent
history, whether opposing Star Wars, the Vietnam War, or providing sanctuary to Salvadoran refugees, some church leaders
have lent their moral authority to war resistance. Over time, the
clergy may have opposed as many wars as they started.

It is as difficult to quantify the effect of organized religion
on human welfare as it is to generalize about the character,
behavior, and beliefs of all religious people, or the virtues of all
religions. We can't even assess the probable effect of a sect simply by examining its values and ideals. Religions offer forums
for personal interactions, as well as particular theologies. (They
are frequently lauded for providing community.) Religions
shape people not simply by the content of their preachings but
by involving them in voluntary associations, which may have
positive, socializing effects, regardless of their teachings. As
political scientist Nancy Rosenblum has observed, even hate
groups, religious and secular, may impart minimal relational
skills; membership in any association generally requires compromise and cooperation.[46] People are affected by the process
of belonging. Of course, they are affected as well by the ideals of
the groups to which they belong. But they have chosen those
groups and their particular belief systems. Religious belief may
well be less a source for good or evil in people than a vehicle for
them. "Religion is only good for good people," Mary McCarthy
wrote, in the days when liberal intellectuals may have deserved
a reputation for skepticism.[47]

It's hard to imagine McCarthy's dismissal of religion's moralizing effect evoking much agreement today, although many believers would be comfortable with the converse notion that religion is only bad for bad people. Even that principle, however, is not applied consistently: political and religious biases are likely to determine whether we attribute acts of terrorism to individual terrorists or the religions that breed them. Americans may blame Islamic fundamentalism for the acts of Iranian terrorists more readily than they'll blame Catholicism or Protestant Fundamentalism for murders at abortion clinics. But absent particular religious or ethnic prejudice, religious belief almost always gets the benefit of the doubt. It's credited for the good that people do and excused for the evils it encourages.

Religion is a source of values, proponents of official school prayer assert; "which religion" and "which values," I always respond. Secularists have values too. (Ask any Unitarian.) I have always been puzzled by the notion that faith, or credulity, is a requisite for goodness. I've always wondered at God's vanity. Why would an omnipotent, omniscient, and essentially benign Deity be offended by disbelief? My favorite God is the one who looks down on us and says, "I wish they'd stop worrying about whether or not I exist and start obeying my commandments."

Of course, whether or not nonbelievers are, in general, better or worse citizens than believers, neither the formation of individual character nor religious belief is the business of government. It has no missionary role. Government is not competent or empowered to ease our existential anxieties; its jurisdiction is the material world of hardship and injustice. It can and should make life a little fair, and in order to do so, it necessarily enforces some majoritarian notions of moral behavior—outlawing discrimination, for example, or a range of violent assaults. But in a state that respects individual privacy, law can address only bad behavior, not bad thoughts, and cannot require adherence to what are considered good thoughts—like love of God: civil rights laws don't deny you the right to harbor prejudices; they deny you the right to act on them. Government can't force you to like people of different races; it can require you to treat them fairly. It can help make people comfortable, ensuring access to health care, housing, education, and the workplace. But government cannot make people good.

The view of government as a purely political not a metaphysical endeavor—the belief that the state has no role to play in the drama of sin and redemption—was enshrined in the Constitution: in addition to the First Amendment prohibition on establishing religion and the accompanying guarantee of free exercise, Article Six provides that "no religious tests shall ever be required as a qualification for any office or public trust under the United States." The wall between church and state erected by Jefferson and Madison did not reflect hostility toward religion so much as a desire to protect it from civil rule and ensure religious diversity. Religious rights would be guaranteed by a "multiplicity of sects" James Madison observed, just as civil rights would be guaranteed by a "multiplicity of interests." So long as the republic comprised a "great variety of interests, parties, and sects," majority coalitions would be more likely to serve general rather than special interests in justice.[48]

Not that an atheist can take much comfort in the prospect that individual sects might cooperate in forming majority coalitions. If you mistrust religion, you have reason to fear ecumenism; divided, religious sects remain relatively weak politically. A private marriage between sects is nearly as threatening as a state alliance with any one of them. To an atheist, all religions are absurd; majoritarian religions are abhorrent, because they impose themselves on unbelievers. Established, mainstream religions are often equally threatening to religious minorities, who tend to be among the most vehement opponents of state endorsement of religion: in this country, that usually amounts to endorsement of sectarian, Christian views.

Whether government must be especially protective of marginal sects, if they are to survive and provide the diversity of belief that Madison extolled, is a question that plagues debates about the relationship between church and state. It is often difficult to distinguish between laws that sponsor religion (in violation of the establishment clause) and laws that respect religion, ensuring its free exercise. Should religious groups be permitted to hold meetings after hours in public schools, if the school rooms are available to nonreligious private groups? Would denial of access to religious groups discriminate against religion, or would a grant of access favor it with state support? The Supreme Court has rightly held that extracurricular religious organizations should have equal access to public school classrooms—just as they have equal access to public streets. Preachers enjoy the First Amendment right to harangue heretics walking down the streets just as construction workers enjoy the right to harass women.

In *The Culture of Disbelief,* Stephen Carter thoughtfully analyzes this problem of distinguishing state accommodation and state establishment of religion.* He advocates an accommodationist rather than a strict separationist approach, arguing that we should extend affirmative action–like preferences to religious groups and abandon the policy of strict government neu-

---

* The introductory chapter of Carter's book, which lamented the proverbial liberal intellectual disdain for religion and our excessively secular public life, probably accounted for its success. But getting past the introduction, you find an intelligent, informative discussion of law and religion

trality toward them; but Carter underscores, nonetheless, the dangers to religion of aligning with the state. He stresses that religion's primary political role is not to join the state but to resist it, providing an alternative (and a higher) moral code. "A religion is, at its heart, a way of denying the authority of the rest of the world." [49]

A similar concern for religious integrity underlay constitutional prohibitions on the establishment of religion. One of America's earliest advocates of secular government, credited with fashioning the phrase "separation of church and state," Roger Williams was a deeply religious, strictly observant Baptist clergyman. (Banished from Massachusetts, he founded the state of Rhode Island.) Williams did not exactly celebrate religious diversity; he believed that Quakers as well as Catholics either came from or were headed for hell. But he did not expect government to save people from sin.

Distinguishing the sacred and mundane, Williams viewed government as a mere worldly endeavor, necessitated by the Fall: It was presumptuous for civil magistrates to claim the spiritual power and purity of priests. He opposed religious tests for officeholders and the general officialization of religion partly because he believed that theocratic states would impede human progress toward salvation. "The only way that civil magistrates could promote religion was to pay no attention to it at all," as Isaac Kramnick and R. Laurence Moore observe in *The Godless Constitution,* a cogent history of the founder's separationist ideals.[50] As Garry Wills has observed, "The secular state came from the zeal of religion itself." [51]

Some one hundred years after Williams articulated the religious need for secular government, Jefferson and Madison made freedom of religion a founding principle of the United States. Like Williams, they presented separation of church and state as a means of protecting religion. In the religious freedom statute Jefferson proposed for the state of Virginia, he declared that religious truth would be best advanced by a laissez-faire policy toward belief: "[T]ruth is great and will prevail if left to herself . . . she is the proper and sufficient antagonist to error . . . errors ceasing to be dangerous when it is permitted freely to contradict them." [52] Or, as Madison wrote, "[F]aith depends on evidence, not on coercion." Madison, an ardent advocate of disestablishing religion, who drafted the First Amendment, argued that both religion and civil society would be harmed by establishment; freedom of religion was essential to a free society: "to deny religious freedom would weaken other rights." [53]

Two centuries later, in 1962, the Supreme Court relied on the Founders' deep aversion to government-sponsored religious activities when it struck down official school prayers: The Constitution reflects the belief "that one of the greatest dangers to the freedom of the individual to worship in his own way lay in the government's placing its official stamp of approval upon one particular kind of prayer or one particular form of religious service," the Court observed. Historically, the state's alliance with religion had always engendered "the hatred, disrespect, and even contempt of those who held contrary beliefs . . . many people lost their respect for religion that had relied upon the support of government to spread its faith." [54]

The Supreme Court stressed that "the First Amendment, which tried to put an end to governmental control of religion and of prayer, was not written to destroy either . . . it was written to quiet well-justified fears . . . arising out of an awareness that governments of the past had shackled men's tongues to make them speak only the religious thoughts that the government wanted them to speak and to pray only to the God that government wanted them to pray to. It is neither sacrilegious nor anti religious to say that each separate government in this country should stay out of the business of writing or sanctioning official prayers and leave that purely religious function to the people themselves and to those the people choose to look for religious guidance."

In what is probably the most frequently quoted line from this landmark decision shoring up the wall between church and state, the Court stressed that the prohibition of established religion (like the disavowal of religious qualifications for office-holders) reflected the conviction "that a union of government and religion tends to destroy government and to degrade religion."

This is not an obscure or overly sophisticated defense of separationism. It is high school civics; the shallowness of governmental religiosity cited by the Court is an obvious fact of American life. Routine references to God, in the Pledge of Allegiance or on our currency, are constitutional precisely because "they have lost through rote repetition any significant religious content," Justice Brennan observed in 1984.[55] That religion is degraded by state endorsement is made clear every Christmas when municipalities combine nativity scenes with plastic Santas, reindeer, and elves. Indeed, the Supreme Court has enunciated what is informally known as the three-reindeer rule in creche cases: the Court has held that official Nativity scenes are constitutional—so long as they are accompanied by secular (or commercial) holiday displays.

Yet the simple principle that Justice Black enunciated in *Engle v. Vitale*—that the state must remain secular to ensure religious liberty and integrity—is either ignored or rejected by critics of secularism who believe that the state must promote religion to secure virtue. "[R]eligion has traditionally played a central role in the development of public virtue," the American Center for Law and Justice, a religious advocacy group, has argued. "Thus, some entanglement of the civil and religious is not only inevitable, but quite welcome."[56]

The Supreme Court's 1962 decision invalidating official school prayer, which should be regarded as an affirmation of the most elementary constitutional ideals, is more often maligned as an assault on American values and even the security of its citizens: right-wing religious rhetoric is apt to blame the abolition of prayer in school for a subsequent rise in crime, associating it, as well, with feminism, homosexuality, out-of-wedlock births, drug use, and other alleged scourges of liberalism. It's as if, in prohibiting official school prayer, the Court had prohibited churches, traditional gender roles, and the nuclear family.

A Supreme Court decision reviewing the Founders' concern for religious liberty and their Lockean view of government as a keeper of peace, order, and justice—not godliness or virtue—has become a casualty to a culture war over values. That measures the tenuousness of our own commitment to freedom of conscience and our insecurities about the power of religion. Surely, if religious teachings are true—if God exists, cares about us, and wants to save our souls—He'll manage without any help from government.

CHAPTER 2

■

THE SECTARIAN PUBLIC
SQUARE

Can government manage without help from God? Politicians
and dollar bills have always invoked God's blessing, acknowledging rhetorically the conventional assumption that America
requires, and deserves, divine support. Presidents dutifully
attend church and sometimes consult with religious leaders
(although if Billy Graham was feted by federal officials, Martin
Luther King was investigated). For most of our history, established religion, notably Protestantism, has shaped social mores
and even laws. The absence of a state religion has never meant
the absence of religious influence on the state.

In recent history, the tacit partnership between religion,
culture, and law was often based on maintaining at least a pre-
tense of nonsectarianism. When my mother was young, she was
required to recite the Lord's Prayer in public school. When I was
in grade school, I recited a brief, bland prayer including only a
simple statement of belief in God and a general request for
assistance. Clearly sectarian activities were respected but con-

ducted after hours or off school grounds: my Catholic classmates were regularly excused from school to attend catechism
classes. Jewish students and teachers were expected to be absent
from school on the High Holy Days. The nonsectarianism of
the time depended partly on the willingness of minority
groups, like Jewish Americans, to assimilate and compartmentalize their own religious practices, but as a reward they were
only expected to profess a generalized belief in God the Father,
and not His son.

Then, in the 1970s, evangelical Christians, including many
fundamentalists, emerged on the national political scene, organized in opposition to momentous social changes that had been
percolating since the 1950s. The fabled quiescence of the '50s
was deceiving: The Supreme Court held that racially segregated
schools were unconstitutional, the Russians launched Sputnik,
and Elvis helped launch rock-and-roll. Mobilized by the abolition of mandatory school prayer in 1962, a new, post-Sputnik
emphasis on science (and evolution) in the classroom, the civil
rights movement, feminism, and the legalization of abortion
(which began in the 1960s), as well as the ascendance of a supposedly relativistic baby boomer generation, conservative
Protestants became a potent political force.[1]

Having been relatively silent for so long, they were probably
more numerous than most liberals realized. As recent, revision-
ist histories have demonstrated, fundamentalism had not been
vanquished in 1925 by the prosecution of science teacher John
Scopes for violating Tennessee's ban on teaching evolution.
(The notorious "monkey trial" was mythologized in the 1955
play *Inherit the Wind*.) Scopes's conviction was eventually over-
turned, and his prosecutor, William Jennings Bryan, may have
been embarrassed and discredited, especially among elites, but
Tennessee's anti-evolution law stood for decades, until the late

1960s. Other states and schools boards throughout the south adopted similar restrictions, which influenced educational publishers nationwide. By 1930, a majority of public high schools (70 percent) did not teach evolution; it did not re-enter the curriculum until the 1960s, when conservatives began protesting secular humanism in the schools, and other sins of modern life.[2]

Right-wing evangelicals were fairly easily organized, through their churches, and they were on a mission—undaunted by doubt. As Jerry Falwell said in 1979, "America was born in her churches, and she must be reborn there as well. The time has come for pastors and church leaders to clearly and boldly proclaim the Gospel of regeneration in Christ Jesus."[3]

This was not a campaign for the fainthearted, who were inclined to extol religious tolerance and the Judaeo-Christian tradition. To people who believed fervently that embracing Jesus was essential to salvation and that all we ever needed to know was inscribed in the Bible, the relative nonsectarianism of the mainline Protestant hegemony must have looked like secular humanism, not religion. An alleged absence of religion, meaning a lack of faith in Jesus, was said to be destroying the nation. Pat Robertson has explained that God "put a hedge of protection around the United States" when it was "governed by the Bible." Because America has rejected God, by banning mandatory school prayer, legalizing abortions, and normalizing homosexual activity (among other sins), "the hedge of protection that has been around the United States is coming down," subjecting us to terrorist attacks, economic collapse, and natural catastrophes. Only faith in Jesus can save us. (Apparently God also told Robertson that He would continue protecting America "as long as Christians are taking the gospel overseas.")[4]

So, while conservative evangelicals targeted secularism rhetorically, they attacked a tradition of nonsectarianism, which was a much more influential force in public life.

The campaign against secular humanism in the public schools, for example, dating back over two decades, targeted the teaching of evolution (in addition to sex education). Not that Darwin's theories are incompatible with religious belief in general, or the Judaeo-Christian tradition; they are incompatible with certain sectarian beliefs including one very literal reading of the Bible. Demanding the teaching of creationism, fundamentalists may have been in a minority nationally. Promoting the most traditional gender roles and standards of sexual behavior, they may have been out of tune with popular culture. Still, they were organizing locally and enjoying some success; efforts to censor secular humanist material in public libraries and schools increased exponentially in the 1970s and have remained high.

The conservative crusade for religious purity was indeed a war against the culture: recent censorship campaigns in public libraries and schools have relentlessly targeted educational material about sex and sexuality. In the early 1980s, anti-ERA activist Phyllis Schafly was denouncing sex education, which Jerry Falwell labeled "filth and perversion."[5] Ten years later, the battle continued: "An unprecedented number of challenges were levelled at health and sexuality education material" in the 1995–1996 school year, according to People for the American Way. In addition to sex education texts, books about teenage sexuality and gay and lesbian literature have been under attack nationwide, along with mass market magazines and generally respected works of literature: In the late '90s, *Seventeen* magazine was banned from a middle school library on Long Island for failure to preach sexual abstinence. A New Hampshire high school teacher was suspended for assigning books by E. M.

Forster and May Sarton that dealt with homosexuality; school officials seized the books from eleventh and twelfth graders while they were reading them in class. Best-selling young adult books by Judy Blume remained perennial targets.

These cases are not anomalous; they're typical. Who was the writer most besieged by the educational book police in 1996? Not the sleazebag semiliterate author of some slasher book. Not even the Marquis de Sade. The author subject to the most censorship attempts in the 1995–1996 school year was Maya Angelou: According to People for the American Way, *I Know Why the Caged Bird Sings* was "the most frequently challenged book in the country." Angelou was one of a group of African-American female authors who were disproportionately targeted by censors. Alice Walker's *The Color Purple* and Toni Morrison's *Song of Solomon* were included on the list of banned books.

Cases involving film censorship also dramatized the sweep of right-wing censorship campaigns. In Oklahoma City, in 1997, the 1979 Academy Award–winning film *The Tin Drum* (an adaptation of the Günter Grass novel about the Holocaust) was removed from the public library and six video stores; and police seized a copy of the film from the home of a private citizen (without a warrant). *The Tin Drum*, a fable about a child in Nazi Germany who refuses to grow up, was labeled pornographic; it includes a scene suggestive of oral sex between a young boy and a teenage girl. (A subsequent federal court decision held that the film could not be considered pornographic.) In Colorado, a high school teacher was dismissed for showing Bernardo Bertolucci's film *1900* about fascism.

From the perspective of the Christian right, secular humanism seemed to be a frighteningly expansive phenomenon. Feminism, homosexuality, extramarital sex, teenage pregnancy, the breakdown of the nuclear family, and an underlying political liberalism constituted its familiar litany of evils. Of course, millions of people who believed in God also believed in feminism, gay rights, and the freedom to divorce, as well as abortion rights. During the 1960s Protestant clergy were active in establishing referral services for women seeking safe, illegal abortions. The social trends that conservatives lamented were not sins of secular humanism; they followed a failure to embrace particular, sectarian interpretations of Scripture.

Neither agnostics nor atheists were able to put up much of a fight against attacks on "humanism" (their ranks have always been small). But right-wing Christians seeking to reverse the sexual revolution and legislate sectarian codes of behavior have had to contend with American ideals of individual liberty and pluralism, which many religious people share. Those ideals shaped the tradition of secular government. The opposition encountered by the religious right wasn't eased by its puritanical attacks on sexually explicit entertainments and extramarital sexual activities, which so many God-fearing people enjoyed.

Still, religious conservatives were not alone in resisting changing gender roles or worrying about violent crime, the rise of alternative family structures, drug abuse, and sex and violence in the media. Bill Clinton, an occasional liberal and committed libertine, championed the censorship of indecency on the Internet, offered up the v-chip to purify TV, defended a very expansive definition of child pornography that included images of adults made to look like children, and continued a highly punitive war on drugs. Political centrism demanded limits on "permissiveness," when it involved children and the use of drugs associated with the counterculture or the ghetto (like marijuana and crack cocaine).

But the mainstream appeal of some traditional mores espoused by the right was qualified, partly by respect for privacy and individual autonomy. Consenting adults might engage in some behaviors considered immoral or antisocial—like excessive alcohol use or extramarital sex—without fearing arrest or other governmental interventions. Even public tolerance for homosexuality increased, so long as it did not involve military service or proximity to children. Legally, lesbians and gay men remained disabled: in 1986, the Supreme Court upheld laws against consensual sodomy, applied to adult homosexuals engaged in consensual sex in their own homes,[6] and by the late 1990s, federal law still did not prohibit job discrimination based on sexual orientation. Yet, state courts were beginning to examine archaic laws that criminalized sex between consenting adults (in 1998, invoking the state constitution, the Georgia Supreme Court struck down the same anti-sodomy law upheld by the U.S. Supreme Court in 1986). Openly gay candidates were running for office and occasionally winning, and homosexuality was gradually gaining social respectability.

So, concerns about privacy collided with anxiety about changing social and sexual mores, and the preservation of childhood innocence. The culture war continued unresolved, with many people drawn to both sides simultaneously. What precisely did the zone of privacy encompass? Where was the boundary between private behavior and public vice, or virtue?

It was President Clinton's misfortune (or his self-determined fate) to force a political resolution of the question. When he lied about the Lewinsky affair and tried to thwart an investigation into his sex life, he invigorated our contradictory desire for moral order tempered by libertarianism. For months, polls showed that the public doggedly insisted on classifying Clinton's affair with Lewinsky as private, and separating it from his performance in office—to the surprise and chagrin of many pundits, as well as conservative Republicans. Leading Republican virtuecrat William Bennett expressed bewildered dismay over the public's apparent disinterest in presidential philandering: "I don't get it," Bennett conceded, after modest Democratic victories in the 1998 congressional elections. "For the first time in my adult life, I'm not in sync . . . What about all these conferences I've been invited to? I mean, values, smalues. I don't get it." [7]

Bennett probably needed to get out more; the right-wing conference circuit is unlikely to provide an accurate, balanced view of public opinion or popular culture. Like many right-wing republicans preoccupied with sexual morality, he had apparently underestimated the value of privacy to many Americans. The tension between public and private concerns that helped shape public opinion on impeachment was consistently reflected in the perspectives offered respectively by Republicans and Democrats: Republicans spoke in general terms about justice (or obstruction of it), honesty, and integrity in government. Democrats stuck to the particulars—lying and extramarital sex—familiar and regrettably normal, private activities to many Americans. Impeachment proceedings finally ended, but the underlying conflict is likely to persist.

Pundits, politicians, and the occasional sociologist like to talk about the American people as if we were a monolith. "The American people are fundamentally decent," or "fundamentally forgiving," or "The American people have a sense of justice," they regularly intone. Which American people, I wonder. It's hard to imagine any homogeneous group of 250 million individuals—and our population is particularly diverse, not simply in terms of race or ethnicity. Consumerism and the mass media may unite us, but American culture still reflects contradictory strains of puritanism and libertarianism, conformity and individualism, freedom and authoritarianism. So while we can identify dominant social trends, they are never simply singular.

The religious and spiritual revival of the 1990s was not, therefore, unmitigated, or undivided by conflicting values and ideals, as the Clinton scandals showed; but it did appear pervasive. Many Americans seemed to be seeking stability and solace in a smorgasbord of religions and newly spiritualized pop psychologies. Indeed, the variety of religious experiences available made a diverse, en masse revival possible.

Attacks on secularism began to enjoy broad appeal. By the mid-1990s, some leaders of the Christian right were endeavoring to tone down the rhetoric of their movement, as they sought common ground with people of other faiths. Pat Robertson, for example, became an embarrassment to more thoughtful, charitable, or simply politic evangelicals, who cringed at his wackier pronouncements—like the suggestion that God would send hurricanes or maybe terrorists to destroy the city of Orlando, Florida, because it allowed rainbow flags, the symbol of the gay rights movement, to hang on city light poles during a weekend event in Disney World.

Conservative Christians remained on the extreme, but their protests began harmonizing with a pervasive yearning for order and divine interventions. Widespread, nonsectarian anxiety about social change, a declining faith in government, and an increasing dependence on angels and other heavenly beings helped generate discussions of civic virtue and demands for new infusions of religion into public life.

Advocates of religiosity were aided by confusion about the separationist ideal, which was wrongly considered hostile to any public professions of faith. Separationism does not require that religious people and organizations remain silent about public affairs. It does not frown upon faith-based movements for social change. How could it? The constitutional prohibition on establishing religion was intended to serve religious liberty. We have undisputed rights to express ourselves in religious language and form social or political affliations with others who share our faith.

Separation of church and state does not desire, much less mandate, the banishment of religious faith from public life, as right-wing rhetoric sometimes suggests. It does prohibit the channeling of public funds to sectarian organizations and purposes. The right of religious people to organize and mount political protests is, in part, a right of private association, which the government is bound to accommodate, but not support. If the agenda of any religious group is a sectarian one, it should not dictate law or policy. Separationism ensures that sectarian beliefs—like the view of contraception as sinful—will not be imposed on a pluralistic society.

Of course, religious beliefs help shape popular notions of morality, which are often translated into law. That is inevitable. Law may properly reflect some sectarian beliefs, so long as it also reflects shared nonsectarian and secular ideals as well. Prohibitions of murder or race discrimination are not invalid because they conform to particular religious beliefs, so long as they also incorporate broadly shared notions of moral behavior. This implies that religious people who seek to shape secular law and policies have a civic obligation, although not a constitutional one, to appeal to shared nonsectarian ideals.

That was one lesson of the civil rights movement. Frequently lauded as a faith-based political movement, it relied as well on a secular, constitutional ideal in demanding an end to racial inequality under law. The inspirational religious rhetoric of civil rights leaders was no more important than appeals to secular justice. The relative success of the movement reflected its success in demonstrating the conflict between stated American ideals of equality and the practices of segregation. Whatever God believed about race discrimination (many white supremacists were convinced He was on their side), the secular ideals on which this country claimed to be based could not be reconciled with Jim Crow.

Members of the Christian Coalition today are free, of course, to base their vision of civil society on particular readings of Scripture and to express it in biblical terms. But they will not and should not succeed in codifying their vision until it is shared by people of other faiths, until it reflects commonly held, nonsectarian principles of democratic governance. This suggests that political success requires some compromise of religious principles: a pluralistic society can't possibly reflect everyone's sectarian notions of morality. When living in the larger culture requires a compromise to their core beliefs, religious groups are free to withdraw, like the Amish. But, ideally, people need only compromise beliefs they consider peripheral to their faith, and it is indeed by virtue of small compromises that people who believe in different gods, or no gods at all, formulate common notions of the public good.

Separationism is premised on the inevitability of religious perspectives entering the public square. It is not a crusade to silence them. I accept as a given that people cannot separate their religious and political lives. Of course they will be guided by their religious convictions when they enter the voting booth and ponder various public policy questions. That's why private religious beliefs are public issues. People who think abortion is murder will oppose its legalization. How could they not? People who believe in the healing power of crystals will support research on alternative medicine. People who belong to a church that posits a collective responsibility to feed poor children will oppose welfare repeal.

The injection of religious perspectives into policy debates is unavoidable; the right to voice a religious belief about public policy is inarguable. At issue are demands that the government adopt and enforce sectarian religious beliefs—compelling the teaching of creationism in public schools or diverting state money to parochial schools. At issue is the notion that secular government cannot function justly or morally without guidance from particular religious denominations.

Hostility toward government increased in the 1980s, and so, not surprisingly, did the desire for religious assistance in governance. Today, demands by religious institutions for government support—funding for parochial schools or sectarian social services—are couched as offers to help government cure our social ills. Approaching the millennium, Americans have sought to improve the effectiveness of government by delegating some of its authority to religion.

The 1996 welfare reform bill, for example, directed federal funds to church-administered welfare programs, which were widely presumed to be more successful than programs that did not address recipient's spiritual needs. Former Carter cabinet member Joseph Califano, now president of the National Center on Addiction and Substance Abuse, asserted that there was "no question about the relevance of God and spirituality" to treatment programs for substance abuse. Princeton-based criminologist John DiIulio declared his faith in faith-based social service programs and set out to lend them academic credibility, with a study of church work in selected cities.[8] National magazines, such as *Newsweek* and *The New Yorker,* heralded the service work of religious groups and the special power of religious faith in inspiring poor people and drug abusers.[9]

Supported by unquestioned assumptions about the value of faith-based services, the channeling of government funds to churches was not hampered by concern about the entanglement of church and state: by the 1990s, conventional wisdom held that secular government was a government of insufficient virtue. Indeed, the biases that underlay reflexive support for faith-based drug treatment or welfare programs engendered general mistrust of a faith-free government. Secularism itself was beginning to be confused with atheism, despite the fact that many secularists are deeply religious and aim to protect religion from the state.

Why are some right-wing Christians today willing to trust the state with religion? Perhaps they don't fear officially established religion because they have no recent history of severe religious persecution; unlike Roger Williams and other colonialists, they haven't witnessed or experienced state-sponsored crusades against dissident Protestants. But they do feel besieged by cultural change; they despair over the relative normalization of abortion and homosexuality, and the recognition by federal courts that individual liberty sometimes prevails over sectarian moral codes. In their view, the state is ruled by an immoral culture, so some attack the basic notion of state sovereignty.

In the ideal world, Christianity would be sovereign, according to crusaders like former Nixon aide Charles Colson (now president of the Prison Fellowship). Christians might be morally bound to revolt against our supposedly godless state (exemplified by the federal courts), Colson wrote, in a controversial 1996 issue of the journal *First Things*. "Only the Church collectively can decide at what point a government becomes sufficiently corrupt that a believer must resist it. But with fear and trembling, I have begun to believe that . . . we are fast approaching this point."[10] Right-wing evangelicals don't have to trust the state with religion, if their apparent aim is a system in which a sovereign religion is trusted with the state.

It's not likely that they will succeed in establishing a theocracy, comparable, say, to the theocratic states in the Middle East. There is too much religious diversity in America and too much democracy to give a would-be ayatollah much hope. But new "partnerships" have formed between church and state, involving the diversion of public funds and delegation of public authority to religious groups. If faith is an inappropriate guide to empirical questions of law and policy, then some of these partnerships are, at least, indirect attacks on reason.

Changing constitutional notions of alliances between church and state were evident by the early 1990s. While the *Wall Street Journal* editorial writers were bemoaning the hostility of judicial elites toward religion, the Supreme Court issued a remarkable decision requiring state support for private religious activities. In *Rosenberger v. University of Virginia*, decided in 1995, the Court held that private religious groups are entitled to direct public funding.[11]

Rosenberger involved a Christian student newspaper at the University of Virginia that was denied funding provided to other student groups precisely because of its religiosity. A state-run institution, the university is subject to the First Amendment strictures imposed on any governmental entity. Reflecting obvious concern about state entanglement in the exercise of religion, the school's funding guidelines prohibited the distribution of student activities funds to religious groups. The guidelines did not discriminate against any particular religion or viewpoint; funds were withheld from any group that "primarily promotes or manifests a particular belief in or about a deity or an ultimate reality."

Arguing that the University of Virginia had an obligation to pay for the publication of this paper, as it paid for other student activities, editors of the newspaper *Wide Awake* sued the school and ultimately prevailed in the Supreme Court, which, like other "elitist" institutions, has become more protective of religion than concerned about its establishment by the state. In a five-to-four decision, authored by Justice Kennedy, the Court held that the denial of funding to *Wide Awake* constituted "viewpoint discrimination." Religion was not "excluded as a subject matter" from fundable student discussions, the Court observed; instead, the university's funding guidelines wrongly excluded discussions of secular issues shaped by "religious editorial viewpoints."

That sounds almost reasonable until you consider the nature of the discussions at issue. As the dissent in *Rosenberger* stressed, *Wide Awake* was an evangelical paper; aimed not at airing ideas about religion, or even religious ideas, its mission was persuading readers to repent and enter into a personal relationship with Christ, reminding them of the alternative—eternal damnation. The paper engaged in pure proselytizing, not a discussion of ideas from a religious perspective; as the dissent observed, "even featured essays on facially secular topics become platforms on which to call readers to fulfill the tenets of Christianity in their lives."

The dissent quoted from *Wide Awake* extensively: A discussion of eating disorders progresses from descriptions of anorexia to a declaration that " 'Christ is the Bread of life' (John 6:35). Through Him, we are full. He alone can provide the ultimate source of spiritual fulfillment . . ." The paper's masthead repeated Saint Paul's warning to "awake from your slumber, because our salvation is nearer now than when we first believed." The paper's mission was not to inform but to cleanse and convert: "The only way to salvation through Him is by confessing and repenting of sin . . . When you get to the final gate, the Lord will be handing out boarding passes, and He will examine your ticket. If, in your lifetime, you did not request a seat on His Friendly Skies Flyer by trusting Him and asking Him to be your pilot, then you will not be on his list of reserved seats . . . You will be met by your chosen pilot and flown straight to Hell, on an express jet (without air conditioning or toilets, of course.)"

It would be tempting to deny state support for publication of this paper on the basis of its puerility. Conservatives who lament the decline of educational standards would surely sympathize with the notion that bad writing should not be rewarded. They would hardly advocate the extension of state entitlement programs to student journals that do not meet standards of "excellence." But when conservative critics of academia complain about a disregard for excellence, logic, and critical thinking skills, they are generally complaining about affirmative action and other efforts to diversify student populations and curricula, for which some like to blame the general decline of Western civilization. Many who would quickly pass judgment on a naive, ungrammatical student essay extolling multiculturalism, would hesitate to dismiss religious proselytizing as clumsy, childish, or utterly irrational.

Sometimes it does seem unfortunate that the First Amendment must be unconcerned with excellence; it extends to unreasonable, unskilled writers and to the most infantile fantasies—about sex or Judgment Day, or the healing power of crystals. In a free society, religious proselytizing enjoys the same constitutional protection as pornography. So *Wide Awake* does not have to merit state funding in order to enjoy it, if funds are distributed to other student activities.

But if preachers have the same rights of access to public streets, classrooms, and other civic forums as pornographers and atheists, they are constitutionally disabled in the competition for direct financial support from the state. The First Amendment's prohibition on establishing religion was partly intended to prevent the levying of taxes to support religious activities, which had become common practice in the Colonies. The student activities funds at issue in *Rosenberger* derived from mandatory student fees that were arguably the functional equivalent of taxes. As the dissent in *Rosenberger* noted, this was the first case upholding (indeed mandating) direct state funding of religious proselytizing.

The majority rationalized this decision by minimizing the evangelicalism of *Wide Awake* and exaggerating its discussion of secular issues. *Wide Awake* is simply a "journal of opinion" distinguishable from "newspapers and magazines anywhere" only in "editorial viewpoint," counsel to Rosenberger argued successfully before the Supreme Court. Counsel's comparison of Christianity to other "secular philosophies, ideologies, and worldviews," adopted by the Court, was crucial to Rosenberger's case.[12] It reduces religion to a mere "viewpoint," which effectively eviscerates the Establishment Clause. Viewpoints are not encumbered by any strictures on state sponsorship.

It is one of the ironies of the church/state debate that this equation of Christianity (and other sects) with worldly ideologies, such as Marxism, supply-side economics, theories of white supremacy, agnosticism, or feminism, has been championed by the religious right. People inclined to worship, who believe that their sect offers access to heaven, are the last people you'd expect to argue that there's nothing special about religion, that it's just another product vying for shelf space in the marketplace, entitled to the same treatment as its competitors. You wouldn't expect critics of secularism to suggest that devout Christians are just additional claimants of individual rights: religion is more often extolled by virtuecrats as an antidote to untrammeled individualism. But, in the 1990s, a new network of Christian advocacy groups (active in the Rosenberger case), modeled after advocacy groups on the left, began portraying practicing

Christians as citizens oppressed by secularism and seeking judicial protection. The American Center for Law and Justice (ACLJ) founded by Pat Robertson was one of the leaders in this movement, borrowing not just most of the acronym but the tactics of the American Civil Liberties Union in a fight for religious "rights."

It is unlikely that the paeans to free speech offered in defense of religion by groups including the Christian Life Commission, Southern Baptist Convention, and National Association of Evangelicals will ever be offered by these groups in defense of pornography, although it surely provides an alternative "viewpoint" on human behavior. (Some feminists argue it provides an ideology.) Not even the notion that religion is merely a "point of view" is promoted consistently: religious proselytizers may feel entitled to receive their share of tax revenues, but, in their organizational capacities, they don't seem to feel obliged to pay them. Critics of the wall between church and state have yet to protest tax exemptions for religious institutions. Churches enjoy tax exemptions partly because, unlike partisan political activities, religions are not simply alternative points of view. They offer all-encompassing, institutionalized belief systems that shape the viewpoints of most Americans. Aligned with the state, religious denominations generally abuse political power, as politicians exploit religious belief.

A godly legislature is a fearful thing. In 1996 the Tennessee state senate passed a bill exhorting people to obey the Ten Commandments and post them at home, in the workplace, in schools, and places of worship, whether or not they partook of the Judaeo-Christian tradition. (The legislators rejected an amendment exempting Hindu, Muslim, and Buddhist houses of worship.) Creationism is also popular among legislators in Tennessee (and elsewhere, particularly in the south.) Seventy years after John Scopes was convicted for violating Tennessee law prohibiting the teaching of evolution, a senate committee on education in the Tennessee legislature passed a bill providing for the dismissal of teachers who describe evolution as fact rather than theory.[13] Across the country, high school science teachers reportedly avoid the subject of evolution, to avoid confrontation with fundamentalist religious groups.[14]

It's worth noting that the fundamentalist attack on evolution relies on the description of religion as "viewpoint" that was central to the *Rosenberger* case. Science is being reduced to a mere viewpoint as well. Evolution is just a "theory," or point of view, champions of creationism assert; they demand equal time for the teaching of "creation science," which is described as an alternative theory, or viewpoint, about the origin of the universe. "If evolution is true, then it has nothing to fear from some other theory being taught," one Tennessee state senator declared, using liberal faith in the open marketplace of ideas to rationalize the teaching of creationism.[15]

So far, the Supreme Court has rejected this view of creationism as an alternative scientific theory. A 1987 case, *Edwards v. Aguillard,* struck down a Louisiana law mandating the teaching of "creation science," describing it as an attempt to inject religion into public schools curriculum.[16] Religious fundamentalists who characterize creationism as a point of view may find some comfort in the Court's more recent holding in *Rosenberger* that religious proselytizing merely expresses a religious viewpoint. But there is a clear difference between injecting sectarianism into a student newspaper, even one supported by public funds, and injecting sectarianism into public school classrooms.

Besides, even conservative and centrist intellectual elites hostile to secularism who champion religion's role in public life generally oppose the teaching of "creation science," although they are likely to ground their opposition in creationism's dubious scientific credibility, not its religiosity. In *The Culture of Disbelief,* Stephen Carter writes that public schools should not teach the biblical account of creation because it is wrong. Like the belief that the earth is flat, or the moon is made of cheese, it is "bad science." That laws challenging the teaching of evolution are "religiously motivated" is irrelevant to Carter; the religious underpinnings of laws prohibiting murder does not invalidate them, he observes.

But religiously motivated laws prohibiting consensual homosexual relations or the sale of alcoholic beverages on Sunday could be considered unconstitutional because they are primarily intended to enforce sectarian notions of bad behavior. It's just that sectarianism is generally overlooked when it reflects majoritarian biases: a law prohibiting the sale of bread during Passover would arouse considerable outrage, unlike laws banning Sunday liquor sales, which have long been tolerated. There were no public objections when President Clinton paid homage to Jesus in a speech commemorating the first anniversary of the Oklahoma City bombing; what if he had referred to Mohammed instead?

Stephen Carter is right to suggest that legislation is often based in religion (which makes you wonder why he complains about secularism). You'd be hard pressed to find a period in American history when majoritarian religious beliefs did not influence law and custom. From the nineteenth century through the twentieth, anti-vice campaigns—against alcohol, pornography, and extramarital or premarital sex—have been overtly religious, fueled by sectarian notions of sin. Domestic relations laws long reflected particular religious ideas about gender roles (which some believe are divinely ordained). But, religion's impact on law is usually recognized and deemed problematic only in cases involving minority religious views: Christian ideas about marriage are incorporated into law, while the Mormon practice of polygamy is prohibited.

The Bible's account of creation may be embraced by nearly half of all Americans, but creationism is not simply a religious doctrine. Like the belief that recreational sex is sinful, it is a sectarian one. People of various faiths share various scientific, religious, and ethical beliefs—that the earth is round and God exists and murder is immoral; but they differ in their beliefs about the origins of the universe. Teaching creationism in the public schools is wrong, not only because it is like describing the moon as a wheel of green cheese but because it is like declaring that Christ was the son of God.

It is practically impossible to inject religion into the public sphere without injecting sectarianism. We don't, after all, simply teach science in the public schools; we teach chemistry, biology, physics, botany, geology, or astronomy. Teaching entails making choices between competing mediums and ideologies. Do we focus an art course on Renaissance painting, Abstract Expressionism, or postmodern sculpture? Do we require students to read the works of Charlotte Brontë, Hemingway, Homer, James Baldwin, Zora Neale Hurston, or Colette? Do we teach them about the Civil War from the perspective of a Klansman or a former slave? However wide-ranging our canon, it will always offend someone because of what it omits, or includes. What should we teach public school students about God? Believers can't even agree on His or Her gender.

Considering the fanciful nature of creationism, or hysteria about "secular humanist" teachings in general, you have to wonder how reason might fare in a system of sectarian schools. In the late 1990s, the evangelical American Family Association (AFA), led by the Reverend Donald Wildmon, challenged an Oregon law that required public school students to pass annual competency tests in order to be promoted. AFA claimed that the law promoted homosexuality, environmentalism, and moral relativism. (A federal appeals court unanimously upheld the law in 1998.)[17] Many religious schools offer rigorous academic instruction, of course, but some may follow Wildmon's lead: faith will trump knowledge, rationalism, and a system of free inquiry. That is one overlooked danger of voucher systems that will shift tax dollars to private religious schools.

The irony is that many people who support vouchers are much less interested in spreading religious teachings than improving the quality of secular education. General disenchantment with overcrowded, underfunded, poorly maintained public schools (and scapegoated, unionized public school teachers), and presumptions about the virtues of religious education helped create broad support for voucher programs.

Core support for them, however, was generated partly by theocratic right-wing Christians who had limited success introducing sectarianism into public schools. Members and supporters of the Christian Coalition did gain seats on local school boards and fought for control of school curriculum. But they encountered significant local opposition. (The Lee County, Florida, school board was bitterly divided for several years over attempts to introduce a fundamentalist Bible class in the public schools.)[18] The difficulties of delivering religious instruction in public schools intensified the campaign for vouchers that would divert public money to religious schools.

But, predictably, conservative advocates of school vouchers have not generally argued that vouchers would help transform us into a more godly, Christian nation; instead they seized upon the rhetoric of choice and equality: lower income parents should be ennabled to choose good private schools for their kids, just like upper income parents, they asserted. The troubled public schools provide dramatically unequal educations compared to the nation's private schools; inequality of education fosters continuing inequality in income and social status.

To liberals, this was hardly a revelation. They had long argued that in a capitalist society, your choices depend upon your income. Of course, poor people can't choose the same schools as rich people; nor can they choose the same health care, housing, groceries, transportation systems, or police protection. That's partly why Franklin Roosevelt once proposed an economic Bill of Rights.

But the liberal response to social inequality was not privatization, as envisioned by school vouchers—the diversion of government funds to private institutions that would serve limited numbers of poor people. The liberal response to inequality was the creation of free public institutions, accessible to all. In an ideal or merely good world, public schools promised to be equal or at least similar in quality to private schools; and for generations, that was a promise partly fulfilled. Public schools did not serve all American children equally well, as the Supreme Court observed in 1954: segregated schools were failing African-Americans.

During the 1990s, the notorious inadequacies of only nominally integrated public school systems, particularly those serving low-income racial minorities, infused the campaign for vouchers with appeals for racial equality. In a 1997 op-ed piece in the *Wall Street Journal*, Alveda King, niece of Martin Luther King, implied that her uncle would have been an advocate of vouchers.[19] Proponents of "school choice" programs are apt to claim the support of a majority of African-Americans: "86% of African-Americans between the ages of 26 and 35" and "70% of low-income African-Americans" endorse vouchers, Democratic Senators Mary Landrieu and Joe Lieberman alleged, lobbying their colleagues for support of a voucher bill for the District of Columbia.[20]

It was difficult for white liberal defenders of public schools to oppose demands for vouchers couched as a campaign for civil rights, although claims of strong majority support for vouchers were questionable: A 1997 *Wall Street Journal* poll found that a majority of all Americans opposed "tax-funded vouchers or tax deductions for parents who send their child to private schools" and that African-Americans opposed these "school choice" programs "by a decidedly larger majority than the rest of the population."[21] In any case, vouchers don't give parents nearly as much choice as politicians promise. A scholarship of a few thousand dollars will not cover the yearly costs of many private schools. Many students whose parents can make the tuition payments will not be admitted to the schools of their choice. Private schools are selective, and they may reject or expel the most troubled kids who need the most help. It's not surprising that private schools appear to foster achievement in kids; they can choose not to deal with failure.

Vouchers promise to worsen educational opportunities for the millions of children left behind in public schools. (There is virtually no possibility that vouchers will create an alternative private system, open and acessible to everyone.) Public schools, which are apt to become repositories for the most troubled kids, will be drained of funds by voucher programs. The cost of vouchers to the public schools is not simply the face amount of the voucher. Public school systems generally lose money allocated directly to them when they lose students. According to the

New York Times, public schools in Milwaukee faced a potential loss of $70 million a year, pursuant to a voucher program approved in 1998 by the Wisconsin Supreme Court (which the U.S. Supreme Court declined to review).[22]

Vouchers seemed destined and maybe designed to harm the public schools. Advocates for vouchers claimed they would actually improve the schools by providing them with competition, but their capacity to compete would hardly be enhanced by the loss of funding. People for the American Way has connected the conservative drive for vouchers with efforts to censor secular humanist materials in public schools and reestablish official school prayer. If this is an accurate description of the voucher movement, it could fairly be said to promise the elevation of faith over reason in the schools.

The sincerity of some conservative appeals to equality of education were, indeed, suspect. Conservatives may have protested the absence of educational choices for the poor, but many remained considerably less sympathetic to all the other restrictions on choice caused by poverty. Indeed, voucher advocates don't generally stress the need to limit tuition assistance to poor families, and large-scale voucher programs are unlikely to be means-tested, if they are to enjoy popular support. They're likely to benefit the middle class. Vouchers seem poised to promote religion, and privatize public services, not correct social inequality.

Vouchers will not significantly expand civil rights—access to equal education and all that it promises, but they will restrict civil liberties. It's true that the government already provides some indirect funding to church-affiliated colleges and universities, through grants and loans to individual students. Vouchers could offer similar aid to students K through 12. But federal loans to college students do not represent a massive drain of resources from essential public education systems. Nor do they involve sectarian efforts to indoctrinate children. By directing government funds to parochial schools, vouchers will entangle government in sectarianism, forcing taxpayers to support religious ideas and practices—and religious bigotry—that are anathema to them.

Religious conservatives often counter that public school curricula violate their religious beliefs. If they are forced to support public schools engaged in teaching "blasphemy," why shouldn't everyone else support parochial schools? You may not share the Christian right's notions of godliness, but if you believe in the free exercise of religion, you have to sympathize with their concerns. Still, there's an important difference between government support of religious proselytizing, the inevitable result of vouchers, and government support of secular teachings that some religious people reject. Indeed, religious conservatives implicitly recognize this when they nonsensically brand secular humanism a religion, just so that they may argue that the First Amendment prohibits government from promoting it in public schools.

But if the rationalism implicit in "secular humanism" will be threatened by a large-scale voucher system, so will the integrity of religious teachings. Financial assistance to religious schools may seem to some believers a sign of respect, but government subsidies will compromise the independence and occasional iconoclasm of religion. If religious schools are being partly supported by public funds, the public will eventually demand some control of school policy and curricula. Conservatives who blame government bureaucrats for the decline of the public schools might think twice about expanding their power over private schools and the teaching of religion. Or, supporters of vouchers may learn the hard way that separation of church and state is essential to church autonomy and religious freedom.

Consider complaints about government-subsidized arts.

Opponents of the National Endowment for the Arts (NEA) have long insisted that public money should not be used to support art that many members of the public find offensive. The sense that government arts programs were unduly coercive and violated the taxpayers' freedom of conscience was captured in the battle over NEA support of performance artist Karen Finley, whose work was labeled "indecent" by the religious right. Imagine the outcry if vouchers are used to support schools established by the Nation of Islam, much less the Church of Scientology.

If voucher programs are widely enacted, sectarianism may defeat them in the end, especially if government money is used to support religious schools outside the mainstream. But, so far, appeals to a tradition of separationism have not been effective in combating the drive for vouchers, and the Supreme Court has upheld the diversion of public funds to religious schools. In a 1997 decision, *Agostini v. Felton,* the Court held that public school teachers may conduct remedial classes in parochial schools.[23] The Court stressed that its decision in *Agostini* did not condone direct, public support of religion: it upheld the disbursement of federal funds to public agencies that provide teachers for all needy students, including those in religious schools. But, as Justice Souter pointed out in his dissent, the Court's ruling allows public school teachers to teach such basic subjects as reading and mathematics in religious schools. This surely constitutes direct, in-kind support for religious education. Approaching the millennium, religious schools and social service programs are developing an unprecedented entitlement to public support.

Many Americans expect religious institutions to focus on both social and spiritual welfare, and they have long obliged, sometimes with the aid of public funds. Traditionally, however, government grants disbursed to religious groups were supposed to be administered in nonsectarian settings, for nonsectarian purposes. Charitable agencies and institutions with religious affiliations received public money, but they were generally governed by independent boards. The state was not supposed to offer direct funding to churches or "pervasively sectarian" institutions.

At times, the rule against government support of sectarianism was observed only rhetorically. In 1988, in *Bowen v. Kendrick,* the Supreme Court upheld a federal law, the Adolescent Family Life Act (AFLA), that provided funding to religious organizations engaged in efforts to keep teenagers chaste, a law that resulted in state support of sectarian education and counseling.[24] As the dissent in *Kendrick* stressed, programs supported by public funds under AFLA included those in which parents and teenagers were taught Catholic doctrine on extramarital sex and birth control. The dissent accused the Court of ignoring lower court findings that the AFLA was, in fact, being used for sectarian purposes by many sectarian programs. But, this was a debate about the facts: the majority in *Kendrick* at least affirmed the principle that government should not fund pervasively sectarian institutions.

Now, under the Charitable Choice provisions of the 1996 welfare reform package, that principle is history. Charitable Choice expressly allows public funding of sectarian institutions: religious organizations do not have to change their "religious character" to qualify for funding, which means the states may disperse federal grants to local congregations for social service programs. Federally funded services now may be delivered directly by a house of worship and within one. Religious service providers have a statutory right to display scriptures, icons, and other sectarian symbols as they serve diverse groups of welfare recipients. Technically, a church, synagogue, or mosque is prohibited from using federal money to proselytize, but this prohibition may be unenforceable. First Amendment guarantees of religious freedom bar states from policing internal church preachings. Technically, welfare recipients have a right to request alternative service providers, but nothing in the law requires that they be notified of their rights—or ensures that they will feel free to assert them.

Social service workers may also lose their religious freedom—or their jobs. The Charitable Choice provisions exempt religious organizations dispensing federal funds from federal antidiscrimination law. In other words, churches serving as welfare providers can fire people for heresy, even if they're essentially on a federal payroll.

Of course, some churches will respect the religious beliefs of the people they hire and serve. Soon after passage of the Charitable Choice bill, the Presbyterian Church issued guidelines for administering federally funded programs, which included a commitment not to proselytize or even subject "staff or clientele" to "sectarian regulations."[25] The guidelines also stressed the dangers to churches of accepting federal aid:

> Government regulation will unavoidably follow government dollars . . . the law requires government audits, oversight of funding of religious activity . . . Therefore, if religious programs are funded, the government will inevitably become entangled in the affairs of otherwise autonomous religious groups, thereby jeopardizing their religious liberty.

The Presbyterian Church originally opposed Charitable Choice, as did the Baptist Joint Committee on Public Affairs, the American Baptist Churches, USA, the United Methodist Church, the Union of American Hebrew Congregations, and the Unitarian Universalist Association. The new welfare bill subtly threatened church autonomy, focused churches on providing material instead of spiritual sustenance, and suggested that the government might be eager to abdicate responsibility for providing social services. Conservative commentator Glenn Loury observed that "as a Christian," he was "troubled by the thought of churches becoming vehicles for funneling billions of dollars into the hands of needy people. Churches should, first and foremost, be about spirituality." [26] A Presbyterian newsletter asked: "Should a state turn its welfare programs over to the religious community. What about the responsibility of government for the social needs of its citizens?" [27]

Questions like this, however, were drowned out by hosannas, as advocates of Charitable Choice called upon the power of faith to provide welfare recipients with spiritual healing, which almost everyone, left and right, assumed that they needed. And by 1999, some three years after religious groups were effectively hired by the government to administer welfare programs, Congress was considering enacting additional Charitable Choice laws, providing additional tax dollars to sectarian institutions involved in delivering a range of social services, like programs for juveniles and seniors. Of course Charitable Choice has been politically popular. It is easier to believe that God is in heaven and all's right with the world than it is to imagine an irreverent politician questioning whether there is a God in heaven or any benefit to prayer.

It's hardly surprising that religion has been touted as the antidote to drug use, crime, or teenage pregnancy. The 12-step movement, started by Alcoholics Anonymous, popularized the notion that substance abuse and other antisocial "codependent" behaviors represented the absence of God: addicts and other practicing codependents were told to surrender to God's will (by embracing their Higher Powers) in order to recover. Religious explanations for the problem of substance abuse, in particular, were common by the 1990s, so religious solutions were inevitable.

Yet evidence of religion's particular utility in treating or preventing social ills is anecdotal and often misleading. The religiously oriented Alcoholics Anonymous, for example, is generally considered the most successful treatment program for alcohol abuse and a model for the faith-based approach, but AA cannot count its failures. How do you track its anonymous and always changing membership? How do you count the people who quit after one meeting because they don't believe in God or any other "Higher Power"?

It is also quite difficult to isolate religion's alleged healing effect. Religious leaders who run successful neighborhood programs, delivering faith-based services, cannot measure how much of their success depends upon religious proselytizing and how much it reflects their active and devoted membership in the communities they are trying to save. You don't have to be religious to minister to people's needs; only conventional wisdom suggests that you have to be religious to succeed.

While belief in God is commonly presumed to inculcate virtue in everyone, welfare recipients and billionaires alike, evidence of religion's auspicious effect on character is scarce. I don't think anyone has ever demonstrated that religious people commit fewer crimes, or sins, than agnostics or atheists, and I'm unaware of any evidence that nonbelievers are disproportionately represented in the nation's prisons. These days, to prove religion's ameliorative effect on crime, believers are apt to cite the number of people who have allegedly defeated their addictions by finding God. But they might also consider some obvious examples of religious offenders: David Koresh and mainstream clergy who've engaged in child abuse, terrorists motivated by religious fervor, and a host of church-going, white-collar criminals.

Still, relatively few people question that religion is good for you—mainstream religion, that is; fringe groups and those all-encompassing religious communities labeled cults are acceptable targets for humor, or dismay—not candidates for federal funds. When *Wall Street Journal* editorial writers exalt faith-based social services, they're not suggesting that we teach troubled teenagers channeling or encourage them to don saffron-colored robes and chant. They're advocating government support of only a few established religious institutions—churches, synagogues, and maybe mosques, or maybe not. While former senator Bob Dole endorsed the Charitable Choice provision establishing churches as welfare providers, exempting them from federal employment discrimination laws, and expressly allowing them to dispense federal aid in sectarian environments, he also excoriated the Clinton administration for hiring the Nation of Islam to police public housing projects. As Jeffrey Rosen noted in *The New Republic*, Dole expressed concern about the Nation of Islam's discriminatory hiring practices and the likelihood of federal funds being used to support religious proselytizing.[28]

Senator Dole's momentary conversion to separationism when confronted with federal support for a radical, minority religion he disdained revealed the majoritarian impulses behind campaigns for faith-based social services and other church/state alliances. Although right-wing Christians have begun presenting themselves as a beleaguered minority in competitions for government support, their demands for state-sanctioned religious practices are often demands for majority rule—reflected in familiar attacks on the Supreme Court's occasional defense of minority rights.

Congress should pass legislation allowing the states to post the Ten Commandments on government property, effectively overturning a 1980 Supreme Court decision keeping the Ten Commandments out of public schools, Dennis Teti argued in a 1997 article in the *Weekly Standard*. There is "a consensus across religious faiths that the Commandments should be publicly respected as the foundation for our constitutional principles," Teti declared, overlooking the constitutional principles that shield individual religious preferences from popular "consensus."[29] And beliefs that are shared "across religious faiths" may be anathema for nonbelievers. Religious freedom is not simply the freedom to worship as you choose; it includes as well the freedom not to worship—a freedom that should surely extend to welfare recipients and patients in federally funded drug treatment programs.

The context for faith-based social services is a campaign to align public policies with majoritarian religious practices and ideals. Consider the outcry against *Romer v. Evans*, the 1995 Supreme Court decision striking down an amendment to the Colorado constitution that would have prohibited the state from protecting homosexuals from discrimination.[30] Like the Court's school prayer decisions, *Romer* was condemned for overruling a majority vote denying equal rights to homosexuals, whose behavior many considered sinful. (*Romer* also fueled demands for a Christian revolt against our godless regime.)

Missing in frequent protests of the Supreme Court's "arrogance" in thwarting the majority's will is any recognition of the fact that the Bill of Rights is intended to protect minorities, even, or especially, when majority rule is based in religious belief. Thirty years ago, when the Civil Rights Act was passed prohibiting race discrimination in public accommodations, it challenged religious beliefs about the sinfulness of integration. For some, white supremacy was considered divinely ordained. As recently as 1977, a Florida school run by the New Testament Baptist Church refused to admit two African-American children, claiming that the tenets of its faith required it to maintain racially discriminatory admission policies. (A federal court found that the school's policy of "non-integration" was a "social policy," not protected by the First Amendment, and mandated the admission of two black children whom the school had turned away.)[31] Not long ago, many believed that male supremacy was a divine right and obligation—a belief that the Promise Keepers has been fighting to revitalize.

It's important to stress, however, that current demands for religiosity in government cannot simply be attributed to the religious right. Left-of-center communitarians share much of the credit or blame for prevailing critiques of secularism and celebrations of majority rule. Communitarians have lauded religious institutions as paradigms of community and sources of civic virtue; they have associated assertions of individual rights with selfishness and anomie; they have given majoritarianism new respectability by calling it a renewal of community. Of course, liberalism has long stood for restraining the market behavior of individuals to promote a greater social good, but it has fought government attempts to control private behavior. Communitarianism extended the liberal critique of individualism in the economic sphere to the sphere of personal relations and civil liberties. It romanticized religious belief and the spiritual power of communities, injecting the left with hostility to existential demands for individual autonomy.

Still, the formation of church/state partnerships would be a

Pyrrhic victory for communitarians who are not generally mistrustful of government. Faith-based social service programs, vouchers directing public funds to parochial schools (opposed by the Clinton administration), and programs assigning public school teachers to parochial schools to conduct classes in basic subjects like reading and math are giant steps toward privatization. "Why not close down the public schools and leave schooling to as many qualified groups as wish to undertake the challenge and provide good quality education," Bishop William F. Murphy asked in 1997.[32]

Religious institutions, after all, don't generally seek partnerships with the state, which would hold them accountable to bureaucrats; they seek access to state funds and control over policy. Their proposed takeover of welfare programs, drug treatment programs, and schools will help justify the government's abandonment of social services and redistribute public funds to private sectarian institutions. It's no coincidence that support for these programs began to flourish at a time of widespread disdain for the federal government, when President Clinton was acting like mayor of the United States, focusing on questionable federal concerns, like school uniforms.

In this climate, appeals to the Founders' ideals of separating church and state and reminders of the threat to minority rights posed by state-established religions will do little to counter anecdotes about recovering addicts who find God or born-again welfare recipients who find the will to work, as well as jobs. If the principles restraining majoritarianism fail us, however, sectarian rivalries may restrain the formation of majorities.

In our increasingly diverse nation, Muslims now outnumber Episcopalians. The vitality of New Age movements has kept interest in Eastern religions alive. The religious majority is no longer entirely secure. In 1998, a new right-wing religious group in Arkanasas, Put God Back in Public School, demanded that the state establish special Christian public schools, but refrained from demanding prayer in all state-supported schools. Apparently God advised the group's founder, Kathy Smith, that Christian prayers might not prevail: "I asked God, 'Do you want me to change the law to put prayer in the schools?' " Smith reported. "He said no. If you do that, kids would have the right to pray to other gods too. They could pray to Buddha. God doesn't want that. There's only one God."[33]

Will right-wing Christians fight to give Muslims the power to conduct prayers in public schools or administer government funds? Will Muslims, Orthodox Jews, or Hindus join Southern Baptists in a fight to post the Ten Commandments in the nation's courts? Historically, religious minorities in America have supported separation of church and state, recognizing in it a grant of religious freedom. But if the majority seems more ecumenical than Kathy Smith, and if minorities begin to feel more threatened by secularism than a theocracy in which a majority rules, with the promise of benevolence toward all believers (and a share of government funds), then First Amendment strictures against establishing religion may fall. We can hope that sectarianism emerges early, to prevent church/state alliances, but it may emerge with a vengeance, too late.

Religion may be a civilizing, moralizing force, but sectarianism is rather vicious. In Alabama, in the late 1990s, state officials advocating the introduction of Christianity into the public schools and courts demonstrated a disrespect for individual, constitutional rights reminiscent of diehard segregationists of the 1950s and 1960s. In the fall of 1997, then governor Fob

James promised to resist a federal court order prohibiting organized, officially sponsored religious activities in the DeKalb County public schools. The court order, issued in *Chandler v. James*, permanently enjoined enforcement of a 1993 Alabama law permitting organized, student-led, "voluntary" prayers at school events.[34] Alabama ACLU attorney Pamela Sumners observed that in defying federal court orders, Governor James "whipped up" religious bigotry the way George Wallace once whipped people into a frenzy over race.

The governor's promised resistance was mostly rhetorical, but it was not without power. He had last been heard threatening to call out the National Guard to protect the prerogative of state court judge Roy Moore to hang a copy of the Ten Commandments in the courtroom, in defiance of the First Amendment and the federal courts. Judge Moore declared the federal court order on prayer in school "an unconstitutional abuse of power," and refused to recognize it as the law in his county. High school students, no doubt emboldened by these pronouncements, protested the court order, marching on City Hall, walking out of class and leaving the stands at football games to pray: "Having Jesus in our school is something that we need. It gives us strength," one student explained.[35]

Advocates of organized school prayer might laud this uprising as a demand for religious freedom, defending the "right" of students to pray. But what was at stake in Alabama was the right not to pray to Jesus, or be subjected to religious indoctrination. The facts of the case that led to the federal injunction on organized prayer in school tell a very different story than the posturings of Alabama officials.

Chandler v. James involved a challenge to the virtual establishment of Christianity in the DeKalb County schools. The case was brought by parents of public school students (including the assistant principal at one school), who protested sectarian prayer and Bible readings organized by school administrators and clergy, conducted in classrooms, at athletic events, and during commencement exercises. Prayer was not voluntary: one teacher required students to pray out loud in class. Students who chose not to pray were forced to appoint surrogate worshipers. Christian devotionals were routinely delivered at school assemblies and other activities during which students were held captive. Gideon Bibles were distributed in school, even in the classroom.

All these practices were clearly unconstitutional and violated numerous federal court decisions, but Alabama does have a history of defying federal law protecting civil rights and liberties. The Chandler decision seemed unlikely to end religious persecution in the Alabama public schools. It clarified no constitutional principles that were not already clear and had not already been rejected by public officials. In fact, after an earlier, preliminary decision in the Chandler case struck down the state's student-led prayer statute, another similar lawsuit, *Herring v. Key*, was brought against the Pike County, Alabama, public schools.

The Herring case involved three Jewish children who had the misfortune to attend the Pike County public schools. They reported being tormented by school officials and classmates because they were Jewish, denied the right to practice their faith, and forced to participate in Christian religious observances. The children, Sarah Herring, Paul Michael Herring, and David Herring, were in the sixth, seventh, and ninth grades, respectively, at the time of the lawsuit, in 1997.

The complaint in the Herring case makes you wonder if Pike County is part of America or Iran. It alleged that: Christian prayers and devotionals were aired over the high school's public address system; the elementary school principal led prayers at assemblies and introduced preachers to captive student audiences; children were required to bow their heads in prayer during assemblies; sixth grader Sarah Herring was expressly ordered by her teacher to bow her head in a "student initiated" prayer (after the federal district court struck down the student-led prayer statute); and ninth grader David Herring was physically forced by a student teacher to bow his head in devotion to Jesus. The children were required to attend Christian sermons; Sarah Herring was once led crying and shaking from an assembly after being told by the preacher that all students who did not embrace Christ as their savior would burn in hell. Eighth grader Paul Herring was required by the vice principal of his school to write an essay on "Why Jesus Loves Me," as punishment for disrupting class. The school principal forbade Paul from wearing the Star of David to school, claiming it was a "gang symbol" (other children were free to wear crosses). School officials tolerated vicious anti-Semitic remarks directed at the children as well as physical assaults. Their possessions were defaced with swastikas, and they were given cartoons about the Holocaust.[36]

Their mother and stepfather, Sue and Wayne Willis, regularly protested the persecution of their kids, with very limited success. Mrs. Willis reported that the high school principal and an elementary school teacher both responded to her complaints "with words to the effect of 'If parents will not save souls, we have to.'"[37]

The Pike County schools had clearly violated the law, and this case was settled out of court, to the satisfaction of the Willis/Herring family. (The settlement did not include any financial compensation: Mrs. Willis says she did not seek money damages because she did not want to feed the biases of people who believe that Jews are naturally mercenary.)

It is tempting to dismiss cases like these as anomalies, but violations of First Amendment prohibitions on establishing religion in the schools are not uncommon, especially but not exclusively in the South. According to the *New York Times,* "Prayer has remained as common as pop quizzes in many [Alabama] schools."[38] In Mississippi, in 1994, a federal court intervened to protect Lutheran children from organized prayer and Bible readings in a predominantly Baptist public school district. (One child was branded a devil worshiper for not participating in sectarian Bible readings.)[39] In West Virginia, prayers were broadcast over the public address system before every home football game at Nitro High School, and everyone in the audience was expected to stand, with head bowed. "They say it's illegal, but we've always done it," Nitro athletic director Patrick Vance told the *Charlotte Gazette.* The *Gazette* also reported that during graduation ceremonies at Herbert Hoover High School in West Virginia, students recited the Lord's Prayer.[40]

Organized, officially endorsed sectarian religious activities in public school are indisputably illegal; but they persist, partly because relatively few people have the strength and courage to challenge them. Members of minority faiths who are most likely to object are also most at risk when they protest majoritarian religious practices. But anyone who publicly complains about illegal, school-sanctioned prayer or goes to court to stop it should expect to be ostracized, harassed, and threatened with physical injury or death, by God-fearing neighbors. After Joann Bell, a member of the Church of the Nazarene, challenged the constitutionality of organized prayer sessions in her child's public school, she was physically assaulted on school grounds by an angry cafeteria worker, and her home was firebombed. Lucille McCord, a member of the Church of Christ who joined in Bell's lawsuit, reported that her son's prize hog had its throat cut after the suit was filed. Both women reported that their children were harassed at school, and upside-down crosses were taped on their lockers. Bell and McCord won their lawsuit but felt compelled to move out of the district.[41]

This is the climate of religious intolerance in which social issue conservatives proposed a constitutional amendment in 1998 intended to legitimize organized group prayer in the nation's classrooms. The amendment, introduced by Oklahoma congressman Ernest Istook (and defeated), would have established a constitutional right to engage in sectarian religious practices on public property, including schools, and given religious groups an entitlement to government funds. The Istook amendment did state that "the Government shall not require any person to join in prayer or other religious activity, initiate or designate school prayers."[42] But the amendment would have authorized student-led prayers, which often involve the de facto endorsement of school officials and can be quite coercive. Anyone doubting the threat to the free exercise of religion posed by student prayers need only attend public school in Alabama.

"I don't want the government involved in the religious upbringing of my son," Michael Chandler, plaintiff in *Chandler v. James*, has explained. "The state has no business telling my child when, where, and how to pray." You'd expect conservatives mistrustful of government to sympathize with Chandler's concern. Instead supporters of a prayer amendment promulgate the dangerous fiction that religion has been exiled from the public schools and students have lost their rights to pray.[43]

In fact, students have the undisputed right to pray individually or in groups during their free time: they can say grace before lunch, drop to their knees on the football field, or pray silently in every class, and, no doubt, many do. Religious associations of students have the same rights as other student groups to meet on school property. In *Chandler v. James,* while the court enjoined organized, official prayer, it expressly affirmed the rights of students to express personal religious beliefs in their schoolwork or during graduation services, engage in religious activities during non-instructional time, announce meetings of extracurricular religious activities over the schools' public address system, or wear religious symbols.[44] The federal courts (and the Clinton administration) have generally made clear that students have the right to exercise their religion in school; what they lack is the power to impose their religion on others.

Religious power, not religious rights, is what supporters of a school prayer amendment seek. In the name of rights, they seek the kind of power that subjects the children of minority faiths to religious persecution in the nation's schools. At least today that persecution is illegal and can be remedied in federal court, when the families at risk persevere. A constitutional amendment permitting organized school prayer would leave every public school student at the mercy of the religious majority. Introduce organized religion in the schools and you introduce sectarianism; and that is a prescription for tribalism, not virtue.

■

POP SPIRITUALITY BOOKS AND
THE GOSPEL OF GOOD NEWS

Experts in personal and spiritual development are apt to consider sectarianism a sign of psychological or spiritual retardation, the New Age equivalent of sin. It doesn't send you to hell—there is none dreamt of in their philosophy—but it may consign you to an arduous and troubled series of lives on earth. Sectarianism divides people. New Agers are preoccupied with unity. Religion is "a force that either creatively or noncreatively separates us," according to Marianne Williamson. "Spirituality is a force that unites us by reminding us of our fundamental oneness." [1]

New Agers tend to mistrust institutionalized religion, regarding it not as a pathway but as an obstacle to enlightenment. It's too restrictive. For over a century, the "consciousness movement" has borrowed freely from Eastern and Western religious traditions, mysticism, spiritualism, occultism, and popular psychology. The notorious nineteenth-century spiritualist Madame Helena Blavatsky, who helped found the Theosophical Society, claimed to have spent seven years traveling in Tibet, acquiring the wisdom of the East, which she offered to an emerging middle class eager for spiritual alternatives. In his review of the rise and fall of theosophy, Peter Washington observed that Blavatsky based her cosmology on sporadic readings of Asian religious texts and the novels of Edward Bulwar-Lytton, which married Eastern religion and Western occultism, two perennial, primary sources of New Age.[2]

Considering the hybrid nature of their philosophies, it's not surprising that New Agers often affirm that there are many paths to God, or Whomever. New Age is ecumenical. We're not supposed to question each other's truths—although most gurus are quick to condemn any critic who questions their teachings. New Age has always been rife with spiritual leaders who expect and enjoy the reverence of consumers, but conventional New Age wisdom dismisses traditional religious institutions as authoritarian, and absolutist. Like nineteenth-century revivalists, who celebrated pietism, "the intuitive religion of the heart," New Agers seek individual relationships with whatever Higher Powers they imagine—direct relationships, unmediated by established churches. As Marianne Williamson clumsily explains, "The highest most spirit filled religious consciousness is a living water. The container through which that water is poured into the world is not the organization of a religion but the human heart."[3]

The personal development movement has long been imbued with a similar brand of ersatz populism. Consumers have been told that they can bypass the mental health establishment and heal themselves—if they follow the expert's advice. Pop psychologists have offered wholesale counseling, billed as self-help, for the mere price of a book or lecture ticket. Dispensing the same advice to what they hoped would be enormous numbers of anonymous readers, they popularized the belief that practically everyone is plagued by the same cutely named syndromes, complexes, and responses.

The personal development culture fostered self-centeredness but very little individuality or distinctions between classes. Intellectual, professional, and political elites were no healthier than the hoi polloi. Neurosis and its most recent incarnation, dysfunction, are great equalizers; and when the recovery movement took hold in the late 1980s, 12-step groups were lauded as peer groups that offered free therapy, unmediated by doctors. "You are all the experts on your own lives," best-selling authors of codependency books used to say, while delivering advice to adoring audiences and millions of readers they'd never met.

Neither the recovery movement nor the New Age consciousness movement to which it contributed have been antiauthoritarian or anarchic, or even nonhierarchal. They've revolved around gurus, from Blavatsky to Williamson and Deepak Chopra, and they have been effectively organized by mainstream, mass-market publishers, as well as a network of nascent, alternative institutions—holistic learning centers and lecture circuits. (At its peak, the recovery movement generated an estimated annual $60 million in book sales.)[4] Yet, at least rhetorically, everyone is accorded her own Higher Power; everyone has her own path to enlightenment, through her own series of lives.

Self-knowledge, rather than moral purity, is considered the engine of personal and spiritual growth. New Age and pop psychology movements are, therefore, naturally relativistic and partake of the postmodern celebration of subjectivism: All we know is what we perceive, and all that we perceive, or feel, deserves "validation." To followers of New Age, recovery, or postmodernism, asking "How do you feel," is often the equivalent of asking "What do you know," and either question may be considered a search for truth. In academia, where the pursuit of knowledge is supposed to be paramount, "holistic education" emerged as a nascent pedalogical fashion of the '90s. Prominent Duke English professor Jane Tompkins began delivering lectures on such subjects as "The Inner Life of Teachers and Students." Advocating a spiritualized approach to teaching that focuses on educating " 'the whole human being'—mind, body, and spirit," Tompkins could be an inspirational speaker on the pop spirituality circuit.[5]

The spectacle of supposedly progressive university professors embracing the hostility toward intellectualism characteristic of pop therapies and New Age is alternately amusing and discouraging. As an indicator of the democratization of culture, it's one argument for elitism. The therapeutic culture has been stupefying. Nurturing New Agers, recovering codependents, and many postmodernists alike, it has popularized the view that the primary obstacle to growth is not self-centeredness, or ignorance, but denial—a refusal to acknowledge what we feel. Questioning the accuracy of what others feel, or intuit, no matter how unreasonable or uninformed they seem, is "abusive."

The problem of ignorance (of science, history, politics, and other worldly realities) is rarely addressed in this spiritualized, therapeutic culture, which focuses instead on repression. Commonly lamented as a primary and very prevalent form of denial, repression is the equivalent of self-abuse: severing people from themselves, it also severs them from God. Thus, in the world of recovery, remembering (by exploring "feeling realities") displaced learning: remembering was the path to salvation. Indeed, borrowing from Freud (among other authorities), the recovery movement taught people to invest memory and the unconscious with godlike power: our visions or revisions of the past supposedly control us and covertly determine our behavior in the present. Retrieving a repressed memory is a religious experience. When you recover and confront your memory, you recover your essential self. You are, quite literally, born again.

Recovery represented the spiritualization of pop psychology. An offshoot of Alcoholics Anonymous, which was rooted in evangelism, the 12-step movement was always religious. The inner child of recovery books was a divine child, untainted by original sin or dysfunction. The ideology of recovery was the ideology of salvation by grace. Counseling surrender to a Higher Power, recovery experts labeled self-sufficiency a form of dysfunction (not unlike preachers who label it a sin). People were discouraged from attempting to overcome their addictions by sheer force of will, without the aid of a program, because addiction was considered a disease of the will. The cure was surrendering to a Higher Power—in other words, relinquishing your will and becoming imbued with the will of God. It was hardly surprising that religious publishers, notably Thomas Nelson, produced a line of codependency books by Christian therapists.

Christian codependency books offered readers the promise of a perfect parent—God (a loving, New Testament God, not the one who tortured Job). But they spoke only to people willing or able to embrace Jesus. Nonsectarian codependency books dominated the market, and reached a much broader range of spiritual seekers; but the comfort they offered was less than absolute. Best-selling celebrity experts might have played parental roles for many readers, but although exalted, they remained less than divine. For all their talk about Higher Powers, most codependency books did not deliver one clear and simple vision of a loving, omnipresent celestial being devoted to our welfare.

Codependency books did, however, illuminate the demand for simple, optimistic spirituality books and helped shape the market for them. The recovery movement addressed readers' preoccupations with guidance or misguidance from above, through vaguely apprehended higher powers or abusive parents—the supreme powers of childhood. Considering the unrelenting complaints about parenting that the movement unleashed, it might have been characterized as a search for kinder, gentler authority figures. Inevitably, publishers supplied them.

By the early 1990s, after nearly ten years of getting in touch with their inner children and recovering from abuse, millions of consumers of personal development had found the perfect parents: Guardian angels watch over each of us, best-selling books about angels proclaimed. Like Superman, they swoop down and save us from sudden death—lifting us out of the way of oncoming cars or catching us when we fall off cliffs. Like Mr. Chips, they nurture and inspire us: "We were given an angel to help us in the creation and writing of this book," the authors of *Ask Your Angels* confide, describing angels as the "social workers of the universe." They give us unsolicited, unconditional love.[6]

Angels are even better parents than the arbitrary, abusive Old Testament God, whom readers of codependency books might diagnose as dysfunctional. Indeed, some recent interpretations of Genesis have relied on modern notions of dysfunctional families. Just as pop psychology has been shaped by religious impulses and beliefs, religion sometimes incorporates therapeutic truths. Angels represent another intersection of religion and the therapeutic culture.

Descending from heaven, or wherever, unbound by the mere material world, angels provide even more than perfecting parenting; they offer proof of immortality, and the comforting belief that there is no death—only some sort of energy transformation—which is confirmed by popular magazines and best-selling spirituality books. By the mid-1990s, instead of stories about codependency, women's magazines, like *McCall's*, routinely published wide-eyed reports of encounters with angels and conversations with deceased relatives, as well as adventures in ESP.

If there were no fear of death, there might be no religion; there would surely be no reason for pop spirituality books. *The Celestine Prophecy* assures us that what we imagine as death is a happy transition to a higher spiritual plane: a new Eden awaits us in the next Millennium.[7] Books about near-death experiences (NDEs) describe the brief sojourns in heaven of people who died but were sent back to earth by God, or God's minions, to complete their missions or simply spread the Word—there is no death. Books about reincarnation assure us that we will live many lives before we achieve spiritual perfection and ascend in the end to—wherever. "(L)ife is endless so we never die; we were never really born. We just pass through different phases," the "Master Spirits" tell past lives therapist, Brian Weiss, author of *Many Lives, Many Masters*.[8] Spiritualized personal development books confirm that death is not an end but a renewal. "(D)eath is always in the process of incubating new life . . . Lady Death represents an essential creation pattern," Clarissa Pinkola Estés writes in *Women Who Run With the Wolves*, a best-selling pop feminist counterpart to Robert Bly's *Iron John*.[9] For Americans worried about the future of this material world, anxious about violent crime, income inequality, inadequate health care, war, global warming, or the decline of the nuclear family, there is incredibly good news about the cosmos.

Publishers of popular spirituality books have already gone to heaven. By the early 1990s, the market for recovery books was "dead," according to one publisher, but, as Clarissa Pinkola Estés might have predicted, it was "in the process" of being reborn.[10] Codependency books transmigrated into books about spirituality; with their casual references to 12-step groups and familiarity with the jargon of recovery, spirituality books clearly targeted recovering readers. Books by unknown, amateur authors who claimed to understand the mysteries of the universe, or simply reported their escapades with angels and extraterrestrials, or their forays into heaven, became sudden, surprise best-sellers.

The Celestine Prophecy, first published privately, was picked up by Warner Books in 1993 and spent years on the *New York Times* best-seller list. (Like many successful personal or spiritual development books, it was followed by a workbook, *The Celestine Prophecy: An Experiential Guide,* a study guide intended to aid readers who are seeking to apply the lessons of *The Celestine Prophecy,* individually or in groups.) *Embraced by the Light,* Betty Eadie's report on her alleged near-death, or after-death experiences, published in 1994, became a number one *New York Times* best-seller.[11] Sales for Sophy Burnham's 1990 *A Book of Angels* were reported to have reached three-quarters of a million.[12] Its success encouraged a spate of angel books, including instructional treatises such as *Angelspeake: How to talk With Your Angels,* and *One Hundred Ways to Attract Angels.* Angel paraphernalia—calendars, mobiles, candles, and neckscarves followed, along with the successful TV show *Touched by an Angel.*[13]

The angel market peaked around the mid-1990s, but people who had established relationships with their guardian angels were invited to move on to communing with God or the spirits of the deceased. In the late 1990s, *Talking to Heaven,* by James

Van Praagh, and *Conversations with God*, by Neale Donald Walsch, ascended to the best-seller lists.[14] The preoccupation with celestial life also included speculations, or convictions, about extraterrestrial visitations. Contemporary interest in UFOs is not new; it dates back to the late 1940s and is frequently associated with the onset of the nuclear age and fears of communist infiltration (although there were also reports of UFO crashes in mid- and late-nineteenth-century America).[15] But the 1980s and 1990s saw a new spate of UFO stories, shaped by the therapeutic culture's focus on child abuse and New Age angelology. (Angels were sometimes associated with other planets and identified or confused with extraterrestrials.) Best-selling books about extraterrestrials included Whitley Strieber's *Communion*, a firsthand account of an alleged alien abduction published in 1987, and *Abduction*, psychiatrist John Mack's 1994 account of his interviews with "abductees."[16]

Like established religions, mass-market spirituality books often differ ideologically—some tell us we only live once, while others preach reincarnation—but they share a general belief in immortality and the existence of extraterrestrial or celestial beings devoted to our welfare, as well as a general disdain for reason, enshrined by the therapeutic culture. Drawing upon popular psychology and notions of recovered memory, experts on angels, aliens, and life after death seek truth in "feeling realities."

In *Abduction*, John Mack writes that he took seriously an alien abduction story if "what has been reported was felt to be real by the experiencer . . . and communicated sincerely"—as if sincerity in these cases might not simply be a measure of delusion. Mack talks about alien abductions the way religious people talk about God, disdaining the skeptic's interest in proving they occurred. Quoting one of his patients, he cautions us not to approach the "abduction phenomenon in narrowly materialist terms . . . trying to find proof for its reality by methods of the physical sciences." This is a familiar message: The truth lies in what you feel, not what you "know in your head," much less what you can prove, personal development experts assert, and people who have talked to their guardian angels, ET, or God, can only agree.[17]

The willingness to believe stories about alien abductions, encounters with angels, and other miraculous occurrences is considered a mark of enlightenment. These are not just tales to send a chill down your spine; they are tests of your character and emotional health. Recounting the respective stories of one woman who had a near-death experience and a meeting with her guardian angel and another who spoke with her dead father (whose spirit was channeled by a psychic), an article in *McCall's* approvingly cited a "healthy willingness" to believe in the supernatural. Skeptics who question stories about angels and other supernatural phenomenon were compared unfavorably with "the open-minded," who were willing to acknowledge their validity.[18]

Spirituality authors who are generally forgiving of most human foibles (suggesting that people aren't bad, only less evolved), take a hard line on intellectualism. Murder they can rationalize: murder victims are spirits who volunteered to be "part of some other soul's enlightenment test," Marlo Morgan reports in *Mutant Message Down Under*. Skepticism they view with contempt, as the refuge of the unenlightened.[19]

"[T]hose who take a strictly intellectual approach to this subject will be the last to 'get it,' " readers are warned in the preface to *The Celestine Prophecy: An Experiential Guide*. To change the world, we must "break through the habits of skepticism and denial."[20]

Like virtually all books of its genre, *The Celestine Prophecy* can confidently demand that readers suspend their disbelief because it tells so many people precisely what they want to hear. Its message is that there is no such thing as a coincidence; there are no chance encounters, no arbitrary events, no reasons for existential angst. There is only cosmic synchronicity to which we become attuned as we evolve spiritually.

The assurance that events are not random, that we live in a universe ordered by a benign omnipotent being (or life force) is repeated in many popular spirituality books. Angels and other supernatural beings are constantly intervening in our lives. Angels "watch over virtually every aspect of human activity." Whatever we consider coincidence is evidence of the Divine, angel experts suggest. "There are *no* accidents . . . Everything in life occurs as part of a spiritual plan," medium James Van Praagh writes in *Talking to Heaven.* "There *is* no coincidence, and *nothing* happens 'by accident,' " Neale Donald Walsch confirms in *Conversations with God.* "Everything has a purpose. There are no freaks, misfits, or accidents." Marlo Morgan agrees. (Reading a slew of pop spirituality books, you may think you've entered an echo chamber.)[21]

We have, then, no reason to worry about the future; it will unfold according to some Higher Power's benevolent plan. We're bound for glory, the experts assure us—sooner rather than later, if we buy their books. According to *The Celestine Prophecy,* we will evolve into a spiritually enlightened culture of peace and harmony in the next millennium. In this new Eden, critical thinking will be unnecessary. (Intellectuals, I suppose, will be extinct.) Truth will be self-evident and accessible to all. People will simply "intuit" the answers to global problems, like pollution, as well as individual ones. "Guided by their intuitions, everyone will know precisely what to do and when to do it."[22] Who would choose the hard work of reason over the serenity of knowledge bred in bone?

So, reason is reduced to a mere developmental stage for humankind. *The Celestine Prophecy* provides a summary history of the past thousand years that earnestly explains that science, born out of the secularization of human culture, was useful in providing us with a map of the material world; but it cannot help us understand the nonmaterial world of interpersonal energy or the spiritual questions that confront us as we approach the millennium. As one of the characters in the book explains, the "particular attitude known as scientific skepticism . . . served us well with the more obvious phenomenon in nature, with objects such as rocks and bodies and trees, objects everyone can perceive no matter how skeptical they are."[23] Psychiatrist and ufologist John Mack apparently agrees. "The Western scientific/materialist worldview has been hugely successful in its exploration of the physical world." But it represents "a restricted way of knowing." We now need a "different kind of consciousness," Mack writes in *Abduction*.[24]

Fortunately, our consciousness is "evolving," spirituality experts assert, meaning that we are replacing rationalism with "feeling and intuition." Einstein helped lead the way, according to a young female scientist in *The Celestine Prophecy*. Thanks to Einstein, we now know that the "basic stuff of the universe" is "a kind of pure energy that is malleable to human intention and expectation . . . our expectation itself causes our energy to flow out into the world and affect other energy systems." Most scientists simply can't take this notion seriously, she laments.[25]

You can hear in this the utter denigration of science coupled with an attempt to appropriate its credibility, which is typical of New Age. (Angel books, for example, talk about doing scientific research into the existence of angels.) Einstein is on the side of *The Celestine Prophecy*, we're told. Most scientists are simply not sufficiently evolved to carry on his work. Most scientists, after all, would not take seriously the assertion that, in the future, human beings will be raised "to higher and higher vibrations."

There is much talk about "vibrations" in pop spirituality books; highly evolved people are usually highly "vibrational." Low vibrations are associated with the body and high vibrations with the spirit: as God explains in *Conversations with God,* "As you undertake to inhabit a physical body here on Earth, your ethereal body . . . lowers its vibrations—slows itself from a vibration so rapid that it cannot even be seen, to a speed that produces mass and matter." [26] *The Celestine Prophecy* reports that as we evolve, vibrating at higher levels, we become invisible to the less evolved among us. As distilled spiritual energy, I think, we achieve virtual immortality.

All these insights into the meaning of everything are delivered in what the flap copy for *The Celestine Prophecy* calls a parable, "a parable filled with vital truths," a description bound to lead an unsophisticated reader to believe that this book is fact, not fiction. It is, however, a dime novel adventure story about a man who goes on a quest in Peru to discover an ancient manuscript containing the nine Insights that will save humankind. The story is told in the first person and the style is testimonial and borrows liberally from popular notions of spirituality and personal development. *Mutant Message Down Under* is equally coy about the veracity of the author's reported adventure with Aborigines: the flap copy labels the book fiction, but in her preface, author Marlo Morgan claims that the book was "inspired by actual experience . . . It is sold as a novel to protect a small tribe of Aborigines from legal involvement." [27] In other words, it's a docudrama, which some readers are apt to consider literally true.

But in the world of pop spirituality, facts are of little import, anyway. In this realm, the difference between fantasy and reality is often merely semantic: fantasies are metaphors that reveal cosmic truths. Fantasies are communications of the spirit, an expert might say. In this realm a concern for factual truth interferes with the quest for actual truth—what spirituality experts might term the soul's truth, "what you know in your heart." When Sophy Burnham tells us eerie stories about the angels and ghosts that she and her friends have encountered, when John Mack recounts the abduction experiences of his patients, they are not operating in the realm of verifiable facts; but Burnham and Mack apparently believe they are recounting truths. People who remain skeptical of their stories are simply less evolved than people who take them on faith. Spiritual correctness deters inquiry into the truth of the experiences the experts report.

Readers are also assured that the experts have rigorously scrutinized their own theories and experiences. Past lives therapist Brian Weiss stresses that he was trained as a scientist in prestigious universities. (He graduated Phi Beta Kappa, magna cum laude from Columbia University and received an M.D. from Yale, we're told at the outset of his book *Many Lives, Many Masters*.) He was taught to consider parapsychology "far-fetched . . . Years of disciplined study had trained my mind to think as a scientist and physician, molding me along the narrow paths of conservatism in my profession."[28] His path has been widened by experience, of course: one of the patients in his care unexpectedly recovered several past lives. Still, he subsequently conducted research into reincarnation, reviewing studies by several supposedly eminent scientists and clinicians. Weiss makes his point: he is a very smart man, who has carefully investigated his claims. If he believes them, so should we.

Not all spirituality experts can brag about their Ivy League degrees (while pretending to trust intuition much more than intellectualism), but others do discuss their intelligence and the process of overcoming skepticism. In *Mutant Message Down Under,* Marlo Morgan repeatedly refers to her "scientific mind." During her initial foray into the desert, "My scientific mind wanted to appease the blankness with a compass."[29] Like *The Celestine Prophecy, Mutant Message* is an adventure story about an American woman who is spiritually adopted by the Aborigines and taken on a walkabout through the Australian Outback. Her Western, "scientific mind" is contrasted unfavorably with the intuitive, otherworldy wisdom of the Aborigines.

Pop spirituality literature generally romanticizes native, premodern societies that exist in opposition to Western culture. (*The Celestine Prophecy* looks to ancient Peruvian civilization, and Native Americans are perennial New Age favorites.) Morgan describes the Aborigines as "real people," while Westerners, like her, are "mutants." The superiority of the former is clear. "Mutants allow circumstances and conditions to bury universal law under a mixture of convenience, materialism, and insecurity . . . Real people close the circle of experience." They know that "all humans are spirits only visiting this earth." Mutants waste much of their "life span" in "artificial, superficial, temporary, decorative, sweetened pursuits. So very few actual moments of one's life are spent discovering who we are, and our eternal beingness."[30]

Why would any reader prefer her own "mutant" version of reality to the vision of the Aborigines? Pop spirituality literature expresses widespread misgivings about America's consumer culture, while making the experts rich and offering readers prepackaged bite-sized bits of spiritual enlightenment.

The appeal of these books is obvious. They promise us bliss—a world of no evil (only spiritual retardation), no fear, loneliness, pain, or death. "Your happy destiny is *unavoidable*. You cannot not be 'saved,' "according to *Conversations with God*.[31] Compare the assurance of New Age prophets that everyone goes to heaven (or the new Eden of *The Celestine Prophecy*) with evangelical Christian visions of the coming apocalypse, which are dramatized in best-selling Christian novels. Only those of us who embrace Jesus as our savior will ascend to heaven, pop Christianity books proclaim; everyone else is destined for hell.

This traditional view of salvation retains considerable power, providing an alternative for those who find New Age excessively relativistic and insufficiently punative. In the late 1990s, a series of Christian thrillers about the final days, by evangelical minister Tim LaHaye and former journalist Jerry B. Jenkins, became best-sellers at specialty Christian bookstores and mainstream discount outlets, like Wal-Mart, Kmart, and Target. The series is supposed to eventually include seven books (the first four were on the shelves by 1999, and sales were reportedly in the millions); the plotlines are based partly on the Book of Revelation.[32]

The first entry, published in 1995 and entitled *Left Behind*, begins with the Rapture: Jesus returns to earth and whisks all true believers off to heaven. Millions of people disappear (leaving neatly folded piles of clothes, and chaos on the highways); millions of skeptics and heretics are left behind. Among those stuck on earth is the hero, Rayford Steele, an airline pilot who scoffed at his wife's born-again religiosity. She disappears in the Rapture, along with their devout twelve-year-old son. He is left behind with their skeptical twenty-year-old daughter. They turn to Jesus, belatedly but in time to be saved, and become leaders in the Tribulation Force, an elite group of believers dedicated to battling the Antichrist. They are primed for seven years of trials and tribulations, and by the end of the fourth book, *Soul Harvest,* the "tribulation saints" have endured global nuclear war, a global earthquake, crashing meteors, tidal waves, and showers of fire and blood.

Meanwhile, the Antichrist—one Nicolae Carpathia—is prospering. A handsome, charismatic Romanian politician, he began his rise to power as secretary general of the UN, preaching global unity, disarmament, and peace. Vigilant right-wingers will, no doubt, recognize the evil in these ideas. While pop spirituality literature tends to avoid politics, pop Christianity books reflect the political convictions of the Christian right, which are, after all, articles of faith: The UN is a satanic instrument of world domination, God is not particularly ecumenical, and abortion is the devil's work. The Antichrist advocates mandatory abortion for less-than-perfect fetuses, establishes one-world government, one-world currency, and a one-world religion, "Enigma Babylon."

With the passion of New Agers extolling spiritual inclusiveness and the rightness of all paths to God, Christian heroes, left behind, exalt religious exclusivity. "Our message flies in the face of a one-world faith that denies belief in the one true God, a God of justice and judgment," one of the Tribulation Saints, a rabbi converted to Christianity, declares. "Those who pride themselves on tolerance and call us exclusivists, judgmental, unloving, and shrill are illogical to the point of absurdity . . . When everything is tolerated, nothing is limited . . . Belief in Christ, however, is unique and, yes, exclusive on the face of it." The former rabbi condemns Enigma Babylon because it "does not believe in the one true God." It does not acknowledge that Jesus is "the only way to the Father." [33]

The *Left Behind* series presents a militant Christianity that glorifies religious wars. It challenges readers to "choose up sides" and "join a team," and prepare to side with God in the final battle. In the meantime, we can proclaim our allegiance and show our team spirit, at least, by ordering T-shirts and baseball caps from the Left Behind Web site; or we can purchase the *People Get Ready* CD: "You're hooked on the series. Now get the songs," the Web site advises.[34]

In the marketplace, even the apocolypse is domesticated. The *Left Behind* series doesn't entirely reject the all-American optimism that defines New Age. It offers an idiosyncratic reading of the Book of Revelation that guarantees all of us second chances. Those who are not swept up in the Rapture can still be saved, if they confess their sins and accept Christ as their savior. God has a sense of fairness, one of the Tribulation Saints suggests, "Hell is judgment for those who don't believe but everyone is given the opportunity."[35]

There is rarely even a hint of hell in New Age books, although not all of them are unremittingly sunny. Brian Weiss is told by the "poet Master" that humans will eventually destroy themselves. But this vision of the apocalypse is fleeting, and we needn't let it worry us. It will not occur in our lifetime, and we will be safely ensconced "on another plane, another dimension when it happens." Weiss acknowledges that our world is plagued with AIDS, the threat of nuclear holocaust, and terrorism; still he promises us a happy ending: "We are immortal. We will always be together."[36]

If the evangelical Christian notion of evil seems excessively simple, doctrinaire, or simply unfair (why should everyone who doesn't worship Christ be damned), it is no more disturbing than the persistent New Age failure even to acknowledge evil. The self-consciously relativistic universe of pop spirituality books provides little possibility for justice. In near-death experience accounts, God or the "Being of Light" who greets us when we die is nonjudgmental. Like a wise but indulgent parent, He, She, or It smiles ruefully upon us when we review our sins, knowing we will do better next time. "Evil is only 'that which you call evil,' " God declares in *Conversations with God.* "[E]ven that I love, for it is only through that which you call evil that you can know good . . . I do not love 'good' more than I love 'bad.' Hitler went to heaven." [37]

Not all spirituality experts would agree that Hitler resides with the angels; but many would assert that he is progressing spiritually, in this world in a new incarnation, or on another plane. Many would have to contend that the Holocaust was part of a cosmic plan, a necessary stage in human evolution. "All experience is for our good, and sometimes it takes what we would consider negative experience to help develop our spirits," Betty Eadie asserts in *Embraced by the Light.*[38]

The denial of coincidence and purposelessness, coupled with the insistence that the universe is governed by a benign Divinity, leads to some startling efforts to rationalize cruelty and human suffering. "Certain souls agree in spirit to experience a natural disaster, or a plane crash and agree to leave their bodies in this matter," James Van Praagh observes in *Talking to Heaven.*[39] We choose our illnesses, Betty Eadie reports, and "Some people choose to die in ways that will help someone else." [40] Both Eadie and Van Praagh echo Marlo Morgan's assertion that murder victims are essentially volunteers, in "agreement on an eternal level," with their murderers.[41] Eadie explains it, like this:

> A person may have chosen to die, for example, by stepping into the street and being hit by a drunk driver. This seems terrible to us, but within the pure knowledge of God, his spirit knew that he was actually saving this driver more grief later. The driver may have been drunk

again a week later and hit a group of teenagers, maiming them or causing greater pain and misery than was necessary, but he was prevented because he was spending time in jail for hitting the person who had already completed his purpose on earth. In the eternal perspective, unnecessary pain was spared for the young people, and a growing experience may have begun for the driver.[42]

If this offensive gibberish seems beneath critiquing, it's worth remembering that *Embraced by the Light* reached the number one spot on the *New York Times* best-seller list. Eadie assembled a sequel, *The Awakening Heart,* and combined sales for both books are over seven million. (Eadie was offered her own imprint by several publishing houses but chose to form her own press instead in 1998.)[43] What I consider nonsensical, others find inspirational. It's worth recalling that *Conversations with God, Mutant Message Down Under, The Celestine Prophecy,* and *Talking to Heaven* were best-sellers as well.

The frequently repeated assertion that there are no involuntary victims (of homelessness or even homicide) apparently has popular appeal. It may partly represent a reaction to the victimism of the 1980s and 1990s, but the belief that we choose our destinies has long been central to New Age and the positive thinking tradition. (It was the message of est, which flourished in the 1970s.) This insistence that we exert exclusive, comprehensive control of our lives ignores "the social nature of human experience," anthropologist Michael Brown has observed in *The Channelling Zone,* his illuminating review of New Age culture.[44] It has helped create a self-appointed spiritual elite of middle-class Americans who are disengaged politically. It also reflects what personal development experts might characterize as denial—an unwillingness to admit that suffering and violent death cannot always be rationalized, a refusal to acknowledge tragedy.

Fatuous optimism is, however, an American tradition, the basis of positive thinking. It shaped nineteenth-century mind-cure movements, characterized by William James as "moon-struck with optimism." Mind-cure represented a "religion of healthy-mindedness," which preached the "all-saving power of healthy-minded attitudes . . . and a correlative contempt for doubt, fear, worry, and all nervously precautionary states of mind." James respected the "practical fruits," of mind-cure, which seemed to have its promised therapeutic effect on many believers. But he ultimately found it "inadequate," as a philoso-phy: "[H]ealthy-mindedness pure and simple, with its senti-mental optimism, can hardly be regarded by any thinking man as a serious solution . . . the evil facts which it refuses positively to account for are a genuine portion of reality." [45]

Contemporary spirituality literature tends to recognize only those "evil facts" that are a portion of unreality. Extra-terrestrials are sometimes evil; they are surely terrifying, abducting and raping their victims. Unlike tales about angels, or the spirits of our great-grandmothers, alien abduction sto-ries are not simple anodynes. Aliens are a lot scarier and more aggressive than other heavenly beings celebrated in popular lit-erature. In some ways, they are evil counterparts to angels; they're the bad parents of recovery books. Indeed, aliens engage in the worst form of parental abuse—sexual molestation of abductees—and abduction stories rely on the reader's belief in "recovered memory syndrome," popularized by the 12-step movement.

In the typical story, the self-proclaimed abductee is plagued by imperfectly repressed memories of aliens, uncovered with the aid of a therapist eager to suspend disbelief. Both therapist and patient follow a script popularized by the recovery movement in its crusade to expose the abuse of children by earthly parents and guardians. That the abuse in some cases is conducted by extra-terrestrials, not human parents, may be mere detail to people who feel victimized by higher powers and consider reason an obstacle to uncovering the truth of crimes perpetuated against them.

Still, there is a new and important plot twist in stories of alien abductions: Extra-terrestrial abuse often turns out to be a form of tough love, or at least a necessity: the aliens are mating with us, creating a higher, hybrid life-form. While tales of alien abductions generally begin in terror, they end with enlightenment—the revelation that we are not alone in an indifferent universe. Usually the aliens want to save us from an impending apocalypse and help us evolve. Usually, as the abductees come to terms with their abduction experiences, they realize that they are part of a spiritual elite, chosen by the aliens to save humankind, or help spawn a new hybrid species.

In the end, there is only good news. It is easy to sell, and the experts confidently rely on classic fallacious arguments. They argue by declaration, which is what makes their books so amusing. In matter-of-fact authoritative tones, the authors tell us how plants and human exchange energy, or they describe what angels look like, whether or how they're gendered, how they communicate with human beings, and how they differ from ghosts. And repeatedly they assure us of our immortality. "Death is ultimately just another transformation, from one configuration of matter and energy to another," best-selling guru Deepak Chopra writes.[46] "How do they know," you might expect readers to wonder.

What makes fantastic declarations believable, apart from the authority of celebrity, is, in part, the vehemence with which they're proffered. In the world of spirituality, as well as pop psychology, intensity of personal belief is evidence of truth. It is very bad form, for example—it is even considered an exercise in abuse—to challenge the veracity of any personal testimony that might be offered in a 12-step group or on a talk show, unless perhaps the testimony itself is equivocal.

Alternative explanations for belief—explanations that don't assume the truth of whatever is believed—are rarely, if ever, considered. Anecdotes about angels or ghosts or mystical out-of-body experiences are presumed to reflect objective realities, not mere imaginings, although the assertion that a supernatural experience was imagined would not shake the faith of many believers: the experts would explain that hallucinations represent hidden aspects of reality. The world of pop spirituality is not simply one in which dreams *come* true; in this world, dreams are true. The "experiential guide" supplementing *The Celestine Prophecy* tells the story of a former "successful businessman," who began having involuntary out-of-body experiences; at first he thought he was mentally ill, the authors report; then he realized the experiences were real and not imagined and wrote books about them, and now he's an expert. In fact, he's now a sort of scientist, doing research on out-of-body experiences, the way others do research on angels. He has found that "The 'second body' of the out-of-body experiences is 'part of another energy system that commingles with the Earth Life System but is out of phase with it.' "[47]

For the sake of argument, assume that this anecdote is true: it describes a man who has devised a belief system, with its own language and rules, to explain what may have been hallucinations, convincing himself, and at least a few readers, that he wasn't crazy. He became an expert instead of a mental health patient because he believed deeply in the literal truth of his experiences. You might praise his equanimity as a "practical fruit" of the will to believe. Still, the story has a troubling moral for anyone with a lingering attachment to reason: The only difference between delusion and expertise is intensity of belief. People who hear voices in their heads are probably more highly evolved than the rest of us, and in touch with the angels.

There are, however, a few exceptions to this notion that sincerity is evidence of truth: if your feelings lead straight to disbelief instead of belief, they're apt to be dismissed as some form of denial. This is not a common problem: usually intellectualism, not "feeling reality," is blamed for disbelief. But, some angel experts suggest, there may be emotional as well as intellectual barriers to belief: Unwillingness to believe in angels can reflect low self-esteem.

Ubiquity of belief is also offered as evidence of truth. *Ask Your Angels* asserts that the references to angels in popular culture in songs like "Teen Angel" and "Johnnie Angel" and in movies, like *It's a Wonderful Life,* constitute evidence that angels exist, as does the popularity of angel books and the willingness of the industry to publish them. John Mack suggests that the similarities of many abduction stories told by different people indicates that the stories are true, ignoring the much less fanciful possibility that different people are influenced by the same stories circulating throughout the culture. In fact, pop spirituality authors gain a lot of credibility from each other: they dispense the same maxims. Popular media disseminate their teachings widely, and help imbue them with authority. James Van Praagh proudly informs us that one of his cases was dramatized on NBC's *Unsolved Mysteries.* "[I]t has become one of the most popular episodes in all of *Unsolved Mysteries* history," he reports, as if the popularity of the episode proved its accuracy.[48] A misplaced populist belief in the wisdom of the market reigns: Whatever sells, whatever many people believe most strongly, must be true.

These are perfectly closed belief systems; the possibility of error is never considered. If you don't see angels or energy fields emanating from your rhododendron, you simply don't know how to look for them. (Sophy Burnham surmises that angels simply don't present themselves directly to people not inclined to believe in them.)[49] The possibility that some people who believe that they commune with angels may be hallucinating, or lying, is given little credence. Like bad detective stories, spirituality books usually discard the most plausible explanations and adopt the most implausible ones for the mysteries they encounter. Rational, alternative explanations for belief don't, after all, assume the truth of whatever is believed.

All these styles of argument—arguing by declaration, arguing from intensity and ubiquity of belief, and arguing from your conclusion—are routinely employed by personal development experts, including codependency gurus and a range of inspirational and motivational speakers (as well as politicians). So it is easy for readers to switch from one belief system to another—to turn from codependency books to books about angels. They all present metasolutions to both global and individual problems: focusing on your spiritual evolution and the evolution of humankind, they're not above giving advice about how to get a better job. Angels can help you with tax audits, according to *Ask Your Angels*. And the experts will not only tell you how to find your own angel wings, they'll tell you how to care for them: "When you have finished using your wings, it is a good idea to pull them back into your body again, so the fibers don't get knotted or tangled."[50]

The appeal of pop spirituality lies partly in its versatility: psychics and gurus are apt to give equal time to helping you lose weight, advance your career, and gain access to past lives. Writing in *McCall's,* actress Demi Moore pays tribute to her psychic and spiritual guide, Laura Day.* How did Day demonstrate her amazing "intuitive abilities"? Moore reports that she predicted the "importance of a particular magazine cover having a profound effect on how people would look at me." [51]

You can find the same preoccupation with the trivial and metaphysical in Norman Vincent Peale, whose best-seller *The Power of Positive Thinking* will cure your existential anxiety and improve your golf game. And, virtually all personal development and spirituality books partake of the positive thinking tradition, which predated Peale by about a hundred years. They also refer back and forth to each other. *Ask Your Angels,* for example, includes a 12-Step Angel Program; *The Celestine Prophecy* talks about codependency and *The Celestine Prophecy: An Experiential Guide* cites Deepak Chopra. Chopra is a classic positive thinker, assuring us that "having an intention is enough to accomplish a result." We needn't be victimized by sickness, aging, or even death, he claims. "Everything that happens to you is a result of how you see yourself." [52]

The power of positive thinking is often intertwined with the power of prayer; in fact, positive thinking is often considered a form of prayer. Thinking positive thoughts is generally considered the equivalent of sending your positive vibrations out into the universe, giving the universe the opportunity to send positive vibrations back. "[P]rayer is nothing more than thought. It is a yearning of the heart," Sophy Burnham writes in *A Book of Angels.* Answers to prayer are practically inevitable, if you pray

* Laura Day, *Practical Intuition and How to Harness the Power of Your Instinct and Make It Work for You* (New York: Villard Books, 1996).

properly (Burnham will tell you how), because "prayer is a law of the universe, like gravity," and "it is the pleasure of the universe to give us what we need." [53]

This suggests that mind and spirit are stronger than matter. We can control events, bringing wishes and dreams to life. *The Celestine Prophecy* makes a similar claim: "When you have acquired enough energy, you are ready to consciously engage evolution . . . to produce the coincidences that will lead you forward." [54]

Virtually all the experts and their books offer membership in a spiritual elite. Indeed, the authors tend to see themselves as messiahs, chosen by aliens, angels, and various "beings of light" to help save the world. A New Age aristocracy, they spread the Word through books and lectures not just for money but out of a sense of noblesse oblige. One hundred years ago, Madame Blavatsky presented herself as the chosen messenger of a secret, immortal Brotherhood of Masters, or Mahatmas, headed by the Lord of the World, who lived in the Gobi Desert. Today Marlo Morgan suggests that she has been chosen by the Aborigines (the real people) to spread their wisdom. Betty Eadie announces that Jesus persuaded her to descend from heaven to earth to complete her "mission." In *Conversations with God*, the Almighty Himself compares author Neale Donald Walsch to John the Baptist. Actually, Walsch is not exactly the author of *Conversations with God*. He is merely an amanuensis. Much of his book purportedly transcribes the Word of God, who sounds a lot like Neale Donald Walsch.

The voice of God, conveyed by Walsch, is unconvincing. If I were inclined to believe in God, I'd expect him to write well and with some originality. Walsch didn't have to converse with God to write this book; he could simply have read an assortment of recovery and pop spirituality books. There are no adages or assertions in his book that I haven't encountered in others. But God is no elitist: He wants His words to be accessible to the least discriminating among us, which is apparently why he chose Walsch. According to God, Walsch is one of an unspecified number of "special messengers . . . gifted with extraordinary insight, and the very special power to see and receive Eternal truth, plus the ability to communicate complex concepts in ways that can and will be understood by the masses." [55]

In a culture preoccupied with self-esteem, megalomania is a virtue, I guess. Authors of pop spirituality books seem to feel inordinately good about themselves, and don't hesitate to share the knowledge of their own superiority. According to past lives therapist Brian Weiss, the Master Spirit has told him that, unlike the average human being, he has "almost succeeded" in achieving spiritual renewal: "You know so much more than the others. You understand so much more. Be patient with them. They don't have the knowledge that you have." Weiss concludes that his mission is to rid us of our fears of death and convince us that the injustices we perpetrate in this life will have to be repaid in the next. "How much less anger and vengeance [we] would harbor," if we only had his knowledge. Thus, if he can make himself heard, Weiss may avert considerable suffering. [56]

Depending on how much power they exercise, people who regard themselves as redeemers range from dangerous to pathetic. The spiritual hubris of experts, whom many regard as authorities, is offensive and reprehensible, but the pretensions of patients and consumers often evoke sympathy. The delusions of grandeur exhibited by people who claim to have been abducted by aliens is especially poignant. One of John Mack's clients explains that aliens kept him company throughout a lonely childhood (which doesn't lead Mack to believe he imagined them). Alleged abductees often observe that they have always felt "special" or "different." Now they know that their alienation was literal.

"I have always known that I was different, that I wasn't from around here. I always wanted to run away. I couldn't figure it out," one of Mack's patients reports. Once, he might have imagined that he'd been adopted; now the culture provides him with a story about extra-terrestrials and his own importance to the human race: He is a prophet; the aliens have given him a vision of the impending apocalypse. Why was he chosen? One woman wonders if "abduction experiencers are chosen because of greater auras or energetic, vibratory fields." [57]

John Mack reports that abductions often run in families, apparently creating a new aristocracy. One patient claims a "dual human/alien identity and [a] role as a healer and a bridge between the two worlds." Like other "abductees," he believes he has "accessed the source of creative energy in the cosmos . . . he has been given, or chosen, a role on Earth to contribute, as an example in his own being of openness and love, to the evolution and transformation of human consciousness." [58] Reading the accounts of self-described abductees, you don't have to wonder why people might indulge in elaborate abduction fantasies, at the risk of being labeled crazy. If there are social costs to insisting you've been abducted by aliens, they are greatly outweighed by its psychic rewards. The abduction story confirms that you're among the chosen few, and so does the prospect of marginalization. Prophets are not supposed to be honored in their time.

Readers may be relieved to learn, however, that you don't have to be raped by an alien, visited by an angel, adopted by the Aborigines, launched into a near-death experience, or contacted by God in order to join the elite. Merely reading these books and being open to their messages is cited as evidence of enlightenment. Studying the books and engaging in the exercises they prescribe will accelerate your spiritual growth. The experts exhibit touching faith in the self-help genre: James Van Praagh reports that he developed his natural talent as a medium by reading how-to books.

Belief systems embraced by pop spirituality books demand very little of us—a good attitude substitutes for good works. Self-absorption is a spiritual imperative. Nineteenth-century revivalists, late-twentieth-century recovery movement experts, and authorities on spirituality tell us that by working on our own religious, psychological, or spiritual evolution, we are working on the world. "Your own willingness to take time to study *The Celestine Prophecy* is part of the evolutionary process. *The amount of consciousness you bring to the collective mind is part of your contribution.*"[59]

Activity is not required. In this world, there is no such thing as a sin of omission. Popular spirituality books involve even less self-help than popular psychology with its exaltation of experts; instead of working through the 12-steps or any other technique, you can now wait for angelic intervention. Action seems futile in any case, if you believe that accidents never happen, that everyone is somehow responsible for his or her plight, and that people never suffer involuntarily or in vain. Marlo Morgan speculates that "street people and the homeless in the United States are allowing themselves to remain victims."[60] But what is equally troubling as the complacency and childlike passivity encouraged by these books is their denigration of skepticism and the habits of unreason they encourage, which carry over into political life. The elevation of personal truths and personal testimony over logic and verifiable fact that links popular psychology and popular spirituality today also infects political belief.

Consider the militia movement. Propaganda of the extreme right (like propaganda of the extreme left thirty years ago) employs the same techniques of argument that you find in popular spirituality books. Propagandists argue by declaration, relying on intensity and relative ubiquity of belief. Genuinely ubiquitous beliefs lose the power of cultism: if the participation of some people in the belief system provides a reality test and a source of solidarity, the participation of many people makes the system less special.

There are also clear analogies between the denial of coincidence that's central to popular spirituality literature and the embrace of conspiracy theories. Conspiratorial thinking has long been popular among UFO fans, who believe that the government has covered up evidence of extra-terrestrial landings. But even the sunniest pop spirituality books that acknowledge no evil, yet insist that there are also no accidents, reflect a yearning for order that underlies the belief in conspiracies. Angel books reflect the need to believe in omipotent, absolute good, and extremist political groups reflect the need to believe in omnipotent evil—in the form of the U.S. government or some New World Order. There are virtually no political accidents in the view of a conspiracy theorist; whatever happens, happens for a reason, and generally happens for the worst.

It's not surprising, then, to find crossovers from New Age to the militias.[61] I know a convert to the militia movement who was once enmeshed in a UFO cult and remains an avid believer in the paranormal. He has always thrived on the presence of enemies, and so, in a way, do popular spirituality authors. If there is no evil, only unenlightenment in the benevolent universe they depict, there are still enemies: notably science, rationalism, and established religion, which is almost always distinguished from spirituality—as doctrine, not feeling. (At the end of *The Celestine Prophecy,* the primary villains are not scientists but priests.) Despite their majoritarian appeal, mass-market spirituality books offer the pleasures of membership in a besieged minority. Like extremist political movements, they shine with moral vanity.

CHAPTER 4

GURUS AND THE SPIRITUALITY BAZAAR

Religion is supposed to make us humble and cognizant of our sins, but many of us seem marked by a belief in our own essential goodness. Seventy-seven percent of Americans surveyed by Gallup in 1990 believe they are bound for heaven.* According to a 1997 Yankelovich survey (for *Time*/CNN), 15 percent of Americans expect an initial sojourn in purgatory, but 61 percent believe that they will "go directly to heaven" immediately after death. It's not clear how many expect a spaceship to transport them. But, from an atheistic perspective, visions of extraterrestrials promoted by cults like Heaven's Gate are no more fantastic or childlike than visions of a celestial paradise that many people share. *Time* reports that most Americans do not consider death the end of life; 81 percent believe that people live forever with God in heaven after they die. Ninety-three percent

---

* Of all survey respondents who professed belief in heaven, 29 percent said they had "excellent prospects of getting in; 48 percent rated their chances of admission "good."

believe that heaven is inhabited by angels; close to half (43 percent) expect to find harps.[1]

Still, in 1997, people shook their heads in wonder over the spectacle of Heaven's Gate's thirty-nine members killing themselves in a San Diego suburb in the expectation that a flying saucer would whisk them to a better place. With no apparent sense of irony, commentators struggled to help us understand the provenance of this absurd cosmology, while millions routinely celebrated Christ's ascent to heaven (the suicides occurred shortly before Easter), or faithfully followed *Touched by an Angel,* one of America's top-rated TV shows.

Equally irrational was the public reaction to the death of Princess Diana. Yet the media endorsed the cultish frenzy that followed her death as much as it denigrated the cult of Heaven's Gate. I'm not comparing a mass suicide to mass mourning over a premature, accidental death. I imagine that most people who wept over Diana dried their tears and went on with their lives. The mourning was excessive, yet somewhat contained, like a ritual; it seemed to represent both ritual and a collective nervous breakdown.

Watching millions mourn the death of Princess Di, I was reminded that the death of Elvis Presley spawned a virtual religion. To many of his devoted followers, Elvis is a Christ figure, who never really died. As journalist Ron Rosenbaum has observed, Graceland is less a theme park than a shrine, remarkable not for tourists who come to gawk but for pilgrims who come to be saved.[2]

The mass hysteria spawned by Diana's death, the tearful protestations of love from her fans, signified the loss of another pop redeemer. Listening to people lament her passing, you'd have thought she was capable of healing the sick as well as comforting them. In death, she was reinvented as a great humanitarian with emerging spiritual power—not just another charitable aristocrat, a '90s Lady Bountiful. Tearfully, people exclaimed that they loved Diana, but you cannot love someone you've never met—someone who is utterly unaware that you exist, except as a member of an undifferentiated mass. You cannot love someone with whom you have no actual relationship. Instead you adore her; you worship her.

Yet the most ardent fans also identify with celebrities and enjoy illusory relations with them—which is why a few of the most unbalanced turn into stalkers; a fan who imagines herself giving love may imagine an entitlement to get some back. The most powerful charismatics are those who simultaneously invite identification and idolatry. They combine transcendent beauty, glamour, or talent with accessibility—providing entrée for fans eager to identify with a higher being. Elvis and Diana had this in common: they seemed both ineffable and utterly familiar. Despite their gifts, they were strikingly ordinary people beset with the ordinary problems of their culture—from drug abuse to self-esteem and familial dysfunction.

Remember how many women explained their attachment to Princess Di: "She had an eating disorder, I had an eating disorder; she was a single mother, so am I." ("Besides," they should probably have added, "I have always fantasized about being a princess.") Yet while she reinforced her membership in the therapeutic culture, Diana also subtly confirmed her rule. Her much publicized yearning to live "normally" did not encompass a desire to reside in a subdivision and hold down a job. Aspiring to be the queen of people's hearts, the Princess was not devoid of grandiosity. That too was a part of her charm.

She was a willing object of reverence, but one with whom people were invited to identify, as well as worship—like Elvis, she was entirely human and entirely divine. That she died partly because she had bad luck with men and the bad judgment to enter a car with a drunken chauffeur underscored the vulnerability that made her seem accessible. That her last meal was a late-night supper in Paris at the Ritz confirmed the distance between the Princess whose photographs adorned the tabloids and the people who read them. They wouldn't have it any other way.

At its most intense, the cultural obsession with celebrities reflects in a very banal form a religious craving for transcendence, which is why fan clubs sometimes resemble cults, and why the death of Diana provoked such intense, ubiquitous, and entirely irrational outpourings of grief. ("I hope the gym facilities are as good in heaven as they are at the Harbor Club. Fondly remembered, Your friend, Mary," one well-wisher wrote in a card left at Kensington Palace on the first anniversary of the Princess's death.) It's not hard to imagine the redemptive pop theology that could develop around Diana. Charles Cameron, an associate of Boston University's Center for Millennial Studies, reports that "the Princess of Wales has now entered millennial discourse." She is alternatively viewed as a saint, a goddess or faerie queen, an angel, or the manifestation of biblical prophecy.[3] "All religion must begin with some anthropomorphism," Karen Armstrong observes in A History of God. "A diety which is utterly remote from humanity . . . cannot inspire a spiritual quest."[4]

Does this demean religion, or elevate the idolization of celebrities? That depends. To an atheist or agnostic, the frenzied reaction to the death of Diana may simply reinforce a jaundiced view of religious belief and ritual as socially sanctioned temporary insanity. To a believer or one who sympathizes with belief, the public's anguish is made comprehensible and lent poignancy by its religiosity.

Why didn't the mass suicide at Heaven's Gate have a similar

poignancy in the popular view? It was surely a religious phenomenon. But if guru Marshall Applewhite (known as Bo) possessed any charisma, it was apparent only to his very small, marginalized group of followers, whose theology conflicted with majoritarian notions of salvation.

Although the United States is a very religious country, it harbors relatively little public respect for the religious impulse, unless it's expressed in a familiar tradition of worship. There is respect, instead, for particular religious beliefs—those that appeal to a critical mass and don't directly conflict with the views of the majority. That was one lesson of Heaven's Gate. In fact, it may have been met with more disapproval among religious people than atheists. The horror engendered by what appears to have been a voluntary mass suicide is partly a reflection of religious beliefs that suicide is sinful or, at least, presumptuous. If you put your faith in individual autonomy, rather than the hope of resurrection, the suicide of thirty-nine people is less disturbing than the murder of one.

The respect accorded mainstream religions is mostly a matter of majority rule. If all the Americans who believed in the sanctity of the Bible believed in UFOs, the mass suicide in San Diego would have been honored more than mourned. But, ask adherents of established faiths to explain why their beliefs about celestial immortality are more worthy of respect than the visions of extra-terrestrial life promoted by Heaven's Gate: baffled by your failure to grasp the obvious, many will explain that their beliefs are true.

That stops the conversation. It is usually futile to point out that other people hold other, contrary truths self-evident. Yet, in our religious culture, the behavior and beliefs of people involved in UFO cults should not be so perplexing. I'm not equating established religions or New Age movements with insular, totalistic religious groups. Of course, millions of well-adjusted people believe in God, while the thirty-nine suicidal members of Heaven's Gate seemed to be misfits and voluntary exiles. But I do want to stress that, as the Heaven's Gate story made clear, the most outré cults are apt to draw upon familiar belief systems—traditional religions, New Age movements, personal development fads, and science fiction. The angels in which a majority of Americans profess belief become extra-terrestrials in the dreams of an even more troubled minority. The extra-terrestrials who abduct and sexually molest their human subjects were prefigured by the abusive parents of codependency books that flourished some ten years ago and gave rise to notions of recovered memory, on which abduction stories rely. Guardian angels are the perfect parents of whom people from dysfunctional families could only dream.

Social issue conservatives often insist that religious belief exists in opposition to popular culture; they demand a greater infusion of religion into social and civic life in order to redeem the culture. But popular culture and religion often prosper in tandem—like crossover Christian rock stars and the music industry. The personal development tradition has always been partly religious. In fact it spawned one indigenous American religion, Christian Science, as well as the career of mid-twentieth-century positive thinker, Norman Vincent Peale. It's no coincidence that fictional evangelist Elmer Gantry dabbled in New Thought between ministries. Today, the foundational principles of popular therapeutic culture are metaphors for religious belief. What was inner child theory but a notion of divinity within?

Popular culture's alliance with religion has been dramatized recently by the increase of religious themes on television and the newfound religiosity of some very materialistic celebrities. Approaching her forties, Madonna began practicing yoga, studying the cabala, and musing about the divinity within everyone: "The more open you are to things, the more you suddenly become aware of people's divine nature," she told the *New York Times*.[5] The more traditional Della Reese, star of the popular TV show *Touched by an Angel*, revealed that she talked to God, who talked right back. God urged her to take on the role of Tess, supervising angel, Reese told James Brady of *Parade Magazine:* "He said to me as clearly as you're talking to me: 'Do this for Me, and in 10 years you can retire.' "[6]

God is a good prognosticator. Reese should be able to retire in style. Shortly after its debut in 1994, *Touched by an Angel* attracted a huge TV audience—an estimated 25 million people—and it won critical acclaim. Leslie Moonves, president of CBS entertainment, explained that the show appealed to the "reverse cynicism" that was apparently sweeping the nation. "Cynicism" is commonly used as a synonym for "skepticism," and Moonves was probably right that "reverse skepticism"—in other words, gullibility—accounted at least partly for the success of this show.[7]

Gullibility is born of desire, and like the pop spirituality books it complemented, *Touched by an Angel* told many viewers exactly what they yearned to believe: Angels roam the earth intervening in the lives of people in crisis. They are sent by God, who manages to hear and consider everyone's prayers, however trivial. God is a perfect parent who keeps busy attending to the details of our lives. He responds to our prayers because He loves us, unconditionally, and He offers each one of us eternal life.

How does God successfully manage the lives of all human beings? He delegates. *Touched by an Angel* chronicles the interventions of three angels: one beautiful young female, Monica, played by Roma Downey, an apprentice angel. She reports to Tess, played with savvy maternalism by sixty-something Della Reese. They are accompanied by a benign, young male angel of death, Andrew, played by the eponymous John Dye. (He also "helps out as a caseworker on various assignments," the network's promotional material notes.) With his long blond hair, Dye resembles the popular image of Jesus.

Every week Monica receives an assignment from Tess (who apparently is in close communication with God). She is to bring faith and a message of God's love to troubled teens, depressed seniors, unemployed people, and people employed in less than honorable professions (like tabloid reporting), who are led to repent. The dialogue sounds as if it were written for children, and it speaks to the fear of death and loneliness that can infantilize the most mature adults. "I am an angel. God made me for a very special purpose . . . to bring the good news that God loves you," Monica tells one of her charges. "Wherever you go, God will be there ahead of you, waiting for you with a miracle." There is nothing to fear, after all. Even when someone dies on the show, the ending is still essentially happy: The dead person walks off toward heaven with Andrew, the comforting angel of death. People have had epiphanies.

What's interesting about the show is its blend of New Age optimism, liberal social attitudes, and old-time religion. God is omnipresent but never judgmental or angry: He only wants you to accept His love. "In God's eyes, you're His beautiful child," Tess assures a gay male on his deathbed, who fears he has disappointed God, as he disappointed his father with his sexual proclivities: "You have not disappointed God because you can't surprise God . . . He never expected you to be anyone but who you are . . . God's love is perfect, and no one can love you better than He does." People who condemn homosexuality represent the "voices of hate and confusion." The man dies, but not before being embraced by his newly enlightened father.

It's not clear what conservatives who praised the show's religiosity thought about the assertion that homosexuality was accepted and maybe even intended by God. Many were more likely to agree with Senate majority leader Trent Lott when he declared in 1998 that homosexuality was a sin. They might have been equally unsettled by God's tendency to be "soft on crime." In another show, a feloniously inclined teenage male is sent to a juvenile detention center and given a liberal dose of rehabilitation: the chance to work with a severely disabled child. Of course, he gradually develops a deep bond with the child, breaks down, accepts God's love and, not incidentally, the love of his mother, and is transformed from a young thug to a role model. Like a good liberal, Tess has insisted all along that love, not punishment, would save him.

Where was Tess when Congress was debating a harsh new juvenile crime bill effectively dismantling state juvenile justice systems aimed at rehabilitation? If *Touched by an Angel* offers us an idealized vision of the universe, governed by a God who understands and forgives everything and believes in second chances, it also offers us an idealized vision of ourselves and our society. Watching this show celebrate a nonjudgmental, loving God, to the apparent approval of 25 million Americans, you'd never know that the public tended to support long mandatory prison terms for nonviolent offenders, while opposing laws extending equal rights to gay people.

Touched by an Angel is Christianity brought to you by Hollywood, not the Bible Belt, which is why it has had such broad appeal. It speaks to grazers at the spirituality buffet—people who sample New Age books about angels and addictions, as well as the occasional church service. CBS's biographies of the show's stars ends with their birth dates, in case you want to know their signs.

If New Age and established religions are separate countries, their borders are permeable and shifting and, with a few exceptions, they're united by the common language of popular culture. But, in general, established religions only accommodate the culture, in varying degrees. New Age seems practically defined by it—while Hollywood, the great purveyor of popular culture, is rife with New Age. And just as celebrities like Princess Di, Oprah, or Madonna become pop divinities, spirituality gurus become celebrities—partly by acquiring celebrity clients. The value of Deepak Chopra's advice is confirmed by the fame of admirers like Barbra Streisand, Donna Karan, Oprah Winfrey, and Demi Moore.

In our culture, fame can sanctify. Since the advent of motion pictures, movie stars have been objects of adoration; and today the mystique of the Hollywood star extends to an eclectic assortment of celebrities—athletes, talk show hosts, television anchors, the occasional pundit and convicted felon, a few politicians, and historical oddities like the Duke and Duchess of Windsor. Fans collect autographs and photos of their favorite stars and mementos (or copies of mementos) from celebrity estates, like acolytes seeking holy relics. Still, while some celebrities may crave attention, they don't generally demand worship so much as incite it. Most remain entertainers rather than authority figures. Madonna is a weathervane, not the wind of cultural change. Even Shirley MacLaine was no guru; she never seemed to be seeking followers so much as an audience for her spiritual adventures.

Sometimes the audience does look like a mob: reviewing images of hysterical teenage girls craving a glimpse of the Beatles or the young Sinatra, you confront the profound irrationalism of a celebrity culture and the ferocious human need for idols. (You're also seeing the effects of hormonal change, but I doubt that hormones create the urge to worship; they just make teenagers less inhibited about expressing it.)

Marry the fan's need to give worship with an idol's need to

receive it, and you risk giving birth to a cult. You're most likely to produce a guru—a charismatic authority figure who answers questions about the cosmos that have bothered you since adolescence. In our consumer culture, gurus may elicit blind, cultish loyalty from some followers, but only occasionally do they establish cults. Most don't demand that you join them in exile to be saved. Instead, they make enlightenment readily available in books, audiotapes, and afternoon "workshops." You can sample the teachings of many seers which are often complementary, if not redundant. The market offers multiple choices to seekers of spiritual wisdom and discourages rigid brand loyalty, which could threaten profits: publishers often include several gurus on their lists, whose cosmologies may differ. New Age conference organizers, like concert promoters, require numerous stars.

The tendency of consumers to consult more than one pop spirituality expert, like moviegoers who regularly attend the films of numerous favored actors, diminishes the power of any one seer. I can't quite imagine everyone rallying behind one best-selling New Age star, to the exclusion of all others, and drinking Kool-Aid on his or her command. But if heeding many spiritual guides is considerably less dangerous than heeding only one, the spirituality bazaar still encourages passivity, gullibility, and a childlike craving for authority. Am I being too harsh? Listening to the purveyors of cosmic truths and observing the interactions between audiences and experts, I've been both amused and dismayed by the painful stupidities that people embrace to ease their fears of death.

At a holistic education center in Cambridge, Massachusetts, trance channeler Kevin Ryerson, self-proclaimed adviser to

Shirley MacLaine, describes the hierarchy of spiritual guides during a lecture on spirit communication, followed by a channeling demonstration. I have signed up for an evening lecture and all-day workshop with Ryerson (who bolsters his authority with frequent references to "Shirley's" faith in him), so here I am learning that Saints are a step below Ascending Masters who are below Angels and Archangels. People listen intently or take notes, in the belief, I guess, that they're receiving information.

They ask questions, assuming that Ryerson has the Answers: "How can you tell if you're channeling a good or evil entity?" Ryerson says that you can only receive a spirit in tune with your own vibrational frequency: "You really can't attract anything to yourself that is not in your vibrations. Charles Manson couldn't speak through any of us because his vibrations aren't aligned with ours."

"Are fairies human beings?"

"They're more in the angelic realm."

"Where are you when you experience déjà vu?"

"You're in the now," Ryerson responds. "Time is a pool out of which you can pull out past, present, and future simultaneously."

"Do spirit guides have a prime directive as in *Star Trek* so that they do not interfere in our free will?" Ryerson predictably assures us that guides respect the prime directive and do not deprive us of our will. "Where do gurus fit in?" Gurus are teachers, Ryerson explains; then he quotes Oprah Winfrey, who once said, he reports, that gurus are here "not to teach us about *their* divinity but to teach us about our own."

I've never sensed any divinity within myself or anyone else, but I defer to Winfrey's understanding of the guru's appeal. Today, business is flourishing, along with religious and spiritual revivalism, as the popularity of Ryerson's nonsensical performance attests. (He isn't a best-selling author, but he has filled the room.) The millennium approaches, and nearly everyone wants to be saved or at least reincarnated. Pop spirituality gurus assure us that we are not mere mortals. They do sometimes demand a show of humility and a stab at confession, in a religious ritual of purification. (The Promise Keepers will reclaim their power after they admit their sins.) But gurus always confirm our essential godliness. They lead by flattery.

Women remain the primary consumers of personal and spiritual development (the audience at a New Age conference I attend is predominantly female), so it's not surprising that gurus commonly praise the stereotypical feminine powers: emotional and spiritual sensitivity and highly evolved relational skills. Women's intuition is frequently invoked, along with their "openness" to psychic experiences. (Men are said to be excessively rational.) Women are praised for forming communities, while men form hierarchies: Women arrange chairs in a circle, one speaker suggests; men arrange them in rows. With its reliance on very traditional beliefs about cognitive and characterological differences between the sexes, New Age feminism is quite regressive. It's difficult to believe in so many sex-based stereotypes and not believe that men and women are destined to play very different social roles.

Feminism has always had a conflicted relationship with gender norms, however; many women have sought to take advantage of the presumed emotional strengths of their sex without admitting its alleged intellectual and physical weaknesses. Or, they've framed an intellectual weakness, like a distaste for rationalism, as a strength, associating it with creativity, the fabled female intuition, and a more acute appreciation of the sacred. So, while some feminists lament the assumption that women are less rational and analytic than men, others celebrate it.

Female chauvinism, which has always infected popular feminism, has flourished within spirituality and alternative-healing movements, which have been dominated by women since the nineteenth century. With its emphasis on holistic perspectives and disdain for "dualism," contemporary New Age thinking appeals to those feminists who believe fervently that women naturally seek connectedness and synthesis, while men analyze, categorize, and strive to maintain boundaries between themselves and the world.[8] One hundred fifty years ago, the allure of spiritualism was not just ideological but practical: the absence of long-established institutions with entrenched male hierarchies provided opportunities for women whose presumptively superior spiritual sensitives enhanced their credibility as mediums and healers. Communicating with the dead, or healing the sick, a woman wasn't violating gender norms, but she was exploiting the limited authority they conveyed.

Conventional feminist wisdom holds that nineteenth-century spirituality movements helped "empower" women and generally advanced the cause of equality. In part, this sanguine view reflects the power that spiritualism retains today, which results in some striking abdications of judgment by feminist scholars. An entry in a recently issued encyclopedia of women's history lauding female religious leaders and spiritualists affirms without question their "recognition" of "the feminine as a higher form of divine consciousness"—assuming both the existence of a divine consciousness and women's privileged relationship to it. Included in the encyclopedia's roster of women who served as "powerful" models of female visionaries, prophets, preachers, and writers are Margaret and Kate Fox, two teenage girls who sparked a craze in spiritualism in the mid-nineteenth century by conducting seances: spirits supposedly communicated with the girls through a series of rapping sounds.[9] In later years, Margaret confessed that she had produced the sounds attributed to the spirits by snapping her big toe inside her shoe.[10]

The Fox sisters were not exactly anomalies. The history of spiritualism is, in part, a history of fraud. Early-twentieth-century master magician and skeptic Harry Houdini made a hobby of exposing fraudulent mediums.[11] That women excelled in this dubious profession and exploited human gullibility as well as men doesn't seem a proud step toward equality.

New Age is generally associated with the political left and challenges to the status quo: in the nineteenth and early twentieth century, it included the then outré preoccupations of the bourgeoisie chronicled by George Bernard Shaw—feminism, spiritualism, and vegetarianism. Today it includes radical environmentalism and transpersonal psychology as well, and is generally associated by critics on the right with the "self-centered" baby-boom generation and the counterculture that arose in the 1960s. In fact, a New Age conference does sometimes resemble a reunion of aging hippies and their acolytes. But despite its identification with progressive causes, New Age is not consistently democratic. It remains infested with spiritual authorities who expect and receive few challenges from their flocks.

The submissiveness expected of New Age consumers is often cloaked in a show of comaraderie by the expert, who consistently reminds her fans that they are as close to God as she, often paying tribute to the presumptively feminine virtues. "Most women I know are priestesses and healers," Marianne Williamson declares in *A Woman's Worth*. "We are all of us sisters of a mysterious order," she adds, inviting readers to identify with her, while they follow—as many fans identified with Princess Di.[12] Williamson simultaneously invites identification and idolatry. Then, if she is divine, so are we.

Like other stars in the universe of pop spirituality, Williamson presents herself as a savior, and many of her fans seem to regard her as one. In 1997, I saw her graciously accept the adoration of an overflow crowd in a large auditorium, along with an award for her "contributions to the world," bestowed by a holistic education center. Promoting her book *The Healing of America,* she was on a mission to redeem or heal the country, with a spiritual awakening.[13]

In her sermon (gurus do not deliver talks), Williamson exhorted members of the "higher consciousness" community to turn their attention from themselves to the world. Pop spirituality experts have generally become sensitive to charges of self-centeredness. "Self-awareness after a while can insidiously move into self-preoccupation," Williamson conceded. In the late 1980s and early 1990s, at the peak of the 12-step movement, recovering codependents accused of excessive self-involvement routinely explained that "you have to work on yourself before you work on the world." By the late '90s, perhaps inspired by a president and vice president with a talent for therapeutic politics, a few gurus have become a bit more concerned with worldly affairs.

Williamson offers herself as a model New Age citizen, intent on marrying spirituality and politics. She says she operates a center that distributes food to the hungry, and she is the founder of the American Renaissance Alliance (ARA), which claims to "provide an organized context for philosophical inquiry and political activism."* (Williamson's cofounder is God's amanuensis, Neale Donald Walsch, author of *Conversations with God.*)

Stressing the need to inject spiritual values into political

---

* The American Renaissance Alliance was supposed to be renamed in 1999, for legal reasons.

debates, the ARA looks like the liberal New Ager's answer to the Christian Coalition. An ARA "training conference" held in Washington, D.C., in November 1998, promised a "weekend of power and discovery" that would draw together "like-minded people from around the country, ready to apply metaphysical principles to the healing of American society." Some four hundred to five hundred people attended; in addition to Williamson's usual sermons about the healing of America, the conference included a basic civics lesson from a constitutional historian and a panel discussion with activists from organizations including Amnesty International, the Children's Defense Fund, and Common Cause. People were encouraged to create their own Citizen Salons when they returned home and to consider the prospects for a powerful third party, which might soon field a president.

On the road, promoting *The Healing of America,* Williamson sounds like a woman who is planning or at least hoping to run for office. When she urges her fans to become involved politically, you have to wonder who she'll urge them to support. Her exhortations seem designed to elicit the response offered by one man sitting behind me at one of her appearances. "Run, Marianne. Run," he yells. It's not surprising that her new organizational vehicle, the American Renaissance Alliance, is not tax exempt, which means it can engage in lobbying.

In her standard sermon on America, Williamson offers a very simplistic, summary political analysis of the last thirty years (contained in her book): Her generation of activists was traumatized by the assassinations of John and Robert Kennedy and Martin Luther King. Baby boomers split into two camps: political people who settled in the East, and the people seeking spiritual enlightenment, who gravitated to California. Simply put, that is the yin and the yang of it. Williamson's goal, it seems, is to lead the spiritual seekers into politics, so that the nation can benefit from their presumed enlightenment.

Her politics are vaguely liberal. She presents herself as an "enthusiastic capitalist," but one with a social conscience who believes that money can't "shield us from suffering." She calls for more funding for public schools and less for the Pentagon, prison construction, or corporate subsidies, but mostly she offers more attitudes than policies: criticizing economic theory, she reminds us that "what goes around, comes around." She begins and ends the evening with a prayer.[14] In her current incarnation, Williamson is like a cross between early-twentieth-century evangelist Aimee Semple McPherson and H. Ross Perot.

Williamson is more charming and attractive than Ross Perot (who helped establish the viability of third-party candidates), but they seem to share the messiah complex common to pop spirituality authors, and it's unsettling to see how well it plays. So many people seem hungry for saviors and eager to be led. Like Perot, Williamson is very prickly, perhaps even a little paranoid. She speaks darkly about the mean-spirited press and its tendency to take down the nation's leaders. "Abuse of leaders is the last unchallenged oppression in the United States," she declares,[15] and I imagine she's thinking of herself. Williamson can't seem to handle criticism: once after I referred to her disparagingly in an aside on *The Today Show,* I received a lengthy, aggrieved, self-aggrandizing letter from her assuring me that she was a very serious person. Hundreds of thousands appear to agree. From what I've seen, she can expect the adoration of her fans. She adores them back, in turn. It's worth remembering that a large body of pop spirituality literature appeals to the reader's sense of being special, or chosen, part of a spiritual elite.

Indeed, the measure of our psychic or spiritual superiority is usually our openness to the guru's teachings. Merely reading a book about codependency or attending a 12-step group distinguished you from people who were in denial, recovery experts once reminded us. Today, when personal development books generally focus on spiritual development and various paranormal phenomenon, consumers of New Age books, workshops, and conferences are assured that they represent the spiritual avant garde who will lead us into the next millennium.

The guru offers us the opportunity to become leaders of our culture by becoming followers of his or her teachings. Gurus frequently renounce any special authority or desire to lead, but that is merely a matter of form. The American personal development tradition demands a nod toward the spirit of egalitarianism: "I'm only an expert on my own life," recovery experts used to say before pronouncing on the lives of others. Gurus may welcome us initially as fellow travelers or pilgrims on a path to enlightenment, but we walk several paces behind. They never fail to fill us in on their credentials—medical degrees or special psychic abilities. And, they are paid to talk while we pay to listen, assuming they have something to say.

I am not disdainful of expertise or the desire to learn from people who possess it. I am wary of experts whose disclaimers of expertise are belied by their behavior and their relationships with fans and followers. How might a guru who professes modesty actually convey it? I've heard Thomas Moore, author of several best-sellers on the soul, acknowledge in passing that all his books are the same and explain that he declines to conduct training seminars on "care of the soul" because they would not be worthwhile. (There is a lucrative lecture/workshop circuit for best-selling New Age authors, which many join.) When asked a question about the soul, Moore responded by referring to the teachings of the neo-Platonic tradition, with which he says he identifies, instead of relying on his own authority. It was a refreshing, but very rare display, which suggests that it's probably unfair to Moore to call him a guru.

Usually, pop gurus claim a great deal of authoritative, personal knowledge and extraordinary spiritual power. I've seen trance channeler Kevin Ryerson slip quickly into a trance and channel "an entity" from ancient Egypt. The entity offered adages about the meaning of life: "There is no such thing as history. There is only the continuity of history," alternating with lame one-liners (about the 1996 presidential race): "That Dole fellow. You talk about mummies; that guy's been around for a while." [16]

But if Ryerson sometimes sounded like a failing late-night comic with mystical pretensions, you could tell that he was in possession of an ancient Egyptian spirit because he spoke stilted English, with a vaguely Asian accent. (When he channeled an Irish spirit, he spoke in a brogue.) Listening to him was like watching an old movie about the French Revolution, in which heavily accented English is the language of eighteenth-century France. I still regret not asking Ryerson why an entity that took possession of his body couldn't take possession of his speech patterns as well. But, at the time, I didn't want to interrupt the proceedings or put him on the defensive.

The audience seemed quite engaged—impressed but not at all shaken or surprised by the sudden appearance of a three-thousand-year-old spiritual entity. The entity is what they have paid to see. Still, their equanimity was striking and more telling than their desire to believe. If an ancient spirit suddenly appeared before you, wouldn't you at least be surprised? What I may have missed most from the audience was any apparent sense of wonder. No one seemed awestruck by Ryerson's transformation. If this is a religious experience, then the sacred has become merely mundane. People asked the alleged spirit about "soul groups" and the lost city of Atlantis, with the air of travelers asking a gas station attendant for directions.

Appearing as himself, Ryerson dispensed his own esoteric wisdom. "We can turn on and off DNA through consciousness alone," he assured us. He was as comfortable explaining the nation's political history as he was expounding on the nature of angels. (They "do not necessarily incarnate." Our own system of checks and balances was derived from the "great law of peace of the Iroquois nation," Ryerson reports.) People seemed to regard him as an authority on grand metaphysical questions: "If you experience the ultimate in heightened consciousness, are you experiencing all your lives simultaneously," someone asked. "Hold that thought," Ryerson responded. I don't recall that he ever responded to a question with a humble "I don't know."

Pop gurus unabashedly explain the mysteries of the universe. Many offer up cosmologies, supposedly grounded in science. At a New Age conference, New Age priest (or "postmodern theologian") Matthew Fox expounds upon the "physics of angels":[17] Angels move at the speed of light, like photons, he claims. Noting current efforts "to connect with extraterrestrial peoples," Fox says that we are better off trying to connect with angels because they move so fast: communications with aliens will be too slow. "It would take 100,000 years for a radio signal to travel from one end [of the galaxy] to the other; 200,000 years until you get a reply." Even sending a message to the nearest star would take 4.2 years, he advises. "Communication with angelic beings, those that can move at the speed of light, would make it across much quicker." Or, maybe we should simply communicate with angels telepathically, he suggests.

Fox does acknowledge some uncertainty: he's not sure whether angels evolve or how they communicate with each other. But he seems confident that angels "operate as organizing principles" of the universe. Angels "help the planets and the universe and the cosmos accomplish its work." There may even be "an angel in the sun." Fox relies heavily on what he calls the "New Science," meaning, I think, quantum physics as understood by New Agers, and any other pseudoscience that rejects the notion of the universe as a soulless machine obeying mathematical laws and confirms the existence of an organizing intelligence.

Thomas Aquinas had an essential understanding of quantum physics, Fox suggests. Aquinas realized that "an angel can move in discontinuous time. An angel can be now and here and there with no time interval in between. When an angel moves, the beginning and the end of the movement do not take place in two instances but rather in one instance." According to Fox, these observations mirror what "physicists are learning about protons. They're here and then there and no time elapses . . . So we find in Aquinas's angelology an entire discourse on quantum mechanics."

People seem to listen intently and very respectfully to Fox's rambling exposition, although I can't imagine they can make much sense of it. Reviewing my notes and a transcript of his remarks, I'm struck by his incoherency. I can't summarize his talk, I can only list some of his points, or declarations: Angels are intuitive ("They don't have to go to school"), and you will encounter them on "the highway of intuition . . . Angels and artists are on the same wavelength, quite literally, the wavelength called intuition." Angels once helped him write a book in six week, Fox confides. Angels are "so interested in the inness of things that they are there when silence is struck." Angels come to people at death. Gustav Mahler's last word was "Mozart," Fox reports, which he takes as evidence that "Mozart came to usher [Mahler] into his next expression of life."

None of this will seem new to people versed in popular angel lore. (Perhaps that's why it needn't make sense.) In this talk on the "physics" of angels, we are a long way from the arcana of science, especially when Fox discusses "the demonic dimension of the angel world." Fox, it seems, is no relativist, hesitant to condemn what he doesn't like as evil. Instead, finding demons in worldly ills or behaviors he disdains, he seems like the leftist mirror image of Pat Robertson: "You know we used to call the demon Satan, Lucifer, and some other names and I think that today we have names like racism and sexism and injustice and militarism and homophobia." Still, I'm not surprised by this particular list of evils (and demonism aside, I don't dissent from it). I am taken aback by his bold condemnation of consumerism.

"Consumerism is a very good example today of the demonic energy," according to Fox. It is "a good word for all the satanic influences." He explains that "consumerism is trying to stuff things down your throat, [and] your throat is your trumpet in which you speak your truth. It lies between your heart chakra and your mind chakra." Condemning consumerism, Fox seems unabashed by the fact that his advertising flyers have been distributed throughout the hall. He seems generally oblivious to the commercial nature of the enterprise in which we are all engaged. Conference registration fees for weekend talks ranged from $265 to $299 and did not include fees for "intensive" sessions on Friday and Monday. They didn't even include a "Saturday vegetarian box lunch" ($10). Fox himself isn't shy about self-promotion. A subsequent talk he delivers on "creation spirituality" is prefaced by a tribute to him from a young man who reportedly quit his job at NYNEX and enrolled in the New Age university Fox has founded—the University of Creation Spirituality, in Oakland, California. A member of the first graduating class, the young man triumphantly reports, "I got my soul back," and I feel as if I'm watching late-night TV.

If anyone notices the contradictions in Fox's presentation, no one mentions them—not that he gives his audience much time for questions or comments. During a brief question-and-answer period, Fox takes up most of the air time, which is typical. Gurus rarely engage in colloquies with their fans.

Attending programs on personal or spiritual development, I have rarely seen an expert leave much time for questions after a talk. On those occasions when queries are allowed, or during a "workshop," I have never heard anyone ask a probing, critical question. Usually people ask for more information—about the nature of angelic presences, or the best technique for accessing a past life and sharpening telepathic powers; they testify to their own otherworldly experiences, or they gratefully praise the expert's wisdom. When, as an anonymous member of the audience, I have respectfully argued with the experts, they have almost always responded with anger and surprise. (Fox reacted rather contemptuously to me when I questioned his attribution of social ills to demons.) The arrogance underlying the gestures of humility typically offered by gurus is evident in their hostility to challenges.

Gurus tend to deter criticism by describing it as a defense against their message and a mark of the unenlightened. Skeptics, meaning people who challenge or debunk the guru's teachings, are met with pity, anger, or contempt for their spiritual blindness. Psychic psychiatrist Judith Orloff condemns naysayers as "witch-hunters." [18] Their resistance to the guru's truth is usually attributed to fear and a reliance on intellect over emotion. (Men are said to be especially resistant to psychic truths.) Injecting spirituality into the personal development movement has only strengthened the familiar command to trust your heart and not your head; now we're encouraged to trust our dreams and longings for transcendence as well. If you imagine a past life, you've probably lived one.

In our therapeutic culture there is an implicit contract between the guru and follower—they accept each other's truths. Judith Orloff regales us with her life story, which includes many eerie psychic experiences (which we're expected to take on faith), and people listen raptly, seek her autograph, and thank her for her "visionary" work. By recognizing her vision, we testify to our own. Audience members with equally fantastic stories are given equal credibility. Stand up during a New Age discussion of spirit guides and describe the life you led in the year 1573, and no one, the guru least of all, is apt to question your account.

The virtual ban on expressions of skepticism discourages us from passing judgment on the morality implicit in personal testimony, as well as its truth. During a discussion of psychic therapy, led by Orloff, one member of the audience who identifies herself as a social worker with psychic powers reports that she has been told that using her powers on clients was immoral: she was "trespassing on their minds." She seems to have been quite shaken by this accusation (her voice quavers as she repeats it), and now, instead of psyching out her clients, she communicates telepathically with the family pets: "They're acting as my cotherapists." She receives a round of applause.

I'm not surprised that people applaud her reported partnership with her client's pets. I do wonder why people who believe in the existence of psychics don't consider it unethical for them to "read our minds" without permission, without even putting us on notice. Don't people here value their privacy? Or do they assume that psychics are like gods who use their power over us only for our own good? Judith Orloff dispenses with any lingering concern about psychic "trespassing" by suggesting that psychics naturally develop integrity as they sharpen their powers and that they either won't have access or won't use access to secrets people would rather not reveal: "I believe there is an inherent integrity to the psychic shielding process."[19]

People appear satisfied with this response; in general, they seem quite eager to trust experts and to bond with their fellow fans. Organizers and participants of this weekend series of lectures and workshops periodically praise the community that those of us in attendance supposedly represent. Yet we are no more a community than people attending a ball game. The self-identified psychic social worker who works with pets told her story after being assured that she was in a "safe place," meaning a place populated only by sympathetic listeners who would not judge her. But she was not, in fact, entirely safe because I was there among her listeners. I've afforded her little sympathy. (I feel sorrier for her clients.)

Yet I don't feel as if I've violated a trust by repeating her story: I haven't identified her (and wouldn't if I could), and I never asked her to trust me. I never agreed explicitly or implicitly not to repeat any testimony I heard. I never entered into a relationship with the psychic social worker, or anyone else in the room. Hundreds of people unknown to each other have signed up for this conference, which is open to the general public. We have no reason to trust the crowd with our secrets.

Many people, however, apparently harbor a need to trust the strangers that surround them. They want to feel part of a spiritually enlightened community. They want to feel free to talk. If they withheld their trust they'd have to withhold their testimony, which some might find intolerable. Besides, experience may teach them that their trust is not horribly misplaced; at least, it doesn't do them harm. Etiquette (and common decency) prevent people like me from challenging other members of the audience. Only the experts are fair game.

Still, the assumption that a room full of strangers is a "safe place" is troublesome. It reflects, in part, the abdication of judgment that leads people to trust the experts, although people do derive at least a short-term benefit from their faith in pop spirituality experts, as they benefit from their faith in each other. If gurus enjoy adoring or at least extremely compliant audiences, not prone to argue with their premises, followers gain sympathetic authority figures who tell them what they want to hear.

"There is no death." That is the primary message of spirituality gurus; it is at the heart of their popularity. Deepak Chopra promises that we can live nearly forever, or, at least, a very long time. Psychiatrist Brian Weiss, author of *Many Lives, Many Masters,* and a popular past-lives therapist, assures us that we have lived before and will live again, and so will the people we love. A taste of immortality is easy to obtain: I've seen Weiss lead an audience of several hundred people back to the womb and then to their past lives in about an hour and a half.[20]

Like many experts in spiritual or personal development, Weiss is on the lecture/workshop circuit. I've attended his "intensive" all-day session on healing and past-life regression. Billed as "North America's leading practitioner of past-life therapy," Weiss will "help us access memories from childhood and prior lives in order to find more peace, health, and joy in the present." And, he will "explore the concepts of soul bonds and show how remembering past lives can transform negative relationship patterns and expand our capacity to love." Some may be inclined simply to revel in the knowledge that there is no death. Weiss will teach you how to use it therapeutically.

You don't need to purchase individual sessions with him. Weiss practices group therapy, on the grand scale. His intensive all-day session on "relationships through time" has attracted several hundred people (in my estimate); we fill a small hotel ballroom. The audience appears to be 80 or 90 percent female, and Weiss confidently predicts that some 50 or 60 percent or maybe even two-thirds of us will have "experiences." Those who don't gain access to a past life or their former selves in utero will still share in the experiences of others, he assures us. "We all share the group's experiences."

How do you retrieve a past-life experience while attending a lecture in a crowd? You allow yourself to be hypnotized. Hypnosis is simply a "state of focused concentration," Weiss assures us; we will never lose control. He then prepares us for the journey back through time by leading us through simple meditation exercises. The lights are dimmed, New Age music plays, and in a soft, soothing voice he tells us to "close our eyes and breathe deeply: "Breathe in the beautiful energy all around you." He tells us to imagine that we're sitting in a pond, that our thoughts are bubbles, which drift off and disappear. Or, "if you have a fear of water, say, for example that you drowned in a past life, and you're a little nervous about water, imagine yourself in a beautiful field and use a helium baloon and just float away."

After a few exercises like this, we are ready for a twenty-minute meditation designed to provide us with our first "experience": "Imagine a beautiful light above your head . . . a healing light . . . a spiritual light connected to the light above and around you . . . Now let the light come into your body, through the top of your head." This "beautiful light" is flowing through our body, he tells us, "healing our hearts." Then he counts backward from ten and we are supposed to let ourselves "go deeper: Go back so deep that your mind is free from the usual limits of space and time, so deep that you can remember everything, every experience that you've ever had in this body, or any body you've ever had or even in between bodies when you've been in the spiritual state."

You get the idea. Eventually, we're told to imagine that we're walking down a beautiful staircase, into a beautiful garden "a sanctuary, a place of complete safety, filled with love, surrounded by light." We're told to recall a pleasant childhood experience. Then Weiss counts backward from five while we "go back, before [we] were born, in utero." What do we remember? Did we choose this life, we're supposed to ask ourselves in utero. "You can remember everything," Weiss tells us repeatedly. "You can remember everything you need and want to remember."

Those of us who "want to go further" are invited "back to other lifetimes or even other dimensions or spiritual states." We can experience "whatever [we] need to experience." It's easy. As Weiss counts backward from five once again, we're supposed to imagine ourselves before a "beautiful door . . . The doorway is a door into pasts, past lives or other dimensions . . . The door will open [and] you'll see a beautiful light on the other side of the door. Go through that door, there is something for you to learn on the other side . . . Go through the door and into the light. And through the light you will see a scene." Don't try to criticize or analyze the scene, he tells us. Don't worry about whether or not it represents a fantasy or metaphor. "Don't analyze, just experience."

"Oh, do not ask 'What is it?' Let us go and make our visit."

Listening to Weiss and watching people participate in this exercise, I recall no in utero experiences and no past lives, but I can't get this line from "The Love Song of J. Alfred Prufrock" out of my head.

Weiss ends the exercise, awakening the audience as he counts to ten. Then he asks for a show of hands. How many people went back in utero? How many returned to a past life? Surveying the raised hands, he estimates that about 50 percent of the audience has enjoyed an "experience." He praises us; we are a "good group," and he predicts that we'll have more experiences by the end of the day.

Soon he us leading us through another exercise, telling us to imagine a particular time period. "Imagine six doors, each leaping into a different time." We're supposed to peer through the each door briefly and choose one. Five of the doors represent respectively the sixteenth, eighteenth, and nineteenth centuries, the year A.D. 25, and the year 500 B.C. "plus or minus a year." If we're not attracted to any of these periods, we can go through the sixth door into the time of our choosing. Soon, people all around me are supposedly recovering their past lives, under Weiss's relentless direction: "How many lifetimes you have had. How wonderful you are," he says. People are told to rest and watch their former selves for several minutes.

Weiss always remains in control. After guiding people to their past lives, he decides when they should return to the present, which doesn't seem fair, or feasible if you believe in reincarnation. Who made Brian Weiss gatekeeper to the previous incarnations of so many souls? But people who asked that question and doubted Weiss's power would not have paid to attend his session.

"Now the images fade away," he says, terminating our supposed sojourn in the past. But on our way back to the mundane environment of a hotel ballroom, he takes us to a "beautiful island, a healing island embedded in the floor of the sea." Although apparently underwater, this "island" boasts a "beautiful" beach. Soon people are swimming with the dolphins in the "beautiful, wonderful water, charged with the healing energy of crystals."

Is this harmless entertainment? Perhaps many of the women here feel relaxed and momentarily at peace when they awake from their reveries. Perhaps a series of meditations with Brian Weiss is the equivalent of a day at the spa. I can't presume to judge Weiss's effect on his audience—but neither can he. He knows nothing about the people in this room; he is utterly ignorant of their histories, expectations, emotional states, or mental health. Will they be helped, harmed, or barely affected by the "experiences" or fantasies he's helped them formulate? Dr. Weiss cannot say.

But if some find Weiss's session therapeutic, I doubt they have "accessed" any prior lives. Of course, I am not inclined to believe in serial reincarnation. Weiss, who seems to take pride in his own skeptical intelligence ("I always take my left brain with me," he confesses), would probably dismiss me as a faux skeptic. A real skeptic, he suggests, would be inclined to believe that someone reporting a past-life experience had merely "tapped into the collective unconscious."

My own skepticism does not include faith in a collective unconscious and my doubts about reincarnation are not only rational but intuitive: I don't feel as if I've lived before. During a break, I explain this to a woman who has just enjoyed an "experience." I wonder if she'll confirm my "feeling reality." She does not. Her feelings prove the truth of her belief that we have all been reincarnated; my feelings mean that I'm "blocked," or in denial. Perhaps. But if I were to entertain seriously the notion that I have lived before, and that my past lives are accessible, I would not expect to encounter them so easily. The prospect of reincarnation is actually less surprising and unsettling to me than the spectacle of several hundred people following Weiss's directions, in the belief that he can lead them en masse to their former incarnations.

Pop gurus offer instant spiritual gratification, clearly designed for a consumer culture. Follow their lead and you will re-experience a past life or converse with a deceased relative in less time than it takes to get a driver's license. The spiritual peace and enlightenment offered by these gurus doesn't require a lifetime of study and discipline or even individual sessions. Attend their lectures and workshops; buy their books and tapes (on sale throughout the three-day conference I attend). They all confirm our immortality—and offer easy access to it.

What's wrong with a phenomenon that brings comfort to so many people? That's a bit like asking what's wrong with a lobotomy, a steady diet of happy pills, or a group like Heaven's Gate. Charismatic authority figures are always disconcerting, especially when they malign rationalism and exhort us to abandon our critical thinking powers in order to realize spiritual growth. Pop gurus prey on existential anxieties and thrive when our fear of being alone and mortal in an indifferent universe is stronger than our judgment. Argue with them. No one who demands worship, however covertly, deserves respect.

CHAPTER 5

—

JUNK SCIENCE

To a skeptic, hubris is a mark of spiritual hucksterism; but to people seeking assurances of eternal life, it's probably a comfort. Asking them to argue with a guru misses the point of being a follower. Spiritual and religious leaders are often expected to offer and embody certainty, not doubt; and some are always happy to oblige. "Has Mrs. Eddy lost her power to heal," Mary Baker Eddy, founder of Christian Science, asked rhetorically a century ago. "Has the sun forgotten to shine, and the planets to revolve around it?" [1]

Not all self-proclaimed saviors are quite as unabashed about their power as Mrs. Eddy, or as quick to imply their own divinity. Sometimes, to buttress their own assertions, they invoke the same secular authorities that they otherwise degrade—namely rationalism and science. As a review of pop spirituality literature shows, the most fanciful assertions are often cloaked in pseudoscience in a bid for credibility. Even the self-assured Mary Baker Eddy called her religion Christian Science.

Ours is often said to be a secular, scientific society, and science retains considerable authority. But popular understanding of science is quite limited, and, in practice, we are much more at home with religious faith. Sunday school is, after all, a lot less taxing intellectually than science class. The combination of respect for scientific expertise, ignorance of scientific principles, and a penchant for religious faith is a perfect prescription for pseudoscience. It's discouraging that some 44 percent of Americans prefer the simple biblical story of creation to Darwin's theory of evolution. But it's not surprising that many creationists call their religious answer to Darwinism "creation science."

The use of pseudoscientific concepts to validate thoroughly unscientific claims dates back to eighteenth-century Europe, when science was beginning to emerge as a powerful source of alternative authority. In the 1700s, Franz Anton Mesmer drew upon nascent understandings of electricity to explain the alleged therapeutic power of animal magnetism. Mesmer, a physician, claimed that a universal force, or fluid, coursed through our bodies and the atmosphere. He posited that illness resulted from fluid imbalances or obstacles to its flow, and preached that exposure to magnets could correct the flow and restore the patient's vital balance. In some cases, it seemed, a healer could effectively harness the vital force within his own body and effect a cure: Mesmer purported to heal people simply by pointing his finger at them, often inducing convulsions, which gradually subsided as the patients apparently recovered. He also practiced hypnosis on his patients and claimed to have "tapped an occult force through which he could influence others." [2]

In his day, Mesmer was effectively debunked by a commission of scientists, headed by Lavoisier, including Ben Franklin, and appointed by the French king, Louis XVI. After conducting their own experiments on the placebo effect, which involved actually treating one group of people with magnets and merely convincing another group that it was being treated with magnets, commission members concluded that the effect of Mesmer's treatments were psychological: "imagination without magnetism produces convulsions and . . . magnetism without imagination produces nothing."[3]

Still, Mesmer's work greatly influenced spiritualists, alternative healers, and positive thinkers who preached the gospel of success. Today, practitioners of therapeutic touch echo Mesmer when they claim that they can scan the body's energy field and redirect or rebalance the energy flow without ever touching the patient. As two critics have remarked, "Therapeutic Touch is, in many respects, Animal Magnetism in modern dress."[4] In the nineteenth century, Mesmer's theories contributed to popular interest in spiritualism, mind-cure, and New Thought movements, which emphasized the redemptive power of optimism or what William James called "healthy-minded attitudes." All these beliefs were premised on the existence of unseen energies that connected us all, living and dead.

Pseudoscientific references to energy and communications systems have rarely been absent from these theologies. They often appropriate the language of reigning technologies. Nineteenth-century spiritualists spoke of a "wireless telegraph" connecting them to the departed. Faith healers regarded themselves as "conductors" of God's healing energy.[5] In the mid-twentieth century, Napoleon Hill, author of *Think and Grow Rich,* based his claim that the desire for wealth was self-fulfilling on a discussion of unspecified mental "vibrations" and magnetic forces: "Our brains become magnetized with the dominating thoughts which we hold in our minds . . . these 'magnets' attract to us the forces, the people, the circumstances of life which harmonize with the nature of our *dominating* thoughts."[6] Today discussions of trance channeling refer to "electromagnetic spectrums." Prayer is likened to a radio transmission: in *The Book of Angels*, Sophy Burnham exhorts us to "Imagine there is a giant radio station out in space, beyond the stars, a receiving station, and all you have to do is to beam your thought, your longing to that station . . ."[7]

Science and spiritualism both flourished in the nineteenth century, and it's not surprising that some spiritualists actually looked to science for confirmation of their claims. (William James, who traversed the boundaries of spiritualism and science with extraordinary grace, was a member of the Society for Psychical Research.) Scientists uncovered unseen immaterial realities, after all. Why was the existence of electricity any more plausible than the virtues of a "universal fluid" that animates and surrounds us? To people just getting accustomed to telephones and telegraphs, mental telepathy might not have seemed strange. It's no coincidence that we refer to the "miracles" of technology. To an inhabitant of the nineteenth century, computers would seem more fantastic than ghosts.

The more limited your understanding of science, the more that scientists resemble masters of the occult, and the more that paranormal phenomenon seem likely to reflect undiscovered scientific truths. (It's often difficult to distinguish science fiction from supernaturalism.) A persistent irony of scientific progress is its encouragement of pseudoscientific claims. Most of us without advanced degrees are ultimately at the mercy of scientific authorities. We take on faith detailed explanations of space travel or even chemotherapy. Why should we doubt equally assured "scientific" explanations of time travel or ESP? Sometimes, the more that people are attracted to supernaturalism and hostile to the skepticism of scientists, the more receptive they are to pseudoscience that buttresses their beliefs. Discussions of energy systems, vibrational frequencies, and meaningless references to quantum physics pervade New Age literature. Deepak Chopra talks about "quantum healing."

Chopra's best-selling book *Ageless Body, Timeless Mind: The Quantum Alternative to Growing Old* exemplifies the use of junk science today in the service of New Age alternative healing. By indiscriminate use of the word "quantum," Chopra appropriates the authority and sophistication of physics, referring offhandedly to the "quantum nature of exercise," or offering to lead you into "quantum space" and even "beyond the quantum." Most of his readers are likely to be unfamiliar with quantum physics, most are eager to acquire the ageless body he promises, so few are likely to question Chopra's silliest "scientific" assertions. Besides, he offers them actual "quantum" experiences. In one typical passage, Chopra guides his readers through an exercise designed to help them imagine that they have crossed into the "fourth dimension," where the body is a mere illusion, and then he assures them that what they have imagined is true:

Study your hand, as if you were examining it through a microscope, he says. Soon you will have "arrived at the boundary between matter and energy . . . Here your hand exists before the Big Bang and after the universe's end in the 'heat death' of absolute zero. In reality these terms are meaningless, for you have arrived at the womb of the universe, the pre-quantum region that has no dimensions and all dimensions."[8] What is he talking about? You can only assume that readers who have no idea what Chopra is saying at times like this simply assume he's saying something. In fact, enigmatic or utterly incomprehensible statements may assure people of his authority. Gurus are supposed to understand truths about the universe that most of us can only sense as mysteries.

Still, a mass-market advice book does not succeed unless its underlying message is mundane, despite the air of mystery with which it is conveyed. The typical best-selling personal development book offers a clearly recognizable philosophy, framed as a series of previously inaccessible or undiscovered truths. In keeping with tradition, Chopra's message is deadeningly familiar to any student of positive thinking: With the right attitude, or "awareness," you can program your body to enjoy good health and an astonishingly long life.

He begins by offering us nothing less than Shangri-la: for $13 (the price of a paperback), Chopra will take us to a land "where old age, senility, infirmity, and death do not exist and are not even entertained as a possibility." We can get there by embracing new possibilities included in (what else?) a new paradigm. Discard the assumptions of the old paradigm, including the belief that sickness, aging, and death are inevitable. "If you change your perception, you change the experience of your body and your world." Like many positive thinkers, Chopra offers wish-fulfillment or magical thinking: "When properly focused . . . awareness has the ability to carry out quite specific commands . . . *intentions automatically seek their fulfillment if left alone.*" [9]

Taken figuratively, in moderation, this is unremarkable advice. Common sense can attest to the value of self-confidence and confirm the concept of a mind/body connection, which Chopra also exploits. The assertion that mental and emotional states have physical consequences is uncontroversial and needn't cloak itself in pseudoscience to gain respectability: a skeptic can accept that stress raises blood pressure and anxiety contributes to indigestion. But mind power has long been spiritualized and imbued with an exaggerated power to heal (rationalized by talk about energy systems). In its magical form, the notion of a mind/body connection is a model of pseudoscience.

Chopra is a descendant of nineteenth-century alternative healers, like Mary Baker Eddy, who also preached that illness was an illusion (what Chopra might call a matter of perception). Compare his assertion that suffering, sickness, aging, and death are not "part of reality" [10] to Eddy's claim that "Sin, sickness, and death are . . . effects of error." "The only reality of sin, sickness, and death is the awful fact that unrealities seem real to human erring belief, until God strips them of their disguise." [11] True to the relativism of popular therapy, Chopra does not seem to be particularly interested in sin, and he prefers talk about mysterious quantum fields or quantum spaces to Mary Baker Eddy's talk about God; but their selling point is the same: sickness and aging are essentially perceptions, or, rather, misperceptions.

Their packaging differs. Although both invoke "science," Mary Baker Eddy relied mainly on traditional religious authority (she refers to Jesus and claimed that she recovered her own health by reading the Gospel), while Chopra presents himself as a scientist, as well as a New Age seer. He accessorizes familiar notions about the mind/body connection with more esoteric references to biology, chemistry, and, of course, physics. The assertion that your attitudes and ideas determine your health is framed like this: "The biochemistry of the body is a product of awareness. Beliefs, thoughts, and emotions create the chemical reactions that uphold life in every cell." [12] Chopra's underlying claim that our bodies are not composed of "solid matter" echoes Mary Baker Eddy's claim that matter is "unreal . . . All is infinite Mind . . . Man is not material"; [13] but instead of describing man (or woman) as spiritual, Chopra says that "our bodies are composed of energy and information," which are "an outcropping of infinite fields of energy and information spanning the universe." [14] *Think and Grow Rich* author Napoleon Hill, who derived many of his ideas from New Thought, might agree.

He observed that the subconscious mind "picks up" the vibrations emitted by "faith blended with thought" and "transmits" them to God, or "Infinite Intelligence." [15]

"Thoughts are things," adherents of New Thought proclaimed long ago, suggesting that things are merely thoughts. That supposedly objective realities are matters of subjective perception is one of Chopra's themes: "The physical world, including our bodies, is a response of the observer. We create our bodies as we create the experience of our world." [16] Chopra might cite a long line of positive thinkers as authority for this assertion, but instead, like Hill, he relies largely on science. The supposedly "new" paradigm he presents is said to be grounded in the discoveries of quantum physics. Chopra's pretends to stand on the shoulders of "Einstein, Bohr, and Heisenberg, and the other pioneers of quantum physics, who realized that the accepted way of viewing the physical world was false. . . . Einstein taught us that the physical body, like all material objects, is an illusion." [17]

None of these references to physics is explained, much less footnoted (which should make any reader suspicious), and scientists tend to regard them with contempt. (As *Time* has observed, "[M]any scientists consider Chopra's assertions about quantum physics 'perverse rubbish.' ")[18] What do Chopra's assertions about the power of subjective perceptions have to do with quantum physics? Not much. Put very simply, quantum physics is the study of atoms and subatomic particles, which, in some ways, behave unpredictably. As science writer Marc Abrahams explains, "when you study subatomic particles close-up, you find that the familiar rules of the physical world don't apply to them. Chopra [and other New Age writers] seem to infer from this that the familiar rules of the physical world don't apply to us. But we're not subatomic particles." [19] In fact, physicists confirm, Newtonian physics, and common sense, "continue to apply on the human scale."[20] (Simply put, Newtonian physics is an approximate description of how all the elements of the physical world, from stars to specks of dust, move and interact.) Chopra's repeated references to quantum experiences, dimensions, or exercises can only make a little sense, at most, if you read them metaphorically, but I think he expects to be taken literally.

Chopra is hardly the first or the only New Age expert to seize upon quantum physics as support for the notion that all reality is relative or subjective (although he has marketed this "theory" more successfully than most). The uncertainty, the mystery of quantum physics seems to appeal to New Agers, who often claim that it demonstrates the power of mind over matter, or the identity of mind and matter, or even the supremacy of alleged metaphysical truths.

Marianne Williams perversely cites Einstein, Bohr, and Heisenberg as authorities for an attack on reason. In her view, quantum physics (which she, like Chopra, cites without explaining) encourages a more "spiritual interpretation of reality."[21] Thanks to the new physics, the medical establishment has begun to explore spiritual healing, she observes. The political establishment supposedly awaits a similar transformation, which Williamson apparently aims to lead.

If there is a God perhaps He or She will save us from the spiritualization of politics and policy. Pseudoscientific claims about healing are often harmless, if they don't encourage people to abandon more realistic therapies; and they may be helpful psychologically. In any case, people are entitled to choose their own medical treatments. So long as health care is widely available, and absent public health concerns about highly contagious diseases, a preference for therapeutic touch over traditional therapies is a private matter. Laws and policies, however, are by definition collective, public questions, and the use of junk science in policy making is a perennial public concern.

Different forms of junk science shape policy debates and personal or spiritual development movements. Pseudoscientific assertions about energy systems and other unseen realities play less of a role in policy making than misuse or misapprehensions of scientific research and foolish stabs at social science. Advocates of official school prayer, for example, are apt to cite statistics allegedly proving that the decline of prayer results in a rise of out-of-wedlock births and violent crime. On the *700 Club*, Pat Robertson has asserted that crime is caused by the absence of mandatory prayer in school. What evidence has he offered: Crime rose in the 1960s, following the Supreme Court decision invalidating organized, official school prayer. Therefore, Robertson has declared, restoring official school prayers would decrease crime. Children who pray together won't prey together.

You don't have to be an atheist or agnostic to question this assertion. All you need are some basic reasoning skills providing an understanding of the difference between correlation and causation: unrelated events often occur simultaneously. In addition to the abolition of official school prayer, America's first manned space flight dates back to the early 1960s. We might just as well blame crime on the space program; instead of forcing children to pray, we might abolish NASA.

Yet, Robertson delivered his message about school prayer like a math or science teacher explaining an equation. (On the *700 Club*, he stood before a graph showing a rising crime line in the 1960s.) It is a common tactic. During his successful campaign for a school board seat in Lee County, Florida, in 1996, one Christian Coalition candidate used a graph to demonstrate a supposed connection between the abolition of school-sponsored prayer and a decline in SAT scores.[22] But there's nothing mathematical or scientific about these claims. You have to take them on faith, and many who believe in the virtue of prayer probably do. Faith, not reason, is the engine of pseudoscience.

Religious faith and spirituality, in general, are not necessarily inimical to real science or rationalism. Sixteenth-century astrophysicist Johann Kepler was a devout Christian, as was Isaac Newton, who took the Bible literally. Nineteenth-century zoologist and botanist Alfred Russel Wallace, who, along with Darwin, developed the theory of natural selection, believed in spiritualism. In addition to several scientific works, Wallace authored *Miracles and Modern Spiritualism*.[23] Thomas Edison was attracted to the occult and various paranormal phenomenon. He believed in psychokinesis (the telepathic control of physical objects), developed an interest in theosophy and the writings of Madame Blavatsky, and tried to invent a machine for communicating electronically with the dead.[24]

Today many scientists apparently believe that they can enter into relationships with God. About 40 percent of scientists responding to a 1997 survey said they believed in a God who communicates with people and may be expected to answer their prayers.[25] As a class, scientists may be more prone to skepticism or agnosticism than the general public: 87 percent of people surveyed by *Newsweek* in 1997 agreed that God answers our prayers (compared to 40 percent of scientists).[26] Still it's clear that the vast majority of Americans who profess belief in God include a number of scientists, and efforts to reconcile science and religion, or at least conduct "dialogues" between scientists and theologians came into fashion in the 1990s. As George Johnson reported in the *New York Times,* the "longing for reconciliation" consists mostly of a religious desire to spiritualize science. It has been facilitated by the well-endowed, religiously oriented Templeton Foundation, which confers the annual Templeton Prize for Progress in Religion, now worth over a million dollars. Templeton has also invested millions in the development of university-based programs on science and religion, and, in June 1997, the Templeton-funded Center for Theology and the Natural Sciences, in Berkeley, California, held a four-day conference on cosmology and religion.[27] Astronomer Allan Sandage reportedly testified that studying the Big Bang helped convince him that God exists.[28]

But if religious belief is compatible with a penchant for science, leaps of faith are no substitute for the scientific method. This is not to suggest that scientists are people of little or no faith. "Faith is synonymous with working hypothesis," William James observed.[29] Science proceeds by hypothesis: scientists discover questions, posit answers, and hope that investigation will prove them to be true. They seek elegant solutions—evidence of order and symmetry. The acute aesthetic sensibilities of physicists were illustrated in a 1998 *New York Times* report on conflicting theories about neutrinos—enigmatic subatomic particles. Dr. John Bahcall, a theorist at the Institute for Advanced Studies in Princeton, sounded so wistful observing that "sterile neutrinos are a very ugly concept."[30]

I can't pretend to understand theoretical discussions about neutrinos, but it's not hard to recognize Bahcall's yearning for evidence of transcendent beauty in the universe: remarking on one explanation of solar neutrinos, he said, "The MSW effect is a beautiful idea. It would seem like a cosmic mistake if nature did not use this solution."[31]

I don't know whether or how much theories about the universe reflect the aesthetics of the theorists. Writer Malcolm

Gladwell has opined that "physicists and mathematicians are really the last intellectuals who get to use beauty as a criteria for assessing the value of knowledge."[32] Yet, beauty is not their criteria for truth. The scientist guided partly by faith and aesthetics in formulating ideas still puts them to the test of reason. Scientists conduct experiments to evaluate the possible truth of their hypothesis, even those that come to mind with the force of revelation.

In the end, faith needs to be contained in the realm of the unknowable. It is an inapt basis for understanding the material world, as reason is inapt in finding God or inadequate in resolving emotional conflicts. We expect therapists to address feelings as well as facts, just as we expect religious and spiritual leaders to rely comfortably on faith, more than reason, when confirming the occurrence of miracles or describing other supernatural realities. But it is unsettling to learn that former First Lady Nancy Reagan relied on an astrologer in advising her husband or that some police departments still use psychics to help them solve crimes (with generally unimpressive results). The New York Police Department occasionally consults alleged psychic Dorothy Allison, although, as the *New York Times* has tactfully reported, "her success rate in cases around the country is difficult to pinpoint."[33] Of course, the NYPD has not abandoned traditional investigatory techniques, and detectives who turn to Mrs. Allison may successfully compartmentalize their irrational belief in her powers: they probably see her as supplementing, not supplanting, an actual investigation. Still, the spectacle of a major metropolitan police force seeking psychic assistance testifies to the reach of superstition into what should be a realm of reason. Secular governance and questions of law and policy surely require reliance on empirical data aimed at discerning objective realities, along with an understanding of how the data should be interpreted.

I'm not denying that many public policy issues also involve ideological or moral choices (as police investigations may involve instinct or intuition). I believe the death penalty is morally wrong, and data strongly suggests that it is ineffective in deterring homicides. Others consider it a moral imperative, regardless of its deterrent effect. But none of us can intuit our way to justice or crime control. To fashion a fair and effective criminal justice system, we need to monitor actual police and judicial practices, consider demographic factors affecting crime, and examine the effect of sentencing policies, or handgun ownership, among other myriad matters. Nor can we intuit our way to welfare reform, relying on what people feel about a link between welfare benefits and teenage pregnancies. We need empirical evidence of any supposed causal relationship between welfare programs and the behavior of recipients.

My point is obvious but often overlooked, partly because the celebration of subjective perception, feelings, and faith that permeates the culture, high and low, has discredited efforts to discern objective realities. The principle of scientific objectivity itself has been attacked by postmodernists, who see only unquestioned biases where others see facts. Even "physical reality" is a "social and linguistic construct," physicist Alan Sokal wrote, parodying the postmodern critique of science. Sokal's parody was taken seriously and published by the editors of the academic journal *Social Text* in a special antiscience issue. Sokal's successful hoax exposed the idiocies of subjectivity and cultural relativism, taken to extremes, which, in academia at least may finally be passing out of fashion.[34]

But when subjectivism is no longer trendy, we will still feel its influence. In the last decades of this century, it has helped shape public policy decisions and our underlying notions of liberty and justice. The therapeutic culture and related New Age "consciousness" movements, for example, have already infected the political sphere with a preference for feelings over facts, partly through their historic influence on feminists. (It's been most evident in debates about sexual misconduct and the notion that a woman who feels victimized—harassed or otherwise abused—has been victimized.) This overweening subjectivism naturally derives from gender stereotypes, including assumptions about women's intuition, that aided nineteenth-century female spiritualists and still thrive today. In late-twentieth-century America, the quasi-feminist, therapeutic culture brought into question the underlying rationale for equality—the notion that women were apt to be as resilient and intelligent as men. It associated feminism with a stereotypically feminine penchant for emotionalism, instead of reason.

Like the relationship of official school prayer to the crime rate, embrace of the naturally feminine virtues is mostly an article of faith. It expresses an emotional truth, not a rational evaluation of evidence, much less respect for individualism. The will to believe, regardless of evidence, which underlies the sense that God exists, can undermine campaigns for earthly justice and efforts to apprehend material realities. It contributes to the most unjust, ineffective public policies—like the war on drugs, which exemplifies the potentially disastrous influence of faith on public policy.

The irrationality of the drug war is matched only by its popularity with politicians, who refuse to consider facts like these: alcohol is associated with much more violent crime than any illegal drug. According to a 1997 study by Columbia University, which confirmed what criminologists have long known, 21 percent of violent felons in state prisons committed their crimes while under the influence of alcohol alone; only 3 percent were high on cocaine, and only 1 percent were using heroin.[35] Violent crimes linked to alcohol use include murder, rape, and domestic abuse. We might add to this list drunk driving, which would not have been covered by the Columbia study of prison inmates, since it doesn't often result in incarceration.

A sensible person reviewing these findings might wonder why we criminalize the use of cocaine and heroin, not to mention marijuana, while we tolerate and even celebrate alcohol consumption. Of course, we learned long ago that prohibition of alcohol was bound to fail. So a sensible person might propose that we consider ending prohibition of drugs like marijuana, cocaine, and heroin, which pose much less threat to the public safety than alcohol, or at least reduce harsh penalties for their use. But sensible people have had little influence over the nation's drug policies.

Listening to bureaucrats and politicians boast about the drug war, you have to wonder what they're smoking. The war on drugs has been one of the biggest public policy disasters of the last twenty-five years. It has not reduced drug use; it has instead increased violent crime attendant on illegal drug trafficking, and police corruption, just as the prohibition of alcohol increased criminal activity and graft in the 1920s. It has eroded civil liberties, particularly constitutional protections against unwarranted searches and seizures. The war on drugs has greatly exacerbated the terrible problem of gun violence. The illegal drug trade not only creates violence; it pays for bigger and better guns. It has helped finance the arms race in the streets.[36]

The war on drugs has also created a crisis in prison over-crowding. People are sent to state and federal prison for long terms, five, ten, or twenty years, for nonviolent, low-level drug offenses. Providing them with in-prison drug treatment programs may be helpful, but it obscures the fact that many drug users should not be in prison at all. The nation's drug laws have turned many ordinary, relatively harmless citizens with ordinary bad habits into convicted felons. What jobs will they find when they're released? What will they contribute to their families or communities? If we imprison people to protect society, we have to ask what society gains in the end from their imprisonment.

I'm not suggesting that the solution to America's drug problem is simple. Decriminalization, legalization, or reductions in sentences imposed on drug users or dealers require careful empirical analysis of costs and benefits. I do want to underscore our failure even to engage in such dispassionate inquiries. Politicians and political appointees risk their careers when they demonstrate willingness to consider alternative approaches to drug abuse. Among the controversial remarks that hastened the resignation of former surgeon general Joycelyn Elders was the suggestion that we study legalization.

We don't ask questions about the efficacy of the drug war, or elect politicians who do, because drug use is generally considered sinful. The war on drugs has been billed as an anticrime measure, but, in fact, it is a faith-based antivice crusade. That's why its failure has not sparked popular protests, or a rational evaluation of its benefits and costs. It is driven by moral fervor, not pragmatism or reason.

Hysteria about drug use has contributed to junk science about its effects. Consider the widely held belief popularized in the late 1980s that babies born to crack-addicted women suffered severe, permanent emotional and mental disabilities. The leading authority on crack baby syndrome was Ira Chasnoff, a Chicago pediatrician and director of a program for drug-addicted mothers at Northwestern University. Undeterred by a dearth of rigorous research, Chasnoff declared in *People* magazine, "These babies can't focus on a human face or respond to a human voice." They reportedly exhibited "gaze aversion," turning away from people observing them. "Crack babies" were said to present some symptoms associated with autism: lethargy, lack of emotion, and inability to form attachments to caretakers. But, they were also described, conversely, as jittery, agitated, and beset with tremors, at least temporarily. An unquestioning press quickly spread this sensational story, acknowledging its shaky foundation only in passing, if at all. The "long-term effects of crack are unknown," *Time* conceded at the end of an article on crack-exposed infants that was marked by pessimism about their future.[37]

Conventional wisdom about these infants became increasingly apocalyptic: they were expected to become practically uneducable and unemployable. According to Coryl Jones, a research psychologist at the National Institute of Drug Abuse, prenatal exposure to crack was apparently "interfering with the central core of what it is to be human." University of California researcher Judy Howard opined that prenatal exposure to crack "wiped out" the part of the brain that "makes us human beings, capable of discussion or reflection." Conservative commentator Charles Krauthamer predicted that "crack babies" would form a new "bio-underclass." [38]

There was, however, relatively little hard evidence of these dire claims, as journalists began to report in the 1990s.[39] Researchers who studied the children of drug users and found no evidence of a crack baby syndrome finally began to be heard. The crack baby myth was not simply perpetuated by journalists who misrepresented research; the research community itself may have been blinded by biases. During the 1980s, papers confirming the crack baby story were more likely to be published than papers refuting it, according to one study. Claire Coles, associate professor of psychiatry at Emory University, a leading critic of the crack baby story, recalled being accused of fabricating data or supporting drug abuse.[40]

Coles pointed out that alcohol use was "considerably worse" for developing fetuses than cocaine use and that babies labeled "crack babies" were sometimes merely colicky. Generally, researchers who "discovered" crack babies did not separate the effects of prenatal exposure to crack from the effects of prenatal exposure to alcohol, tobacco, and other drugs. Nor did they account for the poverty, including poor nutrition and chaotic home environments, that many of these children shared. Perceived developmental problems in infants were blamed on cocaine by people inclined to assume the devastating effects of cocaine on the fetus, just as crime is blamed on the absence of mandatory school prayer by people who assume that prayer makes children behave.[41]

Bad science about the effects of prenatal drug exposure led to bad policy, as well as inappropriate treatment of infants presumed afflicted. "Crack babies" were supposed to be tightly swaddled, kept in dark places, and shielded from direct eye contact with their caretakers. We can only speculate about the effects of this treatment on essentially normal children eager for stimulation and human contact. The effects of crack baby propaganda on national drug policy, as well as race relations, were easier to discern. It played to racist anxiety about a presumptively sociopathic, less-than-human, African-American underclass. It helped antivice crusaders demonize drug use, justify the futile, counterproductive war against drugs, and ignore the poverty that afflicted more children than prenatal exposure to crack. Claire Coles recalled one "crack baby" who had trouble concentrating in school because of persistent hunger, not damage caused by cocaine.

The crack baby scare wasn't science; it was, in part, politics. This is not to suggest that advocates knowingly perpetuated myths about drug-afflicted infants. Rather, many were likely to have been primed by their own prejudices and political agendas to believe that the myths were true. They probably acted in good faith, perpetuating bad science and bad policy.

The uncritical acceptance of research claims that tell us what we want to hear or what we fear has received some critical attention in the media. ABC correspondent John Stossel hosted a 1997 TV special on junk science, which debunked false reports about crack babies and cold fusion and challenged claims about the dangers of breast implants, salty diets, and soil contaminated with dioxen. In assessing the blame for junk science, Stossel identified a host of culprits—government bureaucrats who want to justify their jobs, scientists greedy for fame if not fortune, journalists eager for stories, and mercenary trial attorneys seeking damages. A few hapless purveyors of questioned claims appeared on camera, to their great disadvantage. Stossel demonstrated appropriate contempt for purveyors of junk science, but he might have counted himself among them.

One man's science is another woman's junk. Two years earlier, in February 1995, Stossel hosted a one-hour special on sex difference. Purporting to reveal scientific evidence of biologically determined cognitive and emotional differences between men and women, this show exemplified the reliance on prejudice, preconceptions, and an occasional questionable study that produces junk science—and has always underlain popular sex-based stereotypes.

Junk science about sexual differences is older than the feminist drive for sexual equality. Fanciful scientific research purporting to show that women are a weaker, stupider, more irrational sex has always been used to justify sex discrimination, just as "science" about racial differences justified race discrimination. Indeed, considering its history of sexism, as well as racism, junk science helped create the need for a feminist movement. One hundred years ago, scientists held that males were smarter than females because their brains were heavier, and they warned women that physical exercise would damage their reproductive systems. The history of sexist junk science partly accounts for feminist mistrust of scientific objectivity, which has lately devolved into an ideologically charged embrace of subjective realities. Popular feminism's embrace of "women's intuition" and preference for spiritism over rationalism is one of the sad ironies of modern feminism which was shaped partly by rebellion against male assumptions of female stupidity.

The proof offered by scientists of women's intellectual inferiority makes you wonder how men gained a reputation as naturally smart and rational. To demonstrate the connection between intelligence and brain weight, some scientists around the turn of the century devoted themselves to weighing the brains of famous men. Byron reportedly had a huge brain weighing 2,238 grams, which made him a couple of hundred grams smarter than Turgenev, whose brain weighed 2,012 grams. But, as feminist Helen Hamilton Gardner pointed out, no man's brain outweighed the brain of a whale. If intelligence were determined by brain weight, Gardner observed, "Almost any elephant is . . . perhaps an entire medical faculty." [42]

Gardner bequeathed her own brain to researchers at Cornell University in the belief that scientists should study the brains of "women who think." (In the 1890s, she urged Elizabeth Cady Stanton and Susan B. Anthony to bequeath their brains to science when they were "done" with them.) [43] Gardner might have been pleased with the posthumous press coverage her brain received. In 1927, in an extensive article on the "controversy over mental equality," the *New York Times* soberly reported that Gardner's brain "reveals a wealth of cortical substance, or gray matter, that is only equaled, but not exceeded, by the best brains in the Cornell collection, which includes those of a number of doctors, professors, lawyers, and naturalists."[44]

Scientific knowledge about the human brain has increased considerably in the past 70 years, but junk science about male and female brain power persists. In his television special on sex difference, John Stossel declared that "scientists now know that men and women use different parts of their brain when thinking about the same things." Many people brought up to assume that men are from Mars and women are from Venus probably agreed. But studies showing how scientists "know" this were not cited, much less explained, and skeptical viewers were given no way of evaluating this dramatic claim. In fact, one of the most widely touted recent studies on the way males and females use their brain actually shows more similarities than differences between them.

In 1995 Yale University researchers Bennett and Sally Shaywitz published a study in which nineteen men and nineteen women were asked to perform four cognitive tasks. Brain scans showed that when they undertook *one* task—determining whether nonsense words rhymed—eleven of the nineteen women used different parts of the brain than all nineteen men. The press pounced on this story as evidence of dramatic sex difference, greatly exaggerating its findings. "Men and Women Use Brain Differently, Study Discovers," according to the headline of the front-page story in the *New York Times* that announced the Shaywitz study.[45]

A more accurate headline might have been "Men and

Women Use Brains Similarly." The differences cited by the Shay-witzes appeared only when male and female subjects performed one out of four tasks, and they showed up in only a little more than half of the females. In other words, when performing three assigned tasks, all the men and all the women appeared to use their brains similarly; in performing one task, 42 percent of the women and 100 percent of the men seemed to use their brains similarly. What are the implications of this? Even if you choose to focus on the findings of difference in this study, it tells you nothing about male and female capabilities. There was no showing that the different way in which some female subjects appeared to use their brains affected their performance.

John Stossel is not alone in playing up highly equivocal evidence of difference and ignoring evidence of similarity. Often, scientific caveats about assumptions of difference are buried toward the end of stories that sensationalize any showing of difference. In general, research into male and female brains has shown "an amazing degree of overlap," the *New York Times* conceded at the end of a story, on February 28, 1995, perversely entitled "Brain Studies Point to Difference." According to UCLA biologist Roger Gorski, "[T]here is so much overlap that if you take any individual man and woman, they might show differences in the opposite direction" from what showings of average difference might predict.[46]

It's worth noting that Stossel cited Roger Gorski's work on female rats as evidence of biologically based, behavioral differences between men and women, drawing conclusions that Gorski himself disdained. "[P]eople overinterpret these things," Gorski told the *New York Times*. "The brain is very complicated." After fifteen years of studying sex differences in brains of rats, Dr. Gorski said, he still doesn't understand them and has seen nothing similar in the brains of humans.[47]

What motivates such skewed reporting? Traditional notions of cognitive sex differences remain much more popular than feminist attempts to revolutionize gender roles. Many women, as well as men, are attached to the notion that rationalism and objectivity are essentially masculine, while intuition and subjectivity are feminine. Research that seems to show differences in the way men and women think confirms conventional street-corner wisdom, reflected in popular self-help books, jokes about men who won't ask directions, and a long history of sexually discriminatory laws and policies.

Junk science is often science shaped by politics or ideology, as John Stossel's show on sex difference showed. Like an anti-drug crusader eager to demonize cocaine use, he had a political agenda. His account of difference discredited feminist campaigns for equality, and a broad range of civil rights laws prohibiting sex discrimination. Expressing the same contempt for feminist claims about the capacity of women to compete with men that he directed at junk scientists, and presenting contrary claims about difference with great respect, Stossel declared that we have been misled by "lack of information" about male and female capabilities. "Today there are elaborate and expensive government policies based on the fiction that men and women are interchangeable, that we bring the exact same skills and aptitudes to the table."

Stossel would, however, be hard pressed to find a feminist who actually claims that men and women are exactly the same. Generally, advocates of equality will assert that no two people are the same. That's the point. Sex is not a good and fair predictor of talent or intelligence. There are differences among women, just as there are differences among men. Even if science could find average, cognitive differences between the sexes attributable to biology, which it has yet to do, averages would tell us little about variable, individual aptitude or behavior. If a class of ten students takes an exam and five students receive A's, while five receive C's, the average class score is a B; yet no one student received a B on the exam. The overinterpretation of averages is another mark of junk science, particularly science about differences in the way the sexes think and behave. Some women are better at math and map reading than some men. Some men are more passive than some women.

Of course, my own perspective on research about cognitive sex difference is bound to be colored by my belief in the justice of sexual equality. You have to examine attacks on junk science with the same skepticism that you apply to the science itself. It's hard to know at first glance which is more political—the scientific claims in question or the questioning of the scientific claims.

In the mid-1990s, exposés of junk science were issued by conservative advocates of tort reform, who sought to limit corporate liability for allegedly defective products, like breast implants, and diminish the regulatory power of federal watchdog agencies, like the Food and Drug Administration and the Environmental Protection Agency. Conservatives also used charges of junk science to discredit feminist research about discrimination and sexual violence, which was dismissed as victimology.

This doesn't mean that all their attacks were ill-founded, but they were often oversimplified, as were many highly politicized claims of harm. For example, dramatic claims about the causal relationship between breast implants and illness were persuasively challenged. (In 1998, a panel of scientists appointed by a federal court judge found no definitive evidence that silicon breast implants caused systemic disease.) But even well-founded attacks on the science employed in breast implant cases didn't entirely dispose of the legal issues they raised. Legal standards of proof are different from scientific standards of proof, because law and science serve different purposes. As Joan Bertin, formerly professor of public health at Columbia University, observes, one purpose of tort law is to ensure that companies will take care not to expose consumers to unnecessary risk. Cause and effect can be quite obscure in cases involving the relationship of environmental factors to disease. It may be appropriate for a court to find negligence in the marketing of a product if the manufacturer ignored initial questions about the product's safety, even if subsequent evidence does not support an epidemiological finding that the product actually caused harm.

Do we want to say, as a matter of public policy, that companies should not market products that they have some reason to believe will cause harm, even if that reason does not constitute scientific proof of causation? That is a political, not a scientific question, and it underlies the debate about tort reform. Law does, after all, seek to control the potential for harm. We prosecute people for driving under the influence whether or not they've caused accidents, because driving while drunk is potentially harmful; it's risky behavior. We outlaw selected semiautomatic rifles (labeled assault weapons) absent scientific proof that an assault weapons ban will reduce violent crime, because these weapons scare us and have the potential to cause great harm. In fact, most gun violence involves handguns, not semiautomatic rifles. Many people clamor for stringent control of handguns, even though epidemiologists can't prove that handguns cause crime. Advocates of gun ownership claim that handguns deter crime.

Whether corporations should be permitted to market breast implants, semiautomatic rifles, or handguns (free of liability), whether liquor companies or bars should be liable when consumers drive drunk, whether tobacco companies should be liable to smokers who contract cancer or heart disease are ultimately questions for voters, legislators, jurors, and judges, not scientists. Science should, of course, inform the decisions we make about these and other perceived hazards, but it should not control them.

Political decisions are bound to be inexact and somewhat arbitrary, at best. Politics lacks the precision and fairness ideally offered by science. If the authoritative definitiveness associated with science seems arrogant to some, many find it comforting—especially when it confirms what they believe. The irony is that real science proceeds from a position of uncertainty. The accumulation of scientific knowledge is a painstaking process, requiring the testing of theories, duplication of experiments, and a willingness to admit mistakes.

How can you distinguish science from junk? Science posits hypothesis and tests them. Pseudoscience assumes conclusions and finds evidence to back them up. People who begin with a belief in their ability to communicate with the dead will find proof of their beliefs in the unsubstantiated testimony of others, or nonsensical references to electromagnetic frequencies. People inclined to consider pornography dangerous, or evil, will greatly overstate the findings of laboratory studies purporting to show that porn "causes" aggressive behavior.[48] That scientific proof of a direct causal link between sexually explicit material and sexual violence is about as tenuous as proof that abolition of involuntary school prayer causes crime is irrelevant to true believers. If you somehow lead them to admit that their research is flawed, you will never get them to question their conclusions. Stripped of all evidence, their beliefs will persist. You can tell that people are relying on junk science, when they're not really relying on it at all.

—

CHAPTER 6

THE THERAPEUTIC ASSAULT ON REASON AND RIGHTS

A rational society is one that values argument and considers virtually all points of view subject to debate. It promotes inquiry, experimentation, and empiricism, maintaining some faith in objectivity—which is not the same as certainty. The search for evidence is not a search for indisputable proof. Rationalism is founded on skepticism—a commitment to testing all beliefs, including your own—and a capacity to tolerate doubt. People hungry for absolutes are more likely to choose supernaturalism or unadulterated emotionalism over any system of free inquiry. What is revealed to you in a moment of oneness with your Higher Power is absolutely reliable. What you know "in your heart" is rarely open to question. What you manage to figure out, given the limits of your knowledge and intelligence, is more tentative.

That fundamental religious beliefs are not generally subject to debate is part of their charm, and part of the reason alliances of church and state are so alarming. Public officials who are

absolutely certain of their own rectitude are less likely to tolerate criticism or dissent than officials who are only relatively sure
that their beliefs are true, and just. This does not mean, however, that Hamlet would make a better president than the
pope—or that we have to choose between a sense of infallibility
and paralyzing doubts.

Like atheism, skepticism is often confused with nihilism or,
at least, an inability to adopt principles and to act on them deci-
sively. But uncertainty does not doom the skeptic to pervasive
agnosticism or equivocation. Rationalism requires control of
the emotions and temperamental biases that help shape belief,
but not elimination of them: you take your convictions seriously, and act on them as if they were true. But you acknowledge the possibility of being wrong. So a rational society
tolerates and even encourages dissent (and freedom of expression). It values argument over resolution.[1]

The therapeutic culture shaped by the recovery movement is
profoundly irrational. It seeks truth not in debate but in revelation. It values bolstering people's self-esteem over challenging
their ideas. It assesses proposed truths partly by the passion
with which they are held and partly by their alleged therapeutic
effect. True beliefs are those that help you "heal."

Of course, not all therapists happily participate in this culture. Some disdain pop psychologies and the ideology of recovery, and I don't mean to indict indiscriminately the practice of
therapy or the therapeutic notion of truth. It is sometimes helpful and appropriate within the confines of a therapist's office.
Addressing what pop psychologists call "feeling realities" is the
business of therapy (which some practice with skill and compassion). What feels true to the patient may be more relevant
than empirical or historical truths. Psychoanalysis and other
therapies have been fairly characterized as aesthetic experi-

ences, and they do share a fascination with narrative. You emerge from therapy with a freshly written story about yourself and your family. If the story helps you, does it matter whether it was discovered or invented?

Someone hostile to supernaturalism might be asked a similar question about religious belief. If religion soothes people, protects them from debilitating fears of death, and enables them to endure, does it matter if its stories aren't true? To some extent, we do judge religion, as we judge therapy, by its effects. Major Western religious traditions are celebrated in America because they're considered essential sources of virtue, in addition to peace of mind. The outré beliefs of small minority faiths are disparaged partly because they're likely to be associated with irritating behavior (like chanting and panhandling in airports) and mental or emotional imbalance. The beliefs of Heaven's Gate were denigrated partly because they led to a mass suicide.

Even when their belief systems are not quite so destructive, any groups we label cults are regarded with disdain partly because they attack traditional family life (encouraging members to break away from their families), and partly because outsiders are apt to question the apparent contentment of members. Rightly or wrongly, cults are presumed to threaten society and harm individuals who join them. Mainstream religions are presumed to improve individuals and support the social order.

How do we judge religious beliefs or therapies that allegedly help individuals, at the expense of their families and communities, or the culture? That was one question posed by the recovery movement to those of us who were troubled by its celebration of victimization, hostility toward reason, and absurdly expansive notions of addiction and abuse. While I recoiled from this ideology, countless people testified that it had saved them from the "disease" of codependency. How could I question their feelings of well-being? Lacking carefully structured longitudinal studies of people in recovery, or consumers of recovery books, no one could objectively measure the long-term effectiveness of the books or treatment programs. But assuming that recovery did indeed help some people, we could still examine the ideas of the recovery movement and speculate about their effect on the culture.

One of the more destructive legacies of recovery has been the virtual sanctification of individual testimony of abuse. "Believe the women" and "believe the children" were rallying cries for followers of recovery, including many feminists, who were convinced that incest and other forms of child abuse and family violence were practically ubiquitous. If you questioned a self-proclaimed victim, or tried to reason with her, declining to presume that her story was true, you were likely to be accused of collaborating in her abuse.

Not that feminists lacked all reason for avidly supporting self-proclaimed victims of sexual abuse. For much of our history, family violence was considered a private matter, incest was barely acknowledged, and women who claimed to have been raped were routinely presumed to be lying, unless they fulfilled the most traditional feminine ideals—chastity, modesty, submissiveness, and fidelity. White women were treated with considerably more gallantry than black women, and before the passage of rape shield laws, all rape victims were liable to be brutally interrogated about their own, irrelevant sexual histories. But allied with recovery experts, therapeutic feminism helped mount a defense of self-proclaimed victims that became at least as unreasonable and unjust as the historic attacks on them.

The mandate to believe the victim prevailed even when the victim's story was unbelievable. Accusations of incest, recalled in adulthood, were combined with bizarre tales of satanic ritual abuse and conspiracy theories. According to one self-appointed expert on ritual abuse, the CIA, NASA, the Mafia, and a group of business leaders operate a network of satanic cults, started by Nazi scientists smuggled into the United States after World War II. The aim of conspirators, of course, is world domination. They want to turn people into "mental robots who will do pornography, prostitution, smuggle drugs, engage in international arms smuggling."[2]

Not all believers in the ubiquity of abuse shared this particular view of the impending apocalypse. But, in some quarters, a surprising majority—70 percent of people surveyed by *Redbook* in 1994—believed in the existence of abusive satanic cults. They believed that "at least some people who claim they were sexually abused by satanic cults as children, but repressed the memories for years, are telling the truth." Thirty-two percent of *Redbook's* respondents rationalized the absence of proof by explaining that "the FBI and the police ignore evidence because they don't want to admit the cults exist." An additional 22 percent opined that "cult leaders brainwash their victims so they won't tell."[3] A 1994 government report finding no evidence to substantiate widespread rumors of satanic abuse could easily have been dismissed as a cover-up, like official investigations of UFO sightings.[4]

The crash of an "extra-terrestrial spacecraft" in Roswell, New Mexico, in 1947 was the "biggest story of the millennium. . . . The evidence is overwhelming that planet Earth is being visited by extra-terrestrial spacecraft." . . . according to Stanton Friedman, author of a book about the Roswell phenomenon. He has condemned as a cover-up a 1997 U.S. Air Force report demonstrating that what crashed at Roswell were high-altitude balloons and crash dummies attached to parachutes.[5] Friedman's tenacious belief in UFOs is apparently widely shared. According to a Time/Yankelovich Poll a startling 80 percent of Americans believe that the government is concealing information about extra-terrestrials.[6] An estimated sixty thousand believers flocked to Roswell in July 1997 to celebrate the fiftieth anniversary of the alleged crash.[7] Evidence offered to debunk the Roswell myth seems only to intensify the fervor of its true believers. This too is, in part, a legacy of the recovery movement: denials of deeply felt beliefs—about spaceship crashes or child abuse—are apt to be considered confirmations of their truth.

Mistrust of official reports debunking myths about satanic ritual abuse, or visitations by extra-terrestrials, does not represent healthy, reasoned skepticism of government. Rather it indicates an utter lack of skepticism about fantastic allegations of abuse, or tales of aliens among us. It reflects an unshakable belief in unseen, unsubstantiated evils that control us—until we expose the conspiracy or engage the right therapist and begin to recover. Recovery taught that the external enemy, an abusive parent or alien, creates an enemy within—a buried memory of abuse that separates you from your divine inner child and keeps you from becoming "whole." Frederick Crews has pointed out that the concept of repressed memory is rooted in Freud's theories of the unconscious, and like Freudianism, the recovery movement helped generate faith in the power of utterly unprovable, subjective realities.[8] Originally dedicated to recovering from various addictions (ranging from excessive shopping or worrying to excessive drinking), caused by various forms of childhood abuse (broadly defined as any form of inadequate nurturance), the movement became focused as well on recovering, or recalling, repressed memories of early sexual molestation. (This movement and its consequences—hysteria about satanism and multiple personality disorder—have been thoroughly critiqued in recent years, and my discussion of it here will seem familiar. I don't relish repeating myself, and other critics, but I do want to clarify the connection between this movement and the rise of irrationalism.)

The recovered memory movement valorized paranoia. The mere suspicion that your father had raped you provided entrée into the community of survivors, where you were likely to be praised for your bravery in confronting your abuse, and cutting yourself off from family members who had conspired in it. The best-selling bible of the movement, first published in 1988, by Ellen Bass and Laura Davis, was predictably named *Courage to Heal*. The recollection of childhood abuse was considered heroic. Bass and Davis affirm that the "courage and determination of survivors" was, for them, inspirational.[9]

Commonly cited by self-proclaimed survivors as a catalyst for their "discoveries" of abuse, *Courage to Heal* taught millions of readers that "forgetting is one of the most effective and common ways children deal with sexual abuse . . . Many children are able to forget about the abuse, *even as it is happening to them*." Remembering became an essential rite of passage.[10]

Ellen Bass, coauthor of *Courage to Heal*, has acknowledged in interviews that there was no scientific basis for believing that incest victims completely repress all conscious knowledge of their victimization (even while it is occurring). She based her own unshakable faith in repressed memories on "common sense," or intuition. "Maybe I don't even think a lot about why people repress," she admitted to psychologist Richard Ofshe and writer Ethan Watters. "I can't give you the research proof, but I don't really operate like that in the world . . . My ideas are not based on any scientific theories. As you can hear, I don't have too many theories."[11]

That children routinely bury their worst memories of abuse,

which are recovered years later in therapy, was not an established fact. Indeed, research on memory has thoroughly refuted popular notions of repression. Even common sense (touted by Bass) and a layperson's knowledge of the world might question the belief that traumatic experiences routinely cause amnesia: Holocaust survivors struggle to keep society from forgetting the events they remember too well. Yet, belief in repressed memories became a fundamental article of faith. It implied that the truth was always in hiding.

Logic and reason help obscure it. The truth is in your heart, or your unconscious, not in your head. In the world of recovery, intellectual efforts to analyze and understand yourself, your family, and even society were forms of denial; reason itself was a cover-up. Criticism of recovered memory therapy was compared to Holocaust revisionism—as if our only evidence of the Holocaust were the nightmares of survivors.[12] There is enough irrefutable historical evidence of the Nazi death camps to satisfy the most rigorous skeptic. There is no such evidence of repressed memory syndrome; instead, there are obvious questions about popular therapeutic techniques and assumptions.

Recovery took you through the looking glass. What you saw (a merely imperfect family) was a mirage; what you didn't see or recall (a family history of abuse) was true. To people who believed that child abuse caused amnesia, the absence of any memory of abuse could be evidence that the abuse occurred.

There was, then, no way of refuting the suggestion that sexual abuse was nearly as common as childbirth: the abuse that you remembered had occurred (your memory was evidence of it); the abuse that you forgot was liable to be even worse. This was an utterly nonsensical, self-enclosed belief system. One of the symptoms of repressed memory syndrome was a repressed memory—or denial, the inability to remember abuse.

How else would you know that you had been the victim of abuse you could not remember? You could visit a repressed-memory therapist: therapeutic techniques recommended by experts implanted initial suspicions of abuse. You might be asked by the therapist to imagine or "visualize" your abuse, before you "remembered" it.[13] Or, you could discover your abuse simply by buying a book and diagnosing yourself. Repressed memories, like codependency, supposedly generated vague, varied symptoms, including fear of the dark, feelings of loneliness and alienation, eating disorders (and other compulsive behaviors), low self-esteem, depression, a preoccupation with sex, anxiety, headaches, gastrointestinal ailments, fear of success, relationship problems, parenting problems, a propensity for taking risks, and a propensity for avoiding risks.[14]

These are, of course, common problems, some of which are bound to affect virtually everyone, at least on occasion. How many people never feel lonely or anxious, experience relationship problems or headaches, or fight with their kids? In our culture, how many people aren't occasionally preoccupied with sex? A skeptic reviewing this inclusive list of symptoms would dismiss a resulting diagnosis of repressed memory syndrome as utterly nonsensical.* Like codependency, it's not a disease or syndrome; it's the human condition. But a true believer would counter that the universality of the symptoms proves the ubiquity of the disease. This circular reasoning is familiar to anyone who's studied codependency books: Practically all American families are dysfunctional, experts like John Bradshaw asserted, defining dysfunction so broadly that the assertion came true. It wasn't an insight; it was a tautology.

The diagnosis of codependency was a refuge for people

---

* In response to criticism, a disclaimer was added to the third edition of *Courage to Heal*, noting that this list of symptoms was not an exact diagnostic tool (p. 38).

unable or unwilling to acknowledge that at least occasional unhappiness—marked by anxiety, loneliness, or feelings of alienation—is the cost of self-consciousness. It's no more a disease than growing old. But, as the popularity of plastic surgery shows, we're encouraged to regard even aging as another pathology, which we can and should control. New Age gurus, like Deepak Chopra, optimistically describe it as curable. So is unhappiness, according to personal development experts. Like wrinkles and body aches, unhappiness is said to be unnecessary.

In the culture of personal development, in which unadulterated happiness and success were posited as attainable goals, codependency became an explanation and an excuse for failure and discontent. A diagnosis of repressed memory syndrome, hiding a brutal history of abuse, offered similar solace. Like the existence of God, it accounted for everything.

It's impossible to know how many disturbed women "discovered" that they were victims of child abuse, but by the 1990s, repressed-memory therapy was a highly profitable industry for mental health professionals, costing insurance companies (and ultimately consumers) hundreds of millions of dollars. Publishers sold millions of books about recovered memory. (*Courage to Heal* alone reportedly generated some 750,000 sales.)[15] Television and women's magazines disseminated stories about repressed memories of abuse. Gloria Steinem endorsed recovered-memory therapy, ensuring its place in the popular feminist movement. Anyone who claimed that she'd been the victim of abuse could find validation in the culture. Like political demonstrations in the 1960s, accusations of abuse abounded in the 1980s and 1990s.

It's equally impossible to know how many of these accusations were true and how many imagined, or exaggerated. My purpose is not to minimize the problem of abuse but to point out the irrationalism of the recovered-memory movement. It is not reason but uninformed emotionalism that exhorts us never to question the account of self-proclaimed victims, and leads 70 percent of *Redbook*'s survey respondents to believe stories about satanic cults.

What fueled hysteria about recovered memories, child abuse, and conspiracies of satanic ritual abusers? The rise of the recovery movement coincided with popular anxiety about day care (and the effect of feminism on child welfare). In part, the hysteria represented cultural resistance to women's liberation and changing gender roles. Yet it was also paradoxically encouraged by the feminist movement, from which recovery experts derived their mistrust of traditional family life and their belief in the routine abuse of women and children, as well as concern about pornography and the number of men "addicted" to it. Some feminists, in turn, borrowed recovery's rhetoric about codependency, addiction, and abuse. The recovery movement contributed to the rise of therapeutic feminism, which tended to demonize men and focused on restoring the self-esteem of presumptively fragile, perennially victimized women.

In their supposedly weakened state, women were apt to be wounded by offensive speech as well as abusive behavior; so therapeutic feminism focused partly on policing speech and naturally embraced the crusade against pornography, which was also supported by social issue conservatives and divided women's rights advocates. The anti-porn movement comprised an awkward, de facto coalition of feminists and right-wing Christians; it helped spread stories about satanic cults, often associated with pornography. For those feminists who were convinced that men used sexually explicit material mechanistically in raping, maiming, and murdering women, it was relatively easy to believe in ritual abuse, involving pornography (which for anti-porn feminists included any sexually explicit material they didn't like). Once you believed that abusing women was a virtual religion for many men, it may have been relatively easy to believe in satanism. What other belief system might sanctify such bloodthirst?

A crusade against satanic cults seems even more alluring to some people consumed by their own religious fervor. As Christian fundamentalism and belief in the divinity of Jesus flourished in the 1970s and 1980s, so did fear of the devil. The wrongful conviction and imprisonment of Paul Ingram for ritually abusing his daughters, for example (chronicled by Lawrence Wright), resulted partly from the family's conversion to Pentacostalism.[16] Ingram's daughters were convinced at a church retreat that they had been molested by their father. Some evangelical Christians, outraged by their notion of pornography and other alleged evils of secular culture, seem to believe in the existence of Satan as vehemently as they believe in God. Why shouldn't they?

Thus, several cultural forces converged: feminism, the recovery movement, and the Christian right spread the gospel about sexual abuse, pornography, and recovered memories to disparate constituencies and shaped the *Zeitgeist*. Their colloboration represented no conspiracy, it was merely an unfortunate coincidence.

The result was a widespread cultural delusion that infected public policy and law. In evaluating claims of abuse, religious faith displaced reason—as the infusion of incest stories with supernaturalism made clear. Irrational assumptions about abuse were destructive enough in a therapist's office, where they must have harmed more patients than they helped. But in a courtroom, where facts should always prevail over feelings, blind faith in the truth of virtually all abuse stories was a guarantee of grievous injustice. It led predictably to a series of wrongful prosecutions (often involving charges of satanism and ritual abuse) that have fairly been compared to the Salem witch trials.

The foundation of our criminal justice system—the presumption of innocence enjoyed by the accused—was anathema to the recovered-memory movement, which was founded on the contrary presumption that virtually all accusations and suspicions of abuse are true. Putative experts in recovered memory even advised therapists and family members to believe the "survivor's" abuse story, when she began to doubt it herself.[17] The survivor was encouraged to trust her feelings—when they led her to suspect abuse. Doubts were explained as "a natural part of the healing process."[18] In this world, doubt is not an accessory to reason; it's merely a form of denial.

It's obvious that this is an ideology particularly ill-suited to the trial process, which is supposed to evaluate evidence objectively, absent any preconceptions of guilt. Recovered memory experts demonstrated not just disregard but hostility for rules designed to ensure fair trials, and prevent the convictions of innocent people. The authors of *Courage to Heal* complained that when a survivor pressed her claim in court, she was apt to "be grilled by insensitive defense attorneys or repeatedly forced to face [her] abuser." Never mind that the Constitution gives defendants the right to face their accusers. One advocate for victims actually lamented the fact that "in cases in which there is little hope of proving that the abuse took place, it is unlikely that a trial will result in justice, vindication, or healing."[19]

It is an odd notion of justice that would provide vindication to a victim when she is utterly unable to demonstrate that her claim of victimization is true. But, for a time, from the mid-

1980s to the early 1990s, the recovery movement helped shape legislation facilitating the prosecution of recovered-memory cases, and therapeutic biases infected the justice system.[20]

Recovery's influence on the courts was predictable. Society was generally hostile to the rights of criminal defendants, and outside the recovery movement, a victim's rights movement was flourishing; it helped popularize the notion that criminal prosecutions should help crime victims heal. The confusion of justice and therapy was engendered by right-wing advocacy for victims' "rights" as well as left-wing crusades to protect practically every self-proclaimed victim of abuse.

The rash of trials began in the 1980s with the sensational McMartin case in California, involving a series of improbable accusations of abuse against the operators of a day-care center. Successive trials in this case, one lasting over two years, ended in a combination of acquittals and deadlocked juries; the charges were eventually dismissed, but not before one defendant spent five years in prison awaiting trial.

Similar cases followed. As Debbie Nathan and Michael Snedeker report in *Satan's Silence,* a chilling account of a "modern American witchhunt," hysteria and gullibility about satanic ritual abuse (particularly in day-care centers) resulted in an epidemic of wrongful prosecutions and, in some cases, the imprisonment of apparently innocent people. Generally, the prosecutions were based on sensational, often implausible stories of abuse that emerged from highly suggestive, even coercive interrogation sessions with children who were presumed to have been victimized (although in several cases, the children unaccountably bore no physical scars of the horrendous abuse they were led to describe). False memories were essentially implanted in children by therapists and police officers with ideological or political commitments to "uncovering" stories of abuse.

Documenting and debunking the epidemic of wrongful child abuse prosecutions, often involving belief in satanism and almost always relying on repressed memories, is the subject for another article or book—and several good ones, such as *Satan's Silence,* Lawrence Wright's *Remembering Satan,* and *Making Monsters,* by Richard Ofshe and Ethan Watters, have been written. The press has paid intermittent attention to the scandal of these cases; *Wall Street Journal* columnist Dorothy Rabinowitz has been particularly tenacious in exposing them. The underlying notion of recovered memory has been convincingly discredited by psychologists, notably Richard Ofshe and Elizabeth Loftus. Some, although not all, wrongful convictions have been reversed, and innocent people released after years of imprisonment. Practitioners of recovered-memory therapy have been sued for malpractice by the patients and families they victimized. By the mid-1990s, there was growing recognition that the sensational child abuse cases of the '80s were based on fanciful and fabricated evidence. Like the Salem witch trials, they represented a psychotic episode in the life of the criminal justice system and the culture, and they exemplified the public dangers of faith—therapeutic or religious.

The supernaturalism that infected many child abuse claims exacerbated the hysteria that surrounded them, but absent charges of satanism or flying saucers, what passes for evidence or truth in a therapist's office still has a very limited role in criminal court. In cases involving insanity or diminished capacity defenses, therapeutic truths may be used to illuminate the defendant's state of mind, but it's difficult to rationalize the use of such personal truths as objective evidence of a crime.

Consider the case of George Franklin, convicted in 1990 of murdering his daughter's childhood friend, Susan Nason, in 1969 and sentenced to life in prison. (Nason had been kidnapped and murdered by an unknown assailant.) Franklin's conviction was based on a claim by his daughter, Eileen Franklin-Lipsker, that twenty years after the crime, she allegedly recovered a memory of witnessing it: she "recalled" seeing her father crush Nason's head with a rock. At trial, it was alleged that she recovered this memory suddenly while watching her own daughter play, but Lipsker had alternatively reported recovering the memory while she was under hypnosis, while in therapy, and in a dream. Her accounts of the murder also varied, as an investigation ensued and the trial approached.[21] Franklin's conviction was reversed in 1995, and he will not be retried. Prosecutors determined that they lacked evidence for a conviction, belatedly confirming that a trial is primarily a search for facts, not idiosyncratic feeling realities.

Even in a therapist's office, however, imagined but deeply felt truths about abuse have questionable value: If Franklin's daughter only imagined remembering the murder of her friend, was she served by the fantasy? Is any patient likely to be helped by delusions developed in therapy? Whether or not you have been raped by a member of your family, or subjected to satanic ritual abuse, is a matter of historical truth—a matter of fact rather than feeling, not generally subject to much interpretation. A historical claim like, "my father raped me," is not the equivalent of an emotional truth, like "my parents never gave me what I needed."

When I asked earlier if we should judge the stories that patients fashion about family life by their therapeutic effects or their historical truthfulness, I was begging the question: Are fictional family histories likely to prove therapeutic? In fact, fantasies of abuse are not apt to help people "heal," as exposés of recovered-memory therapy have shown. In a compelling 1998

New Yorker article, Joan Acocella chronicled the disintegration
of a thirty-five-year-old woman, Elizabeth Carlson, convinced
by her psychiatrist, Diane Humenansky, that she suffered from
multiple personality disorder (MPD) and housed over twenty-
five alternate personalities. (Carlson eventually won a $2.5 mil-
lion damage award against Dr. Humenansky.)[22]

In *Making Monsters,* Richard Ofshe and Ethan Watters
explain the fallacies of recovered-memory therapy and describe
the cruelties it visited upon individual patients and their
families: People who entered therapy with normal neurosis,
anxieties, vague feelings of unease, or even postpartum depression—and no recollection of abuse—became practically psychotic in the course of therapy, as they "remembered" their
incest experiences (as Joan Acocella also reported in the *New
Yorker*). In fact, the therapy was designed to make people suffer.
Under hypnosis, patients were encouraged to relive their alleged
abuse, to feel the pain, shame, and humiliation they supposedly
felt as children. Therapy entailed "brutalization and psychological torture."[23]

Patients lost the capacity to function professionally, care for
their children, or relate to their spouses (marriages broke up).
They were encouraged to break off all relations with their parents, after accusing one or both of sexual abuse. (In the prototypical case, the father was accused of perpetuating the abuse
and the mother accused of collaborating in it.) Some patients
were hospitalized. Some became suicidal; in fact, recovered-
memory experts counseled that suicidal fantasies were part of
the recovery process. In the course of therapy, patients learned
to see themselves as victims of a disease even more dramatic
than codependency—multiple personality disorder.

The vast majority of supposed MPD sufferers were middle-
class white women, persuaded that they'd been the victims of

satanic ritual abuse, or at least, more mundane forms of incest, which caused their personalities to fragment. Repression of the abuse was said to involve or require disassociation, which was sometimes likened to an "out-of-body" experience. In extreme cases (which seemed to become the norm), it supposedly led to the formation of new personalities. Some victims of MPD displayed hundreds of "alters," which often emerged under hypnosis and the influence of drugs, prescribed by the therapist.

The notion that hordes of adults abused in childhood are the unwitting hosts of their own alternate personalities, which they cannot control or even recall, is the stuff of science fiction. *The Strange Case of Dr. Jekyll and Mr. Hyde* was not a case history but a horror story, about as realistic as Mary Shelley's dream of Dr. Frankenstein. The tales told by MPD patients were almost equally fantastic—which didn't seem to make them less believable to therapists. Women recovered supposedly repressed memories of being forced by their parents to have sex with animals (and other human beings), and to witness or participate in the sacrifice of their own aborted fetuses. Memories of cannibalism were not uncommon. Women recalled being compelled to eat their own babies, and others; one woman remembered watching a baby being barbequed alive at a family picnic in a public park. Another, convinced she was a high priestess in a satanic cult inhabited by her family since the early 1600s, believed that she had consumed the body parts of two thousand people a year.[24]

Supernaturalism was embedded in the underlying notion of multiple personality disorder, which closely resembled possession. A leading modern multiple personality theorist, Ralph Allison, was also an exorcist who found wisdom in theosophy, a nineteenth-century branch of spiritism. Theories about MPD date back to the late 1800s and have "long had close links with spiritism and reincarnation," as Ian Hacking has observed in his analysis of the multiple personality movement. Nineteenth-century mediums who allegedly channeled the spirits of the deceased were, in a sense, playing host to alternative personalities.[25] Today, people who claim to have recovered memories of their past lives might well feel inhabited by their own multiple, prior selves.

In nineteenth-century America, when strong cultural taboos prohibited women from speaking in public, the belief that people might be possessed by voices stronger than their own had particular appeal to some women's rights activists. The few females who dared to engage in public speaking were likely to be emboldened by faith in their own spiritual powers. The temerity to deliver a public lecture could be explained by the belief that, when she lectured, a woman was not exactly herself.[26] Like spiritualism, multiple personality disorder may have been been a powerful if self-destructive metaphor for women struggling to forge alternative identities, or seeking excuses for their own aggression.

The search for a supernatural excuse for violating gender norms and the promise of supernatural compensations for femininity's restrictions have helped propel women into alternative healing and spirituality movements, for at least 150 years. The mind-cure movement, for example, which promoted belief in the therapeutic and redemptive power of positive thinking, was female dominated. Mind-cure gave restless nineteenth-century middle-class women a world to conquer. But it was a world within themselves that required no active civic or political engagement, and no fundamental challenge to femininity. The mind-cure movement did help a minority of women forge careers as healers or spiritualists, but, from a feminist perspective, their teachings were not terribly progressive.

The same might be said of the late-twentieth-century recovery movement, in all its permutations. It was led partly by females, some of whom became national celebrities, and it served or exploited female patients, who inevitably dominated the ranks of people allegedly suffering from MPD. Recovery had always spoken to dissatisfied women who had been left out of the feminist movement; codependency, supposedly marked by passivity, self-effacement, and a lack of individual autonomy was, in part, a repackaging of the feminine mystique. Codependency books parroted some popular feminist maxims, encouraging women to differentiate from their families and learn to love themselves. Recovered-memory therapy, with its emphasis on multiple personality disorder, was a perversion of a tradition that encouraged women to imagine and audition alternative selves. Unlike mediums or trance channelers, women afflicted with MPD did not control their alters, inviting or invoking their presences. Mediums were the beneficiaries of their presumed powers, while MPD patients were the victims of a disease.

The recovered-memory movement reflected the influence of both popular feminism (with its paradoxical attachment to femininity) and notions of codependency, as well as fashionable irrationalisms. The belief that fathers routinely molested their daughters was the hysterical extension of feminism's critique of the patriarchal family. The assumption that mothers aided and abetted their daughter's abuse was based on the view of women as "enablers," or codependents, popularized by the 12-step movement. The original enablers were women married to alcoholic men, who helped maintain the fiction of normal family life. According to the logic of recovery, wives who collaborated in their husband's addictions and suffered from the "disease" of codependency were likely to collaborate in sexual abuse as well. The notion that incest often involved the collaboration of several family members satisfied a cultural hunger for conspiracy theories.

The demonization of mothers, however, was peculiar to the brand of feminism represented by the recovered-memory movement. Feminists had long protested the tendency of male psychiatrists and psychologists to blame mothers for their children's troubles or inadequacies. They had sought sexual solidarity, within families, between generations of women.

There could be no such solidarity for women recovering from addiction and abuse and uncovering their buried memories of incest. Adults, taught to label themselves "adult children," were encouraged to base their identities in early experiences of victimization, at the hands of their parents. (In 12-step groups middle-aged people routinely complained about their parents, but I never heard anyone discuss their children or the pleasures and challenges of parenting.) Despite its shallow pop feminist appeal, the recovery movement encouraged people to see themselves as children first and adult men or women second.

Women in recovery were not encouraged to identify or even sympathize with their mothers; instead they were taught to see themselves as pioneers who would be the first in their families to "break the cycle" of addiction and abuse—by breaking away from their parents. From this perspective, therapy was appropriately painful, even agonizing, like a particularly turbulent adolescence; it was a traumatic rite of passage that promised rebirth. With the help of their therapists, women were triumphing over their mothers, giving birth to themselves, and sometimes their alters. The divisions between parents and children were stronger than feminist dreams of sisterhood between mothers and daughters.

Yet a critical mass of feminists embraced the recovery movement and infected public policy debates with its irrational deference to personal truths. The notion that sexual discrimination, exploitation, or abuse was a matter of perspective (whatever the self-proclaimed victims declared it to be), and the belief that women didn't lie, exaggerate, or make mistakes in describing their own victimization helped shape discussions of sexual harassment and date rape, as well as child abuse. For many advocates of alleged victims, there was only one side to every story—hers.

Abuse victims were part of a historic political power struggle, one recovery expert declared several years ago, in response to my unremarkable suggestion that accusations of abuse should be questioned and thoroughly investigated. We were on a panel discussing victims' rights, and to the general approval of the crowd she suggested that calling for a neutral fact-finding process in evaluating the claims of a few women who turned to the legal system for help was effectively endorsing and prolonging the victimization of many. The implication was clear: Weighing the details of every victim's story was not nearly as important as acknowledging the larger truths the victims told about oppression. It was as if we were talking about the art of fiction, in which facts are secondary to the "truths of the human heart," not criminal trials.

The victim's side would prove to be the right side of history, the expert insisted. But history has not been quite so predictable. The insistence of some feminists that we "believe the women" eventually proved an embarassment for them when they hesitated to believe Paula Jones. Still, the Clinton sex scandals did not make many therapeutic feminists reconsider their biased approach to sexual misconduct claims by women. Instead they struggled to distinguish accusations against President Clinton from other harassment charges that had elicited reflexive support.

The irony is that the therapeutic culture and therapeutic feminism, which conservative supporters of Clinton accuser Paula Jones had long derided, laid the foundation for her case. Jones based her charge of discrimination largely on her assertion that she sensed the hostility of her supervisor after spurning then Governor Clinton. Her case reflected the elevation of emotion over empiricism, subjective sensations over provable facts. Describing herself as psychologically crippled by Clinton's alleged proposition, she also adopted the pop feminist view of women as permanently traumatized, even oppressed, by sexist behavior and sexual references.

Her objective evidence of discrimination—not receiving flowers on Secretaries Day—was laughable. Her claim of emotional trauma reflected absurdly expansive notions of abuse popularized by the recovery movement—another target of conservative derision. Seven years after the alleged encounter with Governor Clinton, Jones claimed to be suffering from "sexual aversion"—as diagnosed by one Patrick Carnes, a Ph.D. in education and counseling, whom Federal District Court Judge Susan Wright tartly described as a "purported expert," when she dismissed Jones's case. Carnes, who was supposed to be an expert in "sex addiction," met with Jones for three and a half hours some four days before the president filed his motion for summary judgment. Judge Wright sensibly suggested that his diagnosis of sexual aversion wasn't credible.[27]

Imagine if President Clinton had admitted that Jones's allegations were true and claimed in his defense that he had no control over his actions because, as a result of childhood traumas, he was a sex addict. Imagine that he had found a "purported expert," with a Ph.D. in education or counseling, and maybe even a best-selling book, to testify on his behalf and explain Clinton's dysfunctional family history. Conservatives would have been apoplectic, understandably. Paula Jones's claim was rooted in the same culture from which the president might have derived this defense.

Debates about the Jones case were, of course, driven by politics, not principles about harassment and workplace regulation. Hypocrisy reigned on both sides, among therapeutic feminists who denigrated Jones and conservatives who supported her. But, apart from its political impact, her case is worth remembering because in many ways it epitomized the unreasoned excesses of a therapeutic approach to law and public policy.

The cult of victimhood engendered by the recovery movement was frequently and vigorously criticized throughout the early 1990s. There were also many critiques of political and sexual correctness, but relatively little discussion of what they owed the recovery movement, and how recovery helped formulate remarkably restrictive definitions of free speech. You might expect a movement that encouraged people to talk about themselves incessantly to respect the right to speak. Instead, valuing self-esteem and comfort over liberty, argument, and the raucous expression of ideas, the recovery movement helped make censorship seem therapeutic.

Despite all its rhetoric about liberation, recovery proved to be a threat to freedom, partly by equating metaphorical and actual instances of abuse. Failing to distinguish between words and action, between perceptions of abuse and provable events, it provided a justification for the prosecution of thought crimes. Once, on a talk show, I said that being yelled at by your father was not the equivalent of being raped by him, naively expecting that virtually everyone would have to concur. Instead, members of the studio audience hissed at me. "How dare I judge someone else's pain," people said. The therapeutic culture prepared us for the claim that if a woman feels assaulted by a magazine, then, without question, an assault has occurred.

This unreasoned deference to the victim's "pain" influenced left-wing academic theorizing about free speech, as it had influenced therapeutic feminism. Supposedly progressive academics enunciated a rationale for restricting "hate speech" that reflected recovery's romance with victimhood, a preoccupation with the self-esteem of presumptively disadvantaged groups, and the equation of words with actions. "In addition to physical violence, there is the violence of the word," law professor Mari Matsuda wrote, advocating the criminalization of racist speech—when uttered by a "dominant group member" and directed against the member of an oppressed group.[28]

Matsuda called for a "victim's privilege." In her regime, African-Americans would be permitted to hurl racially derogatory epithets against white Anglo-Saxon Protestant Americans—who would be prosecuted for hurling racial epithets back. African-Americans might not, however, be permitted to make racially derogatory remarks to Asian-Americans. Jews would be protected by the "victim privilege," as well, unless they indulged in Zionist speech that included "a statement of generic white supremacy." If, however, their Zionist statements arose out of "the Jewish experience of persecution" and did not resort to the "rhetoric of white supremacy," they would be protected.[29]

No rational, neutral legal principle would guide law enforcement agents trying to determine whether someone should be prosecuted for racist speech. (Legal neutrality is regularly condemned by legal scholars on the left as a tool of the powerful.) Instead, the state would defer to the subjective judgment of the victim or "victim-group members" in deciding whether speech qualifies as racist. This represents the triumph of therapy over fundamental concepts of individual rights and equal justice: the victim's perception of harm becomes the law (providing that the victim is a member of a historically disadvantaged group). Instead of a system based on principles that are supposed to be applied equally to everyone, regardless of group identity, we have a system based on the feelings of people who belong to particular, protected groups.

The threat of this militantly subjective, therapeutic approach to regulating speech became apparent on college and university campuses during the 1980s and 1990s. Speech codes, prohibiting offensive or hurtful speech that targeted selected "victim-groups," proliferated, reflecting and reinforcing hostility to free speech and the unfettered exchange of ideas. In institutions supposedly dedicated to intellectual freedom, professors, graduate students, and undergraduates were prosecuted for speech crimes, thought crimes, and bad attitudes by academic tribunals that offered little due process.* [30]

The celebration of subjectivism among supposedly progressive academics was, after all, selective, and boldly unfair: it only protected the feelings and idiosyncratic perceptions of the presumptively oppressed. The feelings of white males were dismissed as invalid, or even evil. In this context, subjectivism did not lead naturally to relativism and the "anything goes" culture imagined by conservatives. Instead, it led to the moralistic authoritarianism of political correctness.

A generation of college students were taught that they had a "right" not to be offended (if they belonged to victim-groups)

---

* Perhaps the most notorious case involved administrative proceedings against University of Pennsylvania student Eden Jacobowitz, who yelled "shut up, you water buffalo," to a noisy group of African-American females partying beneath his dormitory window. "Water buffalo" was not exactly a familiar racial epithet, Jacobowitz was Israeli, and it was soon revealed that the Hebrew word for water buffalo, *behama*, means unruly person. Still, the university persisted in prosecuting him until adverse publicity persuaded administrators to drop the case, over a year after it had commenced. Jacobowitz's ordeal received a great deal of publicity, but it was not atypical (as Harvey Silverglate and Alan Charles Kors report in *The Shadow University*). [31]

and no right to speak offensively if they were members of a privileged class. Harassment is "making someone feel uncomfortable," students used to say to me, and I'd confess to being a harasser, explaining that I strive to make at least a few people uncomfortable every day.

At the very least, these crabbed notions of free speech were quite illogical. If the First Amendment didn't protect speech that many people find offensive, we'd have relatively little need of it. No group will try to prohibit words or images to which no group objects. The First Amendment protects your right to give offense, and requires that you learn to take it. That is a simple and fundamental principle of democracy, which is rarely polite.

But it's a principle that was lost on people who were taught to regard offensive speech as a virtual assault. In the therapeutic culture, words were considered weapons, quite literally: like sticks and stones, they might break the spirits of vulnerable, codependent people with histories of abuse and post traumatic stress disorders. In our racist society, merely belonging to a group identified as historically oppressed was supposedly traumatic, so members of those groups were as vulnerable as survivors of abuse. Racist words had the power of racist acts. To left-wing censors, like Matsuda, racist speech was an instrument of oppression (an "implement of racism"), like the dogs and firehoses once turned on civil rights activists marching for racial justice.[32] To anti-porn feminists, pornography *was* violence against women, not just an image of violence.

Questioning the effect of pornography, or asking for proof of it, was a callous breach of etiquette. And in this illogical world, it was futile. The harm caused by pornography was likely to be invisible, law professor Catherine MacKinnon asserted. In her view, one of the dangers of pornography was our inability to perceive its dangers in a pornographic culture. MacKinnon explained, "If pornography is an act of male supremacy, it's harm is the harm of male supremacy made difficult to see . . . To the extent that pornography succeeds in constructing social reality, it becomes *invisible as harm*." [33]

There is, then, no way to challenge the view that pornography is evil, just as there was no way to challenge the notion that most families conspire to conceal abuse. Anti-porn feminists employed the irrefutable illogic of recovery experts: Pornography is like incest; at its worst, it remains hidden from us. We are not conscious of its attacks. To believers in repressed-memory syndrome, not remembering your abuse is evidence that it occurred. To anti-porn activists, not seeing the harm of pornography is evidence of its power.

The confusion of metaphor and reality was profoundly irrational, and it limited the opportunities for free inquiry. Freedom of speech rests on the recognition that words are not acts and the state need not and must not protect us from them—as it protects us from criminal behavior. Of course, in some marginal cases, action—like nude dancing—is a form of expression, and words, such as a verbal agreement to kill someone—are subsumed in a criminal act. But in most cases the distinction between speech and action, like the distinction between thought and deed, is sufficiently clear. It's a vital distinction that preserves the freedom to explore ideas and acquire knowledge.

The ironies of drives to regulate individual rights of speech in the name of self-esteem and the vindication of victim-groups are numerous. Without free speech, it is hard to imagine how women and other targets of discrimination might have waged their battles for equality. Anyone committed to social reform should struggle to protect the rights of dissenters, people who challenge, even mock conventional wisdoms—people who make intentionally provocative remarks and advocate policies that deeply offend and anger the majority. In the 1950s, many defenders of racial segregation were outraged by efforts to integrate the nation's public schools. They were appalled by interracial marriages. In fact, it was not until 1967 that the Supreme Court recognized that laws against miscegenation—interacial marrying—were unconstitutional.

That decision came down in an aptly named case involving a black woman married to a white man, *Loving v. Virginia*, which can provide some perspective on the therapeutic disregard for rights. The Lovings had been criminally prosecuted under Virginia law for intermarrying, given a suspended sentence of one year and essentially banished from the state of Virginia for twenty-five years. (Their prison sentence was suspended on condition that they leave the state.) [34]

As the punishment meted out to this couple demonstrated, the feelings of white supremicists against interracial marriages ran deep. Some may have felt traumatized by the sight of interracial couples. They no doubt felt victimized and harassed by civil rights activists. If they had been versed in the language of our therapeutic culture, segregationists who engaged in violence might have claimed that they were suffering from post-traumatic stress disorder (PTSD) brought on by the civil rights movement. Imagine if Byron De La Beckwith, recently convicted after thirty-one years for the 1963 murder of civil rights leader Medgar Evers, had presented a claim of PTSD in his defense.

I'm not suggesting that claims like this should have been honored, or even taken seriously. I am simply pointing out that therapy isn't justice: therapeutic values should not guide the resolution of social conflicts and the allocation of rights. In our public behavior, as opposed to our private lives, we have supposedly agreed to abide by ideals, like equality and free speech, that transcend our personal preferences, and disappointments. Of course we don't always succeed, any more than we always agree on how to implement national principles, which generate inevitable conflicts. But they are, or should be, conflicts about social and political ideals, not hurt feelings. Racial equality guaranteed by the Fourteenth Amendment profoundly offends many white supremacists. Expressions of white supremacy protected by the First Amendment offend many advocates of racial equality, just as expressions of male supremacy offend many feminists. So what.

Social change is forged by people who are not afraid to insult or offend their neighbors deeply and harass upholders of the status quo. That is one important lesson of history. What if feminists did not speak out because they feared offending or intimidating male supremacists? One hundred fifty years ago, when the first women's movement began, many people believed that God wanted women to remain within the domestic sphere. Talk about sexual equality violated some deeply held religious beliefs; worse than insulting, it threatened a kind of Armageddon. Where would the women's movement be if it had been subject to laws against hateful or dangerous speech?

Any system of justice that selectively values feelings over ideals and a dispassionate notion of fairness is bound to be unreasoned, unpredictable, and quite regressive. The power of the civil rights movement and feminism was partly the power of argument. There was not just passion but reason in demands for racial and sexual justice. Given our own professed national belief that all people were created equal, how could we rationalize discrimination? That was the question posed historically by civil rights activists and advocates for women's rights, who demanded that the nation live up to its ideals. Discrimination was eventually prohibited, partly because nondiscrimination was the only answer reason would allow.

CHAPTER 7

■

CYBERSPACY

If reasoning includes debate and the acquisition of knowledge, it will be drastically changed by technology, for better and worse, and in ways we can't predict. Like most revolutions, our migration to a virtual world will surprise the most prescient with its consequences.

Still, we can't help making predictions, and assessing changes already in place. Discussions about the impact of new technologies have abounded. Self-proclaimed Luddites, usually of a certain age, decry the technoboosterism of the digerati. Television and the Internet are making the human imagination obsolete, Kurt Vonnegut has lamented. "The information superhighway will be two lanes loaded with tollgates, and it's going to tell you what to look for. People will just watch the show. We don't need [the imagination] any more than we need to know how to ride horses." [1]

But, across the electronic divide, John Perry Barlow, cofounder of the Electronic Frontier Foundation, has celebrated a "civilization of the Mind in Cyberspace," forming in opposition to the physical world regulated by governments and offering infinite, if rather abstract freedom: "Cyberspace consists of transactions, relationships, and thought itself, arrayed like a standing wave in the web of our communications. Ours is a world that is both everywhere and nowhere, but it is not where bodies live."[2] Like Barlow, Kevin Kelly, editor of *Wired,* delights in the anarchic freedom of the Net, and he confirms that new media expand choices: "[T]he Net and the literary space—the thinking space that it creates—will allow a whole new space for the arts."[3]

Meanwhile, between the doomsayers and utopians, technorealists stating the obvious have staked out the huge middle ground: The changes wrought by technology will be "good and bad." We need to "think critically," about the effect of new technologies. Technorealists are "passionately optimistic about some technologies, skeptical and disdainful of others." Their goal is "neither to champion nor dismiss technology but rather to understand it" and "apply it in a manner more consistent with basic human values."[4]

All sides essentially agree that we're approaching the end of civilization as we know it; they differ as to whether the new world represents salvation or the Fall, neither, or both. With the millennium upon us, technology has the force of a new religion.

I associate Western religions and spirituality movements with a belief in supernatural realities, so I don't label every totalistic belief system, like capitalism or atheism, a religion, as some do. But I'm struck by the religious references of the digerati. "I am the Internet. I am the World Wide Web. I am information. I am *content,*" author and digital publisher John Brockman declares, invoking the mystic's experience of communion—what theologian Karen Armstrong has called "a sense of the unity of all things . . . the sense of absorption in a larger, ineffable reality."[5]

Brockman describes the self-consciously futuristic world of cyberspace in language that would have resonated with nineteenth-century adherents of New Thought, mind-cure, and its most successful progeny, Christian Science. Mind-cure devotees imagined God as Divine Mind; their goal was to merge with the Divine Mind, to share in His thoughts.[6] Brockman finds a strikingly similar sense of communion in cyberspace: "A new invention has emerged, a code for the collective conscious. I call it 'DNI,' or 'distributed networked intelligence.' DNI is the collective externalized mind, the mind we all share."[7] Kevin Kelly refers to the Net as "an emergent, self-governing intelligence."[8]

There are significant differences, of course, between techno-boosterism and the mind-cure movement. Mind-cure discouraged human willfulness (communion was to be achieved through submission), and it envisioned the active human consciousness as a barrier to God. It preached unthinking automatic behaviors, like the mechanistic repetition of affirmations, designed to govern both the conscious and unconscious. It involved "something like hypnotic practice," William James remarked.[9] Mind-cure represented a form of mind control, as historian Donald Meyer explained: "The aim was to fill the subconscious so full of suggestion and lesson and science that it would have no life of its own."[10] The cyber elite do not valorize submissiveness or rote behavior: on the contrary, they tend to celebrate rugged, raucous individualism (although, paradoxically, our evolving relationships with computers can make us feel quite mechanistic). The digital culture has been dominated by men, while in the nineteenth century, mind-cure was especially popular among women. But in offering merger with a collective consciousness, both mind-cure and cyberspace offer some similar visions of transcendence.

William James might recognize interactivity as a variety of

religious experience. Descriptions of it offered by digerati like Kelly and Brockman compare not only to mind-cure but to nineteenth-century spiritualism. It offered women direct access to the Divine: mediums presumed capable of channeling the spirits of the dead bypassed institutional hierarchies and seemed to enjoy profound religious experiences unmediated by churches. The Net is celebrated for providing individuals with direct access to the transcendent collective consciousness of cyberspace. Kevin Kelly imagines "wiring human and artificial minds into one planetary soul." [11]

The new digital culture described by its most enthusiastic inhabitants sometimes looks a bit like a twentieth-century male analogue to spiritualism, as well as mind-cure. (Indeed, Kelly celebrates an "incipient technospiritualism.") [12] As a technological culture, it is grounded in science, not religion. But like the spirit realm, cyberspace is a vast, invisible, immaterial world that encircles all and speaks to each of us. It is an alternative universe involving a revolutionary technology, which is shaping new notions of identity and consciousness.

A child who grows up with a computer begins to experience it as a "second self," Sherry Turkle observed, some fifteen years ago, in 1984. "Computers seemed alive to children because they could think; they were 'aware intelligences,' Turkle wrote. "When children discuss computers, psychological features replace physical ones as the fundamental criteria for aliveness." By now, many adults who are at home in cyberspace similarly regard their computers as extensions of themselves. Computers haven't been humanized so much as humans on the Net are being digitalized. As Turkle noted, we've progressed from seeing ourselves as "rational animals" to considering ourselves "emotional machines . . . the computer is enough like a mind to make analogies between the self and programs plausible." [13]

This means that your relationship with cyberspace is unmediated (like the spiritualist's relationship with the deceased). By identifying with their computers, people on the Net gain direct access to what John Perry Barlow cryptically calls a "context where experience is universal." [14] Whatever "universal experience" may entail, it surely sounds transformative.

Worship of cyberspace doesn't necessarily involve supernaturalism or theism (except when people view the Net as a metaphor for Divine Mind). It does offer a transcendent post-naturalism. William James described religious belief as "faith in the existence of an unseen order of some kind in which riddles of the natural order may be found explained." [15] Instead of explaining the riddles of the natural world, cyberspace, or virtuality, can make the natural world irrelevant. If traditional religions explain nature (as God's creation) and comfort us for nature's cruelties with the promise of eternal celestial life, virtuality enables us to escape from nature entirely. When we envision ourselves as machines, and seek eternal life in artificial intelligence or the creation of digital humanoids that house our brains, we have left the natural world behind.

Does this new virtual universe of our own creation promise a new age of transcendent rationalism to replace the supernaturalisms of old? I doubt it, despite some interesting survey evidence suggesting that irreligious people are more numerous on the Net than in the general population: according to one survey cited in the *New York Times,* 65 percent of on-line users believed in a supreme being (compared to 96 percent generally) and 11 percent of people on-line called themselves atheists (compared to 3 percent generally). [16] People who lack religious faith, however, are not necessarily any more rational than the faithful.

Besides, I can't imagine human beings not believing in gods, or angels, demons, and ghosts: and religion has always benefited from technology, as televangelists might attest. The Bible was the first book fifteenth-century inventor Johannes Gutenberg produced on his revolutionary printing press. New twentieth-century media, radio and television, helped religion permeate popular culture. So will computers.

They are already finding their place in the twilight zone and the realm of the sacred. Paranormal Web sites proliferate on the Web (the Yahoo search engine perversely locates them under the heading "Science: Alternative Paranormal Phenomenon"). Visions of a biblical apocalypse abound: in minutes, you can locate hundreds of Web sites alerting you to the end of the world: some explain the Book of Revelation, the premillennial rapture and rise of the Antichrist; they tell you how to spot the mark of Satan, or offer the assistance of psychics who will help you survive Armageddon. (Alleged instruments of the Antichrist include the World Trade Commission, electronic banking cards, as well as rock stars and the CIA.) As political analyst Chip Berlet observed in the *Boston Globe,* in 1998, "The Internet is a cornucopia of apocalyptic conspiracy theory."[17] For those who prefer the sunny side, however, New Agers and adherents of established Eastern and Western faiths are also on-line, transforming the Net into what *Time* terms a "high-speed spiritual bazaar."[18] If you've had out-of-body experiences, for example, you can find a community on the Astral Projection Home Page. It "provides links to astral projection, out-of-body experiences . . . and lucid dreams resources on the Internet." It assures you that "You are not alone!" The Host of the Astral Projection Page confides that he receives an unspecified number of E-mails daily from other astral travelers, and surmises that they constitute an elite: "Personally, I think we might be a beta release of a new form of astrally enhanced human beings." For those with more traditional tastes in transcendence, a range of Eastern and Western religions have home pages.

While some religious people and institutions view computers as instruments for spreading the Word (like the printing press), or creating virtual religious communities, others consider cyberspace itself a sacred space. "Cyberspace has vast, untapped potential as a creative medium infused with divine presence," Jennifer Cobb declares in *Cybergrace: The Search for God in the Digital World.* Cyberspace is "revealing a novel understanding of divinity" and "has a fundamental role to play in the ongoing movement of soul and spirit through the universe." Cobb suggests that cyberspace has the power to facilitate our spiritual evolution because it demonstrates or embodies spiritual realities so dramatically that even scientists will have to acknowledge them: "Cyberspace drives the first experiential wedge into the hegemony of the modernist perspective of quantifiable matter as the only genuine basis of reality," Cobb writes, meaning, I think, that it provides unique evidence of God.[19]

I wouldn't know, although I'd hesitate to describe cyberspace as offering the first experiential refutation of the modern materialist perspective. Religion has always relied on individual experiences of the Divine. Of course some will find God in cyberspace, but they will have no more or less experiential evidence of God's reality than mystics in predigital times. Putting hyperbole and the grand metaphysical questions aside, I'm interested in simpler, earthly matters: should we expect new communications technologies to introduce more or less reason into the mundane interactions of society?

Cyberspace is bound to change the way we reason, as well as the way we read, and perhaps because I can't envision the New

Rationalism that supposedly awaits us, I'm already nostalgic for the Old. Hypertext will be the death of argument—those tightly structured skeins of logic that require attentive readers, undistracted by linkages. Interrupt an argument repeatedly, and you defeat it.

Is this a lamentable development? Jennifer Cobb, among other digerati, celebrates the illogic of cyberspace and suggests that we may find God in it. "In cyberspace all is connected, all is relational, all is relative," she writes happily. "[W]hen one surfs the World Wide Web, one does not travel in a hierarchal, linear fashion." In her view, cyberspace has its own internal coherency because it is infused with the divine. "Spirit is by definition the force that connects."[20] But you don't need to believe in gods to consider relative, relational thinking progressive. Logical, linear thinking has never been fashionable among postmodernists for whom identity itself is fragmented (or de-centered), and authorship is always collaborative. Legions of college students have already been taught that books are constructed by readers interacting with the writer's text. Truth is considered multiple and labile, like identity. From a postmodern perspective, the death of argument is merely the death of an illusion. Traditional notions of authorship and modes of reasoning are said to represent false assertions of authority and the mistaken belief in the existence of stable realities that logic can apprehend. Hypertext is celebrated as the quintessential postmodern rhetoric: it encourages us to read digressively—the way we supposedly live.

We are not, then, getting stupider; we're getting smarter in different ways, which I cannot appreciate. For me, the threatened loss of argument and logic is an occasion for lamentation. I can't help fear that we're in danger of losing some very useful capacity for sustained rational thought.

It is by now a cliché that the electronic media are leaving us with very short attention spans; we change the subject restlessly, just as we change channels. Students who learn how to write on computers learn to devalue coherency, one of the virtues of linear thinking. This is how the typical writing guide today teaches students how to write essays: "Conceive 5 main points. Construct a sentence and then a paragraph around each, then arrange and re-arrange the paragraphs until you're satisfied with their order." What's lost is the notion of an essay as an integral, organic creation that develops naturally from conception to conclusion, and is not merely a collection of interchangeable paragraphs or parts. What's lost is the pleasure of following ideas as they develop and hearing a writer think.

Abetted by computers, newspaper and magazine editors have contributed to the choppiness and incoherency of much contemporary journalism. I noticed a change in the way my articles were being edited in the mid-1980s, when editors went on line. Suddenly, they had the capability of transposing whole paragraphs in an instant, and some used it promiscuously, with little regard for the internal logic of an article. If a sexy subject appeared in a paragraph toward the end of the piece, they'd move it to the beginning. When I objected, pointing out that the transplanted paragraph was now out of place, that it had nothing to do with the discussion that immediately preceded or followed it, they'd say, "Don't worry. We'll drop a space" (as if consecutive sentences, or thoughts, didn't have to cohere intellectually, unless they were single-spaced).

Maybe readers didn't mind, or notice. As writing has changed, so has reading. I'm periodically approached by people who tell me that they've read one of my books, in part: they describe reading pieces of it haphazardly—glancing at the beginning, jumping to a chapter in the middle that particularly intrigued them, and reading the conclusion. Even when they praise my work, I always cringe and think to myself that they don't yet watch movies in this way, viewing disparate scenes in no particular order. Some movies are constructed with self-consciously hip, purposeful incoherency, but people are still attached to stories, which they want to watch unfold. I suspect they read fiction, the way they watch movies, from beginning to end. Hypertext has not displaced old-fashioned storytelling in popular fiction.[21] But hypertext and other conventions of cyberspace (speed, spontaneity, informality of expression, and interactivity), along with television and talk radio, have influenced the way we approach much nonfiction. Biographies and memoirs are still expected to tell extended stories, but discussions of ideas are, at best, episodic.

In recent years, people have become accustomed to viewing opposing sound bytes as an exchange of ideas. For several years now, the *Crossfire* model has prevailed: Every argument is thought to have only two sides. A debate consists of one side saying "Is too" and the other side insisting "Is not." So, when millions of Americans went on-line, they were well prepared for a cacophonous world of half-finished thoughts and interrupted expositions of ideas. In daily papers and mass-market magazines, paragraphs are short—sometimes consisting of only one sentence. Newspaper columns read like telegrams. Stop. Arguments are not expected to be linear, or particularly coherent. I have always regarded a good argument as a kind of story (the story of an idea)—but I am one of the dinosaurs.

The careful composition of sentences is becoming as obsolete on-line as the composition of arguments. Partly because of the high value placed on spontaneity, writing on the Net is purposefully inelegant and often ungrammatical, intended to sound like ordinary conversation. Formalities, like a disinclination for split infinitives or sentences that end in prepositions, are apt to be considered pedantic and elitist. The disdain for traditional fact gathering and substantiation of sources that characterizes some self-styled cyber-journalism is accompanied by a more pervasive disdain for prose that seems written, not carelessly spoken. At least, thoughtful composition conflicts with the swaggering colloquialism that dominates the Net. Once, an article I contributed to an on-line magazine had some of the grammar edited out of it. I suspect the editor thought it conveyed the wrong attitude. As Kevin Kelly explains, "Net writing is of a conversational, peer-to-peer style, frank and communicative, rather than precise and self-consciously literary."[22] How else might you describe this democratic style? Expression on-line is sometimes rather primitive. "Do you agree, or do you think this sucks," readers are asked at the conclusion of an interactive column.

That's not even the way I talk. Still, I am trying to adapt. While I continue to compose my sentences, I have changed the way I conceive of my books. I digress. I imagine each chapter as an autonomous essay, because I know that people no longer read books about ideas sequentially.

"People don't come on-line to read. They want to interact," entrepreneur Doug Carlston observes. "They don't want to spend more than a minute to read something. They want to do something."[23] This emphasis on the primacy of dialogue, or interaction, is commonplace in discussions about the Net.

Celebrations of the emerging digital culture focus on its potential for democratizing and rationalizing public discourse with dialogue. Former *HotWired* columnist Jon Katz predicts that by providing unprecedented, potentially universal access to information and research, the Net will spawn a new "rational political culture in which decisions are informed not by the gaseous, hypocritical, and pious rhetoric of politics and journalism, but by factual information shared instantly—for the first time in history—with the rest of the world." [24]

As Katz's rhetoric indicates, netizens (denizens of the digital culture) harbor considerable contempt for traditional journalism. Established pundits, whose musings circulate nationally in print and on TV, are dismissed as an insular journalistic aristocracy, still engaged in delivering monologues to audiences that are gradually becoming empowered to talk back. In the view of critics like Katz, the ignorance of old media pundits about the new media is matched only by their fear of it. They are considered on the way to obsolescence, as the interactive digital culture threatens their authority and their jobs.

Politics is expected to change along with journalism. Cyberspace is supposed to reinvigorate democracy, making journalists and politicians less elitist and more responsive to the people (people with computers, that is). Interactivity is heralded as a tool of direct democracy (remember Ross Perot's proposed electronic town hall).

The debate between respective representatives of new and old media is often couched as a conflict between direct and representative democracy. Netizens are cast as populists and the punditocracy as the ruling class. In a 1997 newspaper column Cokie and Steve Roberts wrote that the prospect of electronic town meetings, in which people could vote up or down on national ballot questions, "makes our blood run cold." Electronic democracy would lead to "no more deliberation . . . no more balancing of regional and ethnic interests, no more protection of minority views." [25] Responding in *HotWired*, invoking the spirits of Tom Paine and Jefferson, Jon Katz derided the Robertses as power-hungry elitists, contemptuous of the people and ignorant of the nation's founding principles. (James Madison, one of the champions of representative democracy, who helped draft the Bill of Rights, might disagree.)[26]

Direct democracy on the grand scale isn't necessarily all that democratic. Majority rule always threatens individual rights and the interests of minorities (indeed, recognizing the potential tyranny of majorities, the Founders added the Bill of Rights to the Constitution). Peter Schrag demonstrated the dangers of government by referendum in *Paradise Lost,* a 1998 book analyzing the California experience. Schrag observed that referendums became the tool of affluent whites, disinclined to support public services for less affluent immigrants and racial minorities. White voters represented about half the state's population, but 78 percent of the electorate, and they have been responsible for passing the forty ballot questions approved since 1978. The result has been what Schrag termed the "Mississification" of California: a dramatic decline in public infrastructure and especially public schools.[27]

Cyberlibertarians may applaud this trend, but it virtually disenfranchised entire groups of citizens (not necessarily what the Founders intended). Putting questions about taxation or public school policy directly before the voters left legislators with little if any power to address the needs and protect the rights of minorities.

In any case, numerous referenda cutting back public services and establishing educational policy (banning bilingual education, for example) were not exactly rational. Like most political campaigns, referendum campaigns appealed to emotion, or prejudice, more than reason. Some questions, like "does bilingual education help non-English-speaking students learn?"— are not amenable to simple yes or no answers. Sometimes you can only respond, "It depends." Did it make sense for a relatively uninformed electorate to vote up or down on a question like this? (I'm not chastising people for being uninformed; how much can any one of us be expected to know? Ideally we elect legislators to study issues and solicit the advice of researchers and analysts.) Referenda make misleading appeals to "common sense," which is necessary but not sufficient in formulating policy; sometimes you need uncommon knowledge. The 1998 referendum on bilingual education took an empirical question about pedagogy and transformed it into a question of ideology.

That is a familiar exercise in old politics, not an example of a New Rationalism that Jon Katz anticipates. For all their grounding in technology, champions of the digital culture are sometimes hopelessly romantic about the promise of the Net.

The benefits of cyberspace—interactivity, speed of communication, spontaneity of discussion, access to information and opportunities to disseminate it widely—all have obvious costs. Interactivity can easily devolve into hyperactivity. Spontaneity of expression can be the enemy of thoughtfulness. The power of every individual or group to disseminate facts is also the power to disseminate rumors. That the UN is going to invade the U.S., that weird weather reflects an increase in alien invasions, that gay people regularly engage in bestiality are only a few of the "facts" you can pick up in cyberspace. You don't have to be a Luddite to find the rantings of many denizens of the Net no more worthwhile than the blather of old media pundits.

The ersatz populism of the wired (who are apt to feel infinitely superior to the unwired) interferes with efforts to screen information and publish only what, at least, approximates truth. Matt Drudge, the justly maligned on-line gossip who broke the Lewinsky story, has expressly advocated "populist journalism." In the digital culture, he cheers, "every citizen can be a reporter, take on the powers that be. The Net gives as much voice to a 13-year-old computer geek like me as to a CEO or a speaker of the house. We all become equal."[28] That has a shallow democratic appeal, but it overlooks the fact that while we are all entitled to equal rights, we are not all equal in talent, wisdom, or integrity.

Interactivity has the virtue of democracy, conferring upon everyone with access to a computer the right and opportunity to be heard, but it is also saddled with democracy's vice—a tendency to assume that everyone who has a right to be heard has something to say that's worth hearing. It is a common misconception that plagues the most traditional public forums: people stand up at town meetings and demand that their neighbors respect their opinions, not simply the right to utter them.

It is one of the ironies of democracy that this confusion often turns out to be more subversive than supportive of free speech. When you begin by equating a defense of the right to speak with a defense of one person's point of view, you end by conditioning the right to speak on the perceived value of what is said. You take on the easy fight for freedom of the speech you like, decamping from the struggle to protect the speech you hate.

I'm not suggesting that interactivity will foster intolerance of free speech among netizens. The unusually high value they place on untrammeled free expression, for its own sake, may overcome the impulse to censor. But while interactivity and the commitment to raucous debate is invigorating, it is also apt to produce cacophony and a preference for speaking over thinking.

The Net is not a quiet place, conducive to contemplation. It is tempting to believe that we can retreat from it as we need, that the new digital culture can coexist with a traditional literary one, but the desire to be alone with their thoughts may be bred out of people for whom thinking and reading are by nature interactive. Besides, while we can turn off our computers, it's difficult to escape the electronic media. Solitude and silence, generally devalued in our culture, are becoming scarce commodities. Televisions are omnipresent: in airport lounges, hospital waiting rooms, or hotel coffee shops, they hold us captive. They are the scourge of health clubs, in which you're apt to find several TVs in one room tuned to different channels. Unless you have unusual powers of concentration, it's difficult to read anything more taxing than *People* magazine in the midst of talk shows, commercials, and the chatter of news readers. It's difficult to think.

Of course, you can find quiet in private, but often you're stuck in a public space. Besides, I fear that the taste for quiet, solitude, and long, hard thinking is waning. (The taste for critical thinking may be one that needs to be acquired.) I worry that people don't revolt against the public TVs. I wonder how writing and reading will fare.

For me, writing, like thinking, is an independent, introspective activity, not a collaborative one; it requires quiet solitude. I experience every one of my essays and every book as a conversation with myself. I write partly to discover what I think. Of course, I want to engage readers and provoke debate among them, but while I'm writing, the thoughts of my prospective readers are rarely as interesting to me as my own.

You can accuse me of being arrogant or self-absorbed, but with some exceptions, like pure reportage, writing begins with self-absorption, as every diarist, perhaps most fiction writers, and many columnists or essayists, on or off the Net, can attest. We're always interested in our own opinions. Some of my readers may well be smarter, more informed, or blessed with better judgment than I. Still, I learn much more from doing my work than from heeding reactions to it. In fact, I purposefully avoid showing anyone an essay or book until it's completed: I don't want to be influenced by criticism or praise. I don't want to be distracted.

This doesn't mean that I write without knowing what other people have written and thought about my subject or that I'm cloistered and bereft of interactions. For me, writing is always preceded by reading, and often some historical study. I am not only engaged in a conversation with myself. I'm continuing a public conversation, which, in various guises, predates and may outlive me. I'm contributing one particular point of view, with no hope or desire for resolution. I want my views to be informed, but I don't shape them by a process of consensus. And often my readers do not know more than I do about my subject, because they haven't had the luxury of studying and thinking about it for months, or years.

We read partly to learn, seeking out writers who seem to know more than we do or have thought longer about matters that interest us. The interactivity of cyberspace encourages people to talk more than listen and creates illusions of equal knowledge and expertise. Jon Katz has said that the interactivity of the Web taught him that he was never "completely right"; he was "merely a transmitter of ideas waiting to be improved by people who knew more" (his readers).[29] But if Katz ever thought he was completely right, he was unduly arrogant before he began inhabiting the Web and is unduly modest now. No one is ever completely right, but no writer worth publishing is a mere apprentice to his readers.

This is not an apology for journalistic arrogance. Commentators who pretend to know everything are hardly the only alternative to commentators who know very little. The impatience of new media critics with old media pundits is often refreshing. It reflects the irritating fact that many pundits don't know more than the rest of us; they just talk more. Their authority is unearned. It's not superior knowledge that makes them seem arrogant but the lack of it.

Commentators, however, are not monolithic. Many of us

can probably name at least a few we consider worth heeding. We come to trust particular writers and analysts because we come to know them a little; at least we become familiar with their voices and viewpoints—just as we become familiar with particular magazines, newspapers, and networks. In traditional media, information generally comes with a brand name—like CBS—which is supposed to ensure reliability, as commentators on the digital culture regularly observe. Branding hardly guarantees accuracy, and when media outlets don't live up to their declared standards of truthfulness, their reputations can give misinformation a dangerous credibility. (The Lewinsky affair demonstrated the mainstream media's susceptibility to rumor mongering.) Still, knowing the source helps provide us with context for the opinions and information we receive—essential context often missing on the Net.

In cyberspace, we converse with strangers who may or may not reveal their identities and agendas. We can't know their biases, the sources of their facts or opinions, or the validity of their claims to expertise. Because we don't know the provenance of so much information circulating throughout the digital culture, we cannot evaluate its credibility. How then do we distinguish rumor from fact?

Anonymity is an important civil liberty, protected by the First Amendment. You don't have to identify yourself when you criticize your government. (The Supreme Court has recognized a constitutional right to publish anonymous political pamphlets.) But anonymity does come at a cost; the problem of verbal abuse is minor: democracy requires that all of us grow thick skins. The specter of misinformation is significant. What's worrisome about anonymity is not its intimidation of the thin-skinned but its seduction of the gullible.

Skepticism, even more than branding, would arm people

against anonymous rumor-mongering. The culture of cyber-space is supposed to encourage independent thought and questioning of conventional authorities, but the prototypical netizens seem primarily mistrustful of government and the mainstream media; they assume that politicians and print journalists lie. That's not skepticism; it's nihilism (some politicians and journalists do tell the truth, at least some of the time), and nihilism engenders gullibility, as Hannah Arendt observed. Arendt attributed the power of modern propaganda partly to a popular tendency to believe "everything and nothing," to think that "everything [is] possible and that nothing [is] true." [30] People who automatically disbelieve politicians and journalists may believe instead in angels and UFOs. For those who reflexively assume that government officials always lie, official denials of a report that TWA flight 800 was shot down by friendly fire becomes confirmation of its truth. Sometimes the digital culture seems like one in which Oliver Stone sets the standard for investigative journalism.

How do students learn and conduct research in this misinformation age? Some may use traditional research methods, locating known, reliable sources in cyberspace, or the library. But others send out queries on the Net: "Does anyone know anything about methamphetamines? I'm doing a paper." Perhaps an anonymous self-proclaimed expert will respond with accurate information. Perhaps not.

"We've all got this information, and someone is going to have to decide if it's good information or bad information," columnist John Dvorak has observed. "Reliability is going to be the big issue in the next century." [31] If the Net is going to help rationalize our society, the digital culture will have to adopt some attitudes and practices that the more thoughtless netizens are apt to label elitist, or even oppressive: Matt Drudge celebrates the fact that you can publish on the Net without ever being edited, darkly equating editors with "Big Brother."

As the shoddiness of the Drudge Report demonstrated and as many old and some new media columnists and editors have observed, someone or some trusted person, persons, or organizations are needed to evaluate information on the Net. The problem is obvious. While praising the Net as a "more 'small-d' democratic medium," journalism critic James Fallows has noted that "there is much less of a fact or reasonableness censor on the Internet . . . you still do need editors."[32] *HotWired* columnist Brooke Shelby Biggs has stressed the need to ensure "the new media's integrity. As Internet-based news surges, it begs for a filter that can help the public separate the bunk . . . from mostly accurate news sources." The new media does harbor a few reliable internal critics, Biggs has observed, calling it "its own best critic"; but he has lamented the absences of "enlightened external observers" of the on-line press, similar to independent watchdog organizations (like Fairness and Accuracy in Reporting). Like most new media writers, Biggs has little use for most criticism emanating from old media folk and finds much coverage of cyberspace by traditional media arrogant and obtuse.[33]

Considering the shallowness and inaccuracy of much traditional reporting and the ascendance of celebrity journalism, you may sympathize with defenders of the Net. The occasional unreliability and corruption of the mainstream press was underscored by scandals at the *Boston Globe* in 1998: two star columnists, Patricia Smith and Mike Barnicle, were fired for presenting fictional stories as fact. Smith was caught relatively early in her career, but Barnicle had enjoyed a twenty-five-year tenure at the *Globe*, despite evidence that he plagarized and periodically fabricated quotes.[34] Or, consider the widely publicized case of formerly hot young journalist Stephen Glass, who was fired by *The New Republic* in 1998 for fabricating stories, which were not adequately checked before publication. According to a *New York Times* report, *The New Republic* published six articles by Glass that were complete fictions and twenty-seven articles that were fictionalized in part. Glass also wrote for *Harper's, Rolling Stone,* and *George,* none of which, on second thought, could vouch for the accuracy of his stories. Glass's lies were eventually uncovered, thanks to the efforts of one suspicious journalist—an on-line editor for the Web site *Forbes Digital Tool.*[35]

Yet it's tempting to see Glass himself as a product of the digital culture, not because it necessarily encourages inaccuracy (Glass was, after all, a print journalist caught by a journalist online), but because it trades in merely virtual realities. Identity itself is mutable in cyberspace where role playing is epidemic. As a now famous *New Yorker* cartoon featuring a dog at a keyboard observed, "In cyberspace, nobody knows you're a dog." For many people, cyberspace is a place to act out fantasies. It's an alternative universe of their own creation. (Glass even used the Net to substantiate his fabrications, creating a phony Web site for an imaginary company.) If you're a young, untrained, ambitious journalist who is coming of age with the digital culture, it may not be a great leap from constructing your own multiple identities and telling stories about yourself (as if they were true) to telling stories about other characters you've created. The Net offers freedom from facts and traditional notions of authenticity in constructing your own identity and imagining the world.

People have always lost themselves in stories contained in oral histories, plays, novels, or films. And they have imagined other worlds, populated by spirits, angels, and gods. Yet, before the opening of the electronic frontier, real life was not widely perceived as a mere alternate venue of mortal experience, one that required its own designation RL (real life) to distinguish it from the virtual. Putting aside supernatural realms, RL was the only venue of experience.

Today some people immersed in the digital culture are living alternate lives on-line. Sherry Turkle observes that some "experience their lives as a 'cycling through' between the real world (RL) and a series of virtual worlds." In the words of one celebrant of the virtual, our on-line selves are simply "the selves that don't have bodies," whose experiences are, therefore, not subject to the limitations of the body. Turkle views cyberspace as an arena in which postmodern ideals of fluid, multiple identities are realized. On-line, "many more people experience identity as a set of roles that can be mixed and matched." [36]

The self-consciousness with which people engage in role playing on the Net distinguishes them from designated sufferers of multiple personality disorder, supposed victims of the treacherous unconscious. But it is probably no coincidence that MPD flourished along with postmodernism and the emerging digital culture. It was the pathological manifestation of the multiple self that was beginning to emerge as a cultural norm, and like most diseases, it implicitly defined health, the way vice defines virtue: the disconnect between alters exhibited by MPD sufferers suggested that mental health depended on the integration of multiple identities.

Coherence lingers as a cultural value, although it may be redefined in a virtual world. Turkle suggests that creating a home page, with linkages (a form of hypertext), helps people integrate their seemingly disparate interests and roles. This implies that in cyberspace, free association, not logic, will help us cohere.

If I were a New Age technobooster, I'd say that hypertext and the flourishing of multiple identities represent triumphs of holistic thinking. I'd explain that free association, unlike logic, naturally involves the heart as well as the head. Free association is thinking as play, while logic is serious business, I'd say, hastening to point out that the inner child, source of all our creativity, expresses itself through play.

In fact, while I'm highly skeptical of New Age technoboosterism, I do not question the value of associational thinking (I engage in it when I write). I do want to underscore the unlikely ideological kinship between the therapeutic and digital cultures. Both eschew traditional notions of rationalism and linear thinking. Both envision a colonized self: popular therapies teach us that we are essentially inhabited by the ghosts of family life, or by our own alternative personalities that developed in reaction to early childhood experiences; and, of course, we carry an inner child. In cyberspace, we can learn to view the self as a series of linkages to multiple characters and roles.

People immersed in the spiritualized, emotional realms of recovery, and other personal development movements, may, therefore, feel quite at home in the culture created by new technologies. People ensconced in cyberspace may respond to the popular therapeutic disdain for rationalism and the notion that happiness, success, or recovery can be achieved by a simple reprogramming of the self.

Despite a strong preference for sensibility over sense, despite the relentless glorification of warm emotionalism and denigration of cold logic, the personal development tradition has, paradoxically, promoted a rather mechanistic view of human nature. It is premised on faith in the efficacy of formulaic, technical solutions to idiosyncratic personal or spiritual problems. The 12-step movement has exhorted people to "get with the program" in order to recover from codependency. The positive thinking tradition has long preached that the mere rote recitation of affirmations ("I am a beautiful person. My boss values me. My husband loves me") can change our attitudes and, consequently, our lives. How-to books promise that there is nothing ineffable, much less unattainable about happiness. You can program your life the way you program your VCR, by reading directions—following the recommended steps, adopting the expert's proven technique. "Think with your heart" has always been a rather misleading slogan for a therapeutic tradition that encourages people to practice prescribed techniques unthinkingly.

This was a tradition that easily found a home in cyberspace. If formulaic books can help people heal, so can software programs; on-line therapy has been available since the 1980s. Some programs are virtual shrinks that converse with people; some less interactive programs simply provide the usual advice of experts, just like self-help books and tapes.[37]

Does the growing tendency to identify with the computer, regarding it as an extension of the self, make us particularly receptive to mechanistic therapies? Probably. At least, the computer has become a model for the human brain (it's not uncommon to hear people refer to their own memories as data banks), just as the brain has become a model for new forms of artificial intelligence.[38] The more interesting and rarely asked question is this: Did popular, formulaic therapies, dating back to the nineteenth century, facilitate the development of a digital culture premised on a symbiosis between people and their machines? Perhaps.

Turkle has observed that a resurgent faith in biological determinism and the development of psychotropic drugs helped promote a view of the "mind as program" and eroded the ideal of free will. In recent decades, science has shaped a view of the human animal as a "living machine." [39] But the belief that people could and should be programmed for happiness, success, and even salvation was imbedded in the culture before anyone had ever dreamed of Prozac, by therapies dating back over one hundred years. Mind-cure, the positive thinking tradition, and the recovery movement have always denigrated, even demonized, the human will and offered escape from freedom through submission to techniques.

These supposedly humanistic therapies were essentially dehumanizing—if sense is as precious to human beings as sensibility. Perhaps rational thinking needn't be linear, but it is willful, deliberate, discriminatory, and disinclined to take direction.

The traditional, romantic challenge to the digital culture is to maintain the boundaries between humans and machines. That requires much more than nostalgia for the expressive emotional life, which seems in little danger of disappearing on the Net, so far. It requires jettisoning the baggage of the therapeutic culture, which championed emotionalism and eschewed rationality, only to embrace the mechanistic.

■

CHAPTER 8

THE STRENUOUS LIFE

"The average man doesn't want to be free," H. L. Mencken asserted. "He simply wants to be safe."[1] The misanthropic Mencken had little sympathy for weaknesses he claimed not to share, and his disdain for people who sought refuge from existential terrors or the quotidian struggles of middle-class American life inspired his injudicious wit. I suspect that the average man, whoever he may be, wants both safety and freedom but in times of stress will sacrifice the latter to the former. In fact, Mencken pronounced upon man's preference for safety in 1923, when the country was in the midst of a red scare following the Russian Revolution and the First World War, and political repression in America was relatively high—and tolerated by the "average citizen."

Mencken may have been indulging in hyperbole, but he captured an essential truth about the fear of freedom in a nation supposedly founded on the principle that death is preferable to tyranny. ("Live Free or Die," New Hampshire's license plates say.) Even the NRA, which prides itself on a commitment to individual freedom, thrives on public concern about safety, which drives the desire to own guns. "Average" gun owners fear violent crime much more than they fear the government, and crime is often blamed on freedom. You rarely hear centrist, conservative, or even liberal commentators complain that American society is insufficiently permissive. Whether you consider popular pressure to criminalize socially or politically disruptive speech (like flag burning), popular resistance to affording criminal suspects their constitutional rights, or the popular appeal of formulaic personal development programs, it's hard to deny the powerful allure of order, even when it encroaches upon liberty.

Atheists, like Mencken, are apt to point out that theism is the ultimate retreat from freedom. Religious people who believe that they have found freedom in their love of God would disagree. But they have also found an ordering principle for the universe, whether or not they expect to understand it. Without God, they'd face not just death with no promise of rebirth but anarchy, which few of us feel capable of conquering. If the occasional existentialist fears the existence of God, feeling constrained, and even enslaved by the prospect of a Deity, most seem to fear profoundly God's absence. I do have one devoutly faithless friend who prefers randomness to an order not of his own making. He says he felt liberated and infused with power by the initial realization that he was utterly alone in an arbitrary, indifferent universe; but most flee from such epiphanies.

The freedom and opportunity for inventiveness offered by a godless world is traded for the security of divine benevolent despotism. That is how an atheist might characterize religion's triumph over nonbelievers. Some believers might respond that it was Satan who chose freedom from God. They'd argue that we cannot consistently discern or sustain goodness without God's guidance. Whatever moral authority we exercise derives from "Our Creator," Newt Gingrich suggested in his speech to the House of Representatives following his re-election as Speaker in 1997. "[W]e need to seek divine guidance in what we are doing [or] we are not going to solve this country's problems," he declared.[2] Pat Robertson observes that without God's guidance (and the threat of His wrath), there can be little public morality: "If people do not believe in eternal rewards or eternal punishments, then they readily ask what harm can there be in hedonism?"[3] From the left, Marianne Williamson, too, attributes our ills to a failure of faith: "Our blessings now seem in many ways to have faltered, not because God has abandoned us but because we have abandoned God." Still, she offers hope: "Everytime we pray or meditate, we go home to God . . . We are shown the light that it is then our job to help bring to all the world."[4]

Some seem to feel inspired by such exhortations. I find them soporific, perhaps because the notion of God is irrelevant to me. I don't engage in spiritual practices and don't spend much time imagining an Almighty or wondering about the origin and end of the universe. Perhaps I am insufficiently curious, but I've put concern about the nature and meaning of life in the category of things I can't worry about. "Ah, that is a metaphysical speculation, and like most metaphysical speculations has little reference at all to the actual facts of real life, as we know them," Oscar Wilde wrote, in *The Importance of Being Earnest*. I don't care if there is no supernatural authority behind my own moral sensibility. Doubting the existence of God has never led me to doubt that murder is wrong. Considering religion's checkered history and reviewing contemporary pop spirituality literature does make me question, instead, the assertion that people turn to God for moral guidance. In general, the literature tends to be amoral and focused on the promise of eternal life, religions respect their professed moral principles inconsistently, and, as Mencken observed, self-interest has always facilitated religious belief: Religion gives "man access to the powers which seem to control his destiny, and its single purpose is to induce those powers to be friendly to him."[5]

Besides, science can explain our ethical impulses, as well as religion. In *Descartes' Error,* an intriguing study of the relationship between emotion, reasoning, and moral judgment, neurologist Antonio Damasio suggests that there are "biological mechanisms behind the most sublime human behavior."[6] (You will be guided by these mechanisms whether or not you believe that God designed them.) Common sense tells us that parental nurturance, as well as a vision of the Divine, also helps make people good. It is possible, after all, to instill respect for justice and generally accepted notions of ethical behavior in children without encouraging them to believe in God. Acknowledging that there are no gods on their side, it may be easier to imbue children with tolerance and moral modesty. Or, maybe not. Tribalism and sanctimony may come as naturally to people as religious belief.

Some fervent atheists do deny the existence of God with the self-righteousness and intolerance of religious zealots. Certain only of their doubts, agnostics are less prone to evangelicism. The challenge for atheists is to make the case for not believing in God without falling into the pit of moral certainty squirming with believers. After all, generalizing about the benefits of atheism and character of atheists is as difficult as generalizing about religious faith and the faithful. You can't accurately claim that atheists are particularly virtuous or intelligent or even courageous: some are just resigned to their existential terrors.

But you can, at least, acknowledge what atheism, along with agnosticism, are not: They are not inherently nihilistic, as many believe; they do not automatically deprive you of moral standards, or instincts. Except for the sadomasochistic among us, childhood lessons in the Golden Rule may serve as well as fables about God handing Moses a tablet of commandments. (In fact, sadomasochists are apt to feel more at home with some religions, given their habits of authoritarianism and self-flagellation.) Nor does disbelief in God encourage hedonism. The conviction or suspicion that there is no cosmic justice can fuel a commitment to the cause of earthly justice. They deny you the luxury of believing that the wrongs of this world are merely illusory, or will be avenged in the next, or remedied by the intervention of guardian angels.

Without faith in the supernatural, people tend to celebrate reason, an underrated quality in these pre-millennial years. This does not mean that they disdain emotionalism, like Dickens's Mr. Gradgrind, in the belief that human beings are like computers. Atheists and agnostics are as likely as believers to be ruled by temperamental biases, especially in the conduct of private life, but they are probably less likely to consult their horoscopes seriously or suppose they've been abducted by aliens. Temperament, as well as supernaturalism, is one source of passion, and ideals. "[T]here is no opposition between [intelligence] and emotion," John Dewey wrote. "There is such a thing as passionate intelligence, as ardor in behalf of light shining into the murky places of social existence . . ."[7]

The point is simple: that secular purposes can inspire moral fervor and that sentiment, or instinct, in addition to reason, guide us all. To answer moral questions, a nonbeliever will consult "his own heart," Bertrand Russell observed. These questions "belong to a realm . . . of emotion and feeling and desire . . . a realm which is not that of reason though it should be in no degree contrary to it."[8] If you put your faith in earthly justice, faithlessness in God can make moral choices harder but no less true; the absence of a higher power demands an active inner life as well as a capacity for empathy and engagement with the world. Empathy itself entails reason; actively imagining another's plight requires the capacity to process knowledge of an experience utterly different from your own, as well as the inclination to care about it.

The contrary assertion that religion is essential to virtue, or moral discrimination, reflects an understandable mistrust of human nature. History hardly testifies to a consistent human propensity to be good; but it provides little reason to believe that we are better when we consider ourselves allied with God. You can condemn the effort to formulate ideals without the aid of God as an exercise in hubris. Or you can welcome the acknowledgment that your values lack divine sponsorship as an expression of humility. Charles Colson has remarked that when we remove the Ten Commandments from the courtroom or classroom wall, we are left with the proverbial barroom question, "Says Who." [9] Exactly. He laments the question. I celebrate it. Isn't the endeavor to define a set of shared moral values, without reliance on divine authorities, the challenge of a free, democratic society?

It includes a commitment to argument and unending political strife. Democracy is not for utopians. It promises us no earthly paradise, no ultimate resolution of conflict, no assurance of absolute rectitude, no rest. It presumes a perennial willingness to make hard moral choices. Democratic ideals of liberty and equality conflict: racial and sexual equality, for example, require restricting the freedom to discriminate. Unlike totalitarian systems, democratic states do not promise perfection. If justice in a democratic society entails compromise—the balancing of conflicting values like individual freedom and collective, social justice—then it entails an ability to tolerate loss, a willingness to approximate ideals. It requires energy. Democracy offers one variation of the "strenuous life" in which William James sought transcendence. "Not the absence of vice, but vice there, and virtue holding her by the throat, seems the ideal human state," he opined.[10]

The strenuous effort to forge moral consensus in a diverse society is hardly a celebration of relativism, or subjectivism. It assumes, instead, that we can agree upon a set of sufficiently objective, core values—like racial and sexual equality or religious freedom. It accepts that at times we will disagree bitterly over fundamentals—the morality of reproductive choice or the right to die. The values we fashion and ultimately codify are likely to be influenced by religious teachings, of course, but they should be shaped democratically, by the human intellect reflecting on experience, not handed down from on high. The anticipated answer to Charles Colson's question "Says who," is a collective, "Say we."

That was the secularist ideal articulated by John Dewey in the early twentieth century. Writing at a time when rationalism and science were ascendant among intellectuals, he disdained supernaturalism and believed that religion had "lost itself in cults, dogmas, and myths." Convinced that "all morality is social" (not divine), the result of social interactions and demands, he considered each of us responsible for shaping and respecting our own ideals: "Considerations of right are claims originating not outside of life, but within it. They are 'ideal' in precisely the degree in which we intelligently recognize and act upon them . . ."[11]

Dewey was a secularist but no relativist. He spoke readily of good and evil and criticized religion partly because of what he considered its deleterious effect of "moral faith." The conversion of human ideals into divine mandates evinced a lack of "moral faith," he wrote: Theology transforms "faith that something should be in existence as far as lies in our power" to the conviction that "it is already in existence." [12] In other words, religion posits a moral code divinely ordained that exists regardless of our efforts and beliefs, inadvertently encouraging intolerance and passivity: Tell people that a divine moral order already exists in "some supernal region" and they are bound to assume that their own beliefs reflect it. When earthly realities do not meet supposedly divine ideals, the realities can be dismissed as mere "appearances," or temporary, even momentary inconveniences. "The pain we experience on earth is just a moment, just a split second of consciousness in the spirit world, and we are very willing to endure it," best-selling, formerly deceased author Betty Eadie writes. [13]

Dewey wanted to preserve the religious impulse—the impulse to be governed or absorbed by a transcendent ideal—but to dispense with theology and supernaturalism. Collectively, we would become our own authorities, he hoped, seeking transcendence in progressive, co-operative human endeavors that served human ideals—like truth, affection, and justice. "It is admitted that the objects of religion are ideal . . . What would be lost if it were also admitted that they have authoritative claim upon conduct just because they are ideal . . . An unseen power controlling our destiny becomes the power of an ideal." [14]

The assertion that transcendent ideals of justice, compassion, equality, and freedom are not derived from God but from human history and "concrete" human relations resonates with me; but I don't imagine that Dewey's vision will ever be realized. For a pragmatist, he seemed hopelessly unrealistic in assessing the allure of supernatural realities. The good society he proposed might have provided people with transcendence and order, but it would not have alleviated their fear of death or accounted for experiences and emotions that some would consider intimations of the divine.

To believe that society can successfully rid itself of religious belief, you have to regard faith as essentially voluntary, and I suspect it is more like an instinct or reflex, a reflection of taste and temperament. I've never regarded religious faith as a choice, but rather as a talent, or gift. It's obvious that belief in God is a unique and essential comfort, with some social benefits. People believe in deities because they would find life unbearable without them. Disbelief has its own advantages— no fear of hell—but most believers apparently expect to go to heaven anyway. Sometimes, especially in adolescence, living without God seems heroic—the moral equivalent of war—but religious faith too has surely inspired heroism. Some consider faith in God essential to moral courage.[15] I suspect that it inspires roughly equal measures of courage and cruelty.

Moral absolutism is, of course, the central strength and weakness of religion. It would exert considerably less market appeal if it did not provide us with an ultimate Authority, but it would also offer less incentive to kill in His name. Some will argue that religious absolutists who control heresy with violence and other forms of persecution do not represent the "true" religious spirit, but the absolutists, of course, would disagree. Their beliefs seem true enough to them and so are never subject to debate. You can't argue or reason with the one true faith, as relatives of cult members discover.

I'm not suggesting that all or even very many religious people are glassy-eyed, relieved of all doubt, or bereft of the capacity to question. If a minority of people embrace visions of God with frightening, fanatical zeal, many incorporate belief into their lives without being carried away by it. And, religions don't generally demand that believers withdraw from the secular world, with all its temptations and challenges. Even the Hasidim and more cloistered Amish communities interact cautiously with society. Cults—those insular, occasionally totalistic groups that thrive partly on their own otherworldliness—are exceptions. People enter them and sometimes exit disillusioned, but they don't move freely between the cult and society. Cults are for in-patients. Denominational religions and New Age movements treat people on an outpatient basis. But ultimately religions do rely on a tendency to shed or at least overcome reasonable doubt and embrace the inexplicable. Ultimately, religious beliefs are not supposed to be justified or explained; the ways of God are supposed to be a mystery.

Is theology mere detail? If you focus solely on the propensity for worship and the craving for miracles, immortality, and unconditional love, all religions and pop spirituality movements are the same. Of course, even the least dogmatic, most ecumenical believers don't blithely dismiss theological differences as different strokes for different folks. Religious dogmas would exert little appeal if they were considered accidental, not absolute. Still, for people of different faiths, moments of revelation often seem to feel the same; at least, their descriptions are strikingly similar.

Considering the apparent similarities between mystical experiences, acid trips, and various mental disorders, you might well view religion as one socially acceptable form of psychosis, like falling in love. Or, you might praise both some established and New Age religions for keeping people sane. In addition to a belief system, they offer communities of believers and social institutions, which provide a great many people with emotional stability. Education and relative material comfort do not immunize people from the allure of the utterly, all-consuming irrational. That was one lesson offered by Heaven's Gate; like many cults, it drew from the middle class. Consumerism is sometimes glibly described as an American religion, and it does distract us from our existential terrors; but it doesn't soothe them. In many ways, it makes people more anxious.

Cult members sometimes display a preternatural calm, but it is as unsettling to outsiders as the desperation it may mask. It seems to reflect a belief system that deprives followers of all reason, unlike some New Age and mainstream faiths, which are integrated into a larger, pluralistic society and only demand the subordination of some reason. And, whatever reason established religion jettisons is probably absent in most people anyway.

Psychologist James Alcock has observed that virtually everyone, including professional skeptics, have a natural propensity for magical thinking. We need to acknowledge the appeal of the supernatural, he suggests, partly to arm ourselves against it: People who most vehemently deny the possibility of supernatural realities and are averse even to fantasies of divine or occult phenomena are most vulnerable to conversion experiences. They cannot integrate visions or sensations that their rigid belief systems cannot explain. Magical thinking can only be tempered, not eliminated, by teaching critical thinking skills, which do not come naturally to most of us.[16] If the great lie driving crusades for public piety is the assertion that we are an excessively secular nation, the great lie of pop spirituality experts is the insistence we need to learn how not to be rational.

I'm not suggesting that we should only be rational. I don't regret a childhood spent reading fairy tales. Skeptics sometimes lack a sense of whimsy; they take too seriously the pleasure that people find in ghost stories, astrology, dreams, or experiments in ESP. Virtually all of us harbor superstitions. The trouble is that some people are apt to be ruled by them. From one agnostic perspective, the value of religion may lie in its ability to ritualize and contain the ravages of faith.

To a religious person, that's a bit like suggesting that the value of school is keeping children off the street. Religion is supposed to shape our characters as well as save our souls. Its teachings are supposed to be integral to daily life. Indeed, people who engage in periodic religious practices without consistently adhering to religious principles are liable to be scorned as hypocrites. People are supposed to believe in God daily, not just on Sunday; and many do; and that is both a blessing and a curse, if I am right about the dangers posed to reasoned public discourse by faith.

No religion can simply be trusted to balance faith with reason; but regular social rituals, like attending church or New Age lectures, and private rituals, like prayer, or maybe even watching *Touched by an Angel* once a week, can provide people with the opportunity to compartmentalize their beliefs, so as not to be consumed by them. Some atheists will make the counter argument that religious rituals endorse and encourage irrationalism. You can hardly praise religion for keeping people sane, they say, when it sanctifies their delusions. But that wrongly assumes that it is possible for us to rid ourselves of all supernaturalism. I'd treat religious cravings homeopathically. The cure is the disease, in small doses.

NOTES

—

INTRODUCTION

1. William James, *Varieties of Religious Experience* (New York: Penguin Books, 1982), 31.
2. Ibid., 10–12.
3. William James, "The Sentiment of Rationality," in *The Will to Believe and Other Essays in Popular Philosophy* (New York: Dover Publications, 1956), 92.
4. James, *Varieties of Religious Experience*, 79–123.
5. See Brian L. Weiss, *Many Lives, Many Masters,* (New York: Simon & Schuster, 1988). Judith Orloff, *Second Sight: A Psychiatrist Clairvoyant Tells Her Extraordinary Story . . . And Shows You How to Discover Your Psychic Gifts* (New York: Warner Books, 1997).
6. John Dewey, *A Common Faith* (New Haven, Conn.: Yale University Press, 1934), 48.
7. James, *The Will to Believe and Other Essays in Popular Philosophy,* 97.

1. PIOUS BIASES

1. Thomas Moore, *Care of the Soul* (New York: HarperCollins, 1992), xi.

2. "America and Religion," *The Economist,* July 8, 1995, 19. Ari L. Goldman, "Religion Notes," *New York Times,* February 27, 1993, sec. A, 9. *The Gallup Poll Monthly,* January 1998, no. 388. Jeffrey L. Sheler, *U.S. News & World Report,* April 4, 1994, 48–59. *Gallup Poll,* November 1990, survey no. 122008.

3. Robert Wuthnow, *Experimentation in American Religion* (Berkeley: University of California Press, 1978), 71. *Gallup Poll,* 1990, survey no. 922011. Princeton Survey Research Associates, Newsweek Poll, June 29, 1996. Michael F. Brown, *The Channelling Zone: American Spirituality in an Anxious Age* (Cambridge: Harvard University Press, 1997), 6.

4. "Why Discourage Religion," *Wall Street Journal,* December 23, 1993, sec. A, 10.

5. Quoted in Robert Wuthnow, *Christianity and Civil Society* (Valley Forge, Pa.: Trinity Press International, 1996), 27.

6. Judy Mann, "Getting Back to the Heart of Things," *Washington Post,* November 18, 1994, sec. E, 3.

7. "Drugs and God," *Wall Street Journal,* March 6, 1996, sec. A, 20.

8. Robert Bork, *Slouching Toward Gomorrah: Modern Liberalism and American Decline* (New York: Regan Books, 1996), 294.

9. Kathleen Kennedy Townsend, "A Rebirth of Virtue: Religion and Liberal Renewal," *Washington Monthly,* February, 1989, 36.

10. Stephen Carter, *The Culture of Disbelief: How American Law and Politics Trivialize Religious Devotion* (New York: Anchor Books, 1993).

11. Amy Waldman, "Why We Need a Religious Left," *Washington Monthly,* December 1995, 37–43, at 39.

12. Bork, *Slouching Toward Gomorrah,* 294.

13. Barnaby J. Feder, "Ministers Who Work Around the Flock," *New York Times,* October 3, 1996, sec. D, 1.

14. Annetta Miller, "Corporate Mind Control," *Newsweek,* May 4, 1987, 38.

15. Stephanie Armour, "Conflict Grows Between Bosses, Devout Workers," *USA Today,* November 12, 1997, sec. B, 1.

16. Diego Ribadeneira, "Viewers' Interest in Faith Prompts TV Networks to Get Religion," *Boston Globe,* April 25, 1998, sec. B, 2.

17. John Meroney, "Religion Is Ready for Prime Time," *Wall Street Journal,* December 27, 1996, sec. A, 6.

18. Patrick Flaherty, "Believing in the Blessedness of Audrey," *Boston Globe,* August 10, 1998, sec. B, 1.

19. See Saul Levine, *Radical Departures: Desperate Detours to Growing Up* (San Diego: Harcourt Brace Jovanovich, 1984).

20. Mark Twain, *Letters from the Earth* (New York: Harper Perennial, 1991), 7.

21. H. L. Mencken, *Treatise on the Gods* (New York: Alfred A. Knopf, 1930), 271.

22. H. L. Mencken, *A Mencken Chrestomathy* (New York: Vintage Books, 1982), 81.

23. Mencken, *Treatise on the Gods,* 260.

24. Mencken, *A Mencken Chrestomathy,* 80–81.

25. Bertrand Russell, "A Free Man's Worship," in Robert E. Egner and Lester E. Denonn, eds., *The Basic Writings of Bertrand Russell* (New York: Simon & Schuster, 1961), 67.

26. Michael Kelly, "Saint Hillary," *New York Times Magazine,* May 23, 1993, 22. Martha Sherrill, "Hillary Clinton's Inner Politics," *Washington Post,* May 6, 1993, sec. D, 1.

27. Walter Lippmann, *Public Opinion* (New York: Macmillan, 1950), 197.

28. Anita Sharpe, "More Spiritual Leaders Preach Virtue of Wealth," *Wall Street Journal,* April 5, 1996, sec. B, 1.
29. Sally Jacobs, "The Guru Wore Armani," *Boston Globe,* May 23, 1995, 73. (Lenz committed suicide in 1998, leaving an $18 million estate.)
30. J. Gordon Melton, "New Thought and the New Age," in James R. Lewis and J. Gordon Melton, eds., *Perspectives on the New Age* (Albany: State University of New York Press, 1992), 18.
31. "God and Drugs, *Wall Street Journal,* March 6, 1996, sec. A, 20.
32. John T. McQuiston, "Woman Who Called Daughter Possessed Pleads Not Guilty to Her Murder," *New York Times,* January 28, 1998, sec. B, 5.
33. Quoted in Jonathan Rauch, *Kindly Inquisitors* (Chicago: University of Chicago Press, 1993), 107.
34. Betty Eadie, *Embraced by the Light* (New York: Bantam Books, 1992), 84.
35. Wuthnow, *Christianity and Civil Society,* 41.
36. Herbert McCloskey and Alida Brill, *Dimensions of Tolerance: What Americans Believe About Civil Liberties* (New York: Russell Sage, 1983), 130–132, 124.
37. Wuthnow, *Christianity and Civil Society,* 78.
38. Harvey Cox, "Bill the Baptist," *The Nation,* October 5, 1998.
39. Gayle White, "Searching for Forgiveness," *Atlanta Constitution,* September 26, 1998, sec. D, 1.
40. Tom Perrin and Tim Engle, "Religious Leaders Urge Forgiveness," *Kansas City Star,* September 14, 1998, sec. A, 1.
41. Richard Rorty, *Achieving Our Country* (Cambridge: Harvard University Press, 1997).
42. Garry Wills, *Under God: Religion and American Politics* (New York: Simon & Schuster, 1990), 21.

43. Alison Mitchell, "Lott Says Homosexuality Is a Sin and Compares It to Alcoholism," *New York Times,* June 15, 1998, sec. A, 24.

44. Dewey, *A Common Faith,* 7.

45. See *Brown v. Dade Christian Schools,* 556 F2d 310 (1977), holding that a church school was not exempt from federal antidiscrimination laws, despite its claim that admitting black children violated the school's religious precepts.

46. Nancy Rosenblum, *Membership and Morals: The Personal Uses of Pluralism in America* (Princeton: Princeton University Press, 1998).

47. Mary McCarthy, *Memoirs of a Catholic Girlhood* (New York: Harcourt Brace, 1946), 23.

48. James Madison, *The Federalist Papers,* no. 51 (New York: Penguin Books, 1961), 324–25.

49. Carter, *Culture of Disbelief,* 41.

50. Isaac Kramnick and R. Laurence Moore, *The Godless Constitution: The Case Against Religious Correctness* (New York: W. W. Norton, 1996), 57.

51. Garry Wills, *Under God,* 352.

52. Quoted in Wills, *Under God,* 352.

52. Ibid., 365.

53. Ibid., 375.

54. *Engle v. Vitale,* 370 US 421 (1962).

55. *Lynch v. Donnelly,* 465 US 668 (1984).

56. Brief of the American Center for Law and Justice, *Rosenberger v. University of Virginia,* no. 94-329, 9, 15.

2. THE SECTARIAN PUBLIC SQUARE

1. See Wills, *Under God,* 115–17.

2. Daniel J. Kevles, "Darwin in Dayton," *New York Review of*

Books, November 19, 1998, 61. See also Wills, *Under God,* 108–14.

3. Quoted in James Risen and Judy L. Thomas, *Wrath of Angels: The American Abortion War* (New York: Basic Books, 1998), 129.

4. Pat Robertson, *Pat's Perspectives:* "Is America Headed for Judgment," CBNonline, www.cbn.org.

5. Stacey Burling, "Falwell Antisex-Education Letter Decried," *Virginia Pilot,* November 17, 1980.

6. *Bowers v. Hardwick,* 478 US 186 (1986).

7. Melinda Heenenerger, "Many on Right Give Up Goal of Clinton's Ouster," *New York Times,* December 3, 1998, sec. A, 22.

8. Joe Klein, "In God They Trust," *New Yorker,* June 16, 1997, 40–48.

9. John Leland, "Savior of the Streets," *Newsweek,* June 1, 1998, 20. See also Klein, "In God They Trust."

10. Charles Colson, "Kingdoms in Conflict," *First Things,* November 1996, 34–38, 37.

11. *Rosenberger, v. University of Virginia,* 515 US 819 (1995).

12. Brief for Petitioners, *Rosenberger v. University of Virginia,* no. 94–329, 19, 21.

13. "In Fact," *The Nation,* March 25, 1996, 7.

14. Peter Applebome, "Creationism Fight Returns," *New York Times,* March 10, 1996, sec. A, 1.

15. Ibid.

16. *Edwards v. Aguillard,* 482 US 578 (1987).

17. "Oregon Tests Survive Religious Right Challenge," *Church and State,* July/August 1998, 21.

18. Rob Boston, "Florida's Bible Battle," *Church and State,* January 1998, 4.

19. Alveda C. King, "Fighting for School Choice," *Wall Street Journal,* September 16, 1997, sec. A, 14.

20. Mary Landrieu and Joe Lieberman, "Letter to Democratic Colleagues," September 9, 1997.
21. Sarah McBride, "Education Is the Top priority Among Public Policy Concerns, A Benefit to Democratic Party," *Wall Street Journal,* September 19, 1997, sec. R, 2.
22. "Breaching the Church-State Wall," *New York Times,* June 12, 1998, sec. A, 20.
23. *Agostini v. Felton,* 117 Sup. Ct. 1997 (1997).
24. *Bowen v. Kendrick,* 487 US 589 (1988).
25. "Implementation of Charitable Choice," Presbyterian Church (U.S.A.), Washington Office, January 13, 1998.
26. Glenn C. Loury, "Legal Limits," *The New Republic,* February 23, 1998, 16–17.
27. Elenora Giddings Ivory, "Questions About Charitable Choice," *Washington Report to Presbyterians,* January/February 1998, 3.
28. Jeffrey Rosen, "Big Church," *The New Republic,* December 11, 1995, 6.
29. Dennis Teti, "The Ten Commandments and the Constitution," *Weekly Standard,* July 21, 1997, 21–24.
30. *Romer v. Evans,* 517 US 620 (1996).
31. *Brown v. Dade Christian Schools,* 556 F2d 310 (1977).
32. William F. Murphy, "Real School Choice," *The Pilot,* July 24, 1997.
33. "Religious Right Group in Arkansas Has Confusing Agenda," *Church and State,* July/August 1998, 20.
34. *Chandler v. James,* 985 F. Supp. 1062 (1997).
35. Kevin Sack, "In South, Prayer Is a Form of Protest," *New York Times,* November 8, 1997, sec. A, 9.
36. Amended Complaint, *Herring v. Key,* United States District Court, Middle District, Alabama, CV97-D-1179-N.
37. Ibid.
38. Sack, "In South, Prayer Is a Form of Protest."

39. *Herdahl v. Pontotoc County School District*, 933 F. Supp. 582 (1996).
40. "Graduation Prayer Common in West Virginia," press release, American Civil Liberties Union, May 30, 1997. "West Virginia Imposes Organized Prayer at Football Games," press release, American Civil Liberties Union, October 15, 1997.
41. Rocky Scott, "Settlement Reached in School Prayer Case," UPI, October 15, 1986.
42. Katherine Q. Seelye, "Religion Amendment Is Introduced," *New York Times*, May 9, 1997, sec. A, 26.
43. "Americans United and ACLU of Alabama Sue School Districts to Halt Egregious Violations of Separations of Church and State," press release, American Civil Liberties Union, February 1, 1996.
44. *Chandler v. James*, 985 F. Supp. 1062 (1997).

3. POP SPIRITUALITY BOOKS AND THE GOSPEL OF GOOD NEWS

1. Marianne Williamson, *The Healing of America* (New York: Simon & Schuster, 1997), 76–77.
2. Peter Washington, *Madame Blavatsky's Baboon; Theosophy and the Emergence of the Western Guru* (London: Secker & Warburg, 1993), 36–38.
3. Williamson, *The Healing of America*, 76.
4. Margaret Jones, "Getting Away from the 'R' Word,'" *Publishers Weekly*, July 5, 1993, 42.
5. Alison Schneider, "Jane Tompkins's Message to Academe: Nurture the Individual, Not Just the Intellect," *Chronicle of Higher Education*, July 10, 1998, sec. A, 8.
6. Alma Daniel, Timothy Wyllie, and Andrew Ramer, *Ask Your Angels* (New York: Ballantine Books, 1992), 4, 98.

7. James Redfield, *The Celestine Prophecy: An Adventure* (New York: Warner Books, 1993).

8. Brian L. Weiss, *Many Lives, Many Masters* (New York: Simon & Schuster, 1988), 112.

9. Clarissa Pinkola Estés, *Women Who Run With the Wolves: Myths and Stories of the Wild Woman Archetype* (New York: Ballantine Books, 1992), 132.

10. Jones, "Getting Away from the 'R' Word," 42.

11. Betty J. Eadie, *Embraced by the Light* (New York, Bantam Books, 1994).

12. Sophy Burnham, *A Book of Angels: Reflections on Angels, Past and Present and True Stories of How They Touch Our Lives* (New York: Ballantine Books, 1990).

13. Linton Weeks, "Practically Flying Off the Shelves," *Washington Post,* December 16, 1995, sec. F, 1.

14. Neale Donald Walsch, *Conversations with God: An Uncommon Dialogue* (New York, Putnam, 1996.) (Walsch has published two sequels to this book.) James Van Praagh, *Talking to Heaven: A Medium's Message of Life After Death* (New York: Dutton, 1997). A sequel to Van Praagh's book has also been a best-seller.

15. Robert E. Bartholomew, "Before Roswell: The Meaning Behind the Crashed-UFOP Myth," *Skeptical Inquirer,* May/June 1998, 29.

16. Whitley Streiber, *Communion: A True Story* (New York: Avon Books, 1987). John Mack, *Abduction: Human Encounters with Aliens* (New York: Ballantine Books, 1994).

17. Mack, *Abduction,* 16, 256.

18. Deidre Martin, "Tales from Beyond the Grave," *McCall's,* October 1996, 74.

19. Marlo Morgan, *Mutant Message Down Under* (New York: Harper Perennial, 1995), 175.

20. James Redfield and Carol Adrienne, *The Celestine Prophecy:*

An Experiential Guide (New York: Warner Books, 1995), xi, xiii).

21. Daniel, Wyllie, and Ramer, *Ask Your Angels*, 4. Van Praagh, *Talking to Heaven*, 68–69. Walsch, *Conversations with God*, 51–52. Morgan, *Mutant Message Down Under*, 51.

22. Redfield, *The Celestine Prophecy*, 223.

23. Ibid., 41.

24. Mack, *Abduction*, 408, 388–89.

25. Redfield, *The Celestine Prophecy*, 42.

26. Walsch, *Conversations with God*, 181–82.

27. Morgan, *Mutant Message Down Under*, xiii.

28. Weiss, *Many Lives, Many Masters*, 10.

29. Morgan, *Mutant Message Down Under*, 20.

30. Ibid., 77, 93, 78.

31. Walsch, *Conversations with God*, 115.

32. Tim LaHaye and Jerry B. Jenkins, *Left Behind: A Novel of the Earth's Last Days* (Wheaton, Ill.: Tyndale House Publishers, 1995). Tim LaHaye and Jerry B. Jenkins, *Tribulation Force: The Continuing Drama of Those Left Behind* (Wheaton, Ill.: Tyndale House Publishers, 1996). Tim LaHaye and Jerry B. Jenkins, *Nicolae: The Rise of AntiChrist* (Wheaton, Ill.: Tyndale House Publishers, 1997). Tim LaHaye and Jerry B. Jenkins, *Soul Harvest: The World Takes Sides* (Wheaton, Ill.: Tyndale House Publishers, 1998).

    See also Laurie Goodstein, "Fast Selling Thrillers Depict Prophetic View of Final Days," *New York Times*, October 4, 1998, sec. A, 1.

33. LaHaye and Jenkins, *Soul Harvest*, 327–29.

34. Web site: www.leftbehind.com.

35. LaHaye and Jenkins, *Nicolae*, 361.

36. Weiss, *Many Lives, Many Masters*, 159, 164.

37. Walsch, *Conversations with God*, 61.

38. Eadie, *Embraced by the Light*, 67.

39. Van Praagh, *Talking to Heaven*, 69.
40. Eadie, *Embraced by the Light*, 68.
41. Morgan, *Mutant Message Down Under*, 175.
42. Eadie, *Embraced by the Light*, 68.
43. Karen Angel, "Inspirational Author Finds Her Own Press," *New York Times*, July 13, 1998, sec. D, 5.
44. Michael F. Brown, *The Channelling Zone: American Spirituality in an Anxious Age* (Cambridge: Harvard University Press, 1997), 68.
45. William James, *Varieties of Religious Experience*, 94–96, 363–64, 163.
46. Deepak Chopra, *Ageless Body, Timeless Mind: The Quantum Alternative to Growing Old* (New York: Harmony Books, 1993), 280.
47. Redfield and Adrienne, *The Celestine Prophecy: An Experiential Guide*, 257.
48. Van Praagh, *Talking to Heaven*, 142.
49. Burnham, *A Book of Angels*, 110.
50. Daniel, Wyllie, and Ramer, *Ask Your Angels*, 163.
51. Quoted in Martin, "Tales from Beyond the Grave," 78.
52. Chopra, *Ageless Body, Timeless Mind*, 99, 37.
53. Burnham, *A Book of Angels*, 222–23.
54. Redfield, *The Celestine Prophecy*, 154.
55. Walsch, *Conversations with God*, 143.
56. Weiss, *Many Lives, Many Masters*, 122.
57. Mack, *Abduction*, 158.
58. Ibid., 231–32.
59. Redfield and Adrienne, *The Celestine Prophecy: An Experiential Guide*, 28.
60. Morgan, *Mutant Message Down Under*, 130.
61. Michael Kelly, "The Road to Paranoia," *New Yorker*, June 19, 1995, 60–75.

4. GURUS AND THE SPIRITUALITY BAZAAR

1. *Gallup Poll,* November 1990, survey no. 122008. David Van Biemer, "Does Heaven Exist," *Time,* March 24, 1997, 71–78, 73.

2. Ron Rosenbaum, "Among the Believers," *New York Times Magazine,* September 24, 1995, 50–64.

3. Charles Cameron, "She Became an Icon: The Life and Death of Princess Diana in Millennial Discourse," Center for Millennial Studies, http://www.mille.org.

4. Karen Armstrong, *A History of God: The 4,000 Year Quest of Judaism, Christianity, and Islam* (New York: Ballantine Books, 1993), 48.

5. Ann Powers, "New Tune for the Material Girl: I'm Neither," *New York Times,* March 1, 1998, sec 2, 34.

6. James Brady, "In Step with Della Reese," *Parade Magazine,* November 9, 1997, 22.

7. Eric Mink, "The Divine Secret Behind Angel's Success," *Daily News,* March 13, 1997, 104.

8. Mary Farrell Bednarowski, "The New Age Movement and Feminist Spirituality: Overlapping Conversations at the End of the Century," in Lewis and Melton, eds., *Perspectives on the New Age,* 167–77.

9. Irene S. M. Makaruska, "Religion," in Wilma Mankiller, Gwendolyn Mink, Marysa Navarro, Barbara Smith, and Gloria Steinem, eds, *The Readers Companion to U.S. Women's History* (Boston, Mass.: Houghton Mifflin, 1998), 506.

10. Barbara Goldsmith, *Other Powers: The Age of Suffrage, Spiritualism, and the Scandalous Victoria Woodhull* (New York: Alfred A. Knopf, 1998), 426.

11. Massimo Polidoro, "Houdini and Conan Doyle: The Story

of Strange Friendship," *Skeptical Inquirer*, March/April, 1998, 40. See also, Loren Pankratz, "Rose Mankenberg: Crusader Against Spiritual Fraud," *Skeptical Inquirer*, July/August, 1994, 28.

12. Marianne Williamson, *A Woman's Worth* (New York: Random House, 1993), 8.
13. Talk by Marianne Wiliamson, November 14, 1997, Boston, Massachusetts.
14. Ibid.
15. Ibid.
16. My report on Kevin Ryerson is based on an evening and day-long session with him that I attended on September 24 and September 25, 1996, at Interface, a holistic learning center in Cambridge, Massachusetts. (Interface has since relocated to Watertown, Massachusetts.)
17. Lecture by Matthew Fox, on "The Physics of Angels," presented in Boston, Massachusetts, September 20, 1997, at "Body and Soul," a three-day New Age conference sponsored by Interface and *New Age Journal*, September 19–21, 1997.
18. Remarks by Judith Orloff, "Body and Soul," conference, Boston, Massachusetts, September 20, 1997.
19. Ibid.
20. My report on Brian Weiss is based on an "intensive" day-long workshop that I attended at "Body and Soul," conference, Boston, Massachusetts, September 19, 1997.

5. JUNK SCIENCE

1. Mary Baker Eddy, *Miscellaneous Writings, 1883–1896* (Boston: Trustees under the Will of Mary Baker G. Eddy, 1896), 54.

2. Kay Alexander, "Roots of the New Age," in Lewis, Melton, eds., *Perspectives on the New Age*, 31.
3. Thomas S. Ball and Dean D. Alexander, "Catching Up with Eighteenth Century Science in the Evaluation of Therapeutic Touch," *Skeptical Inquirer*, July/August 1998, 31–34.
4. Ibid., 31.
5. Alexander, "Roots of the New Age," 45.
6. Napoleon Hill, *Think and Grow Rich* (New York: Fawcett Books, 1960), 29.
7. Sophy Burnham, *A Book of Angels*, 223.
8. Chopra, *Ageless Body, Timeless Mind*, 42–43.
9. Ibid., 3, 6, 99.
10. Chopra, *Ageless Body, Timeless Mind*, 4.
11. Mary Baker Eddy, *Science and Health* (Boston: Trustees under the Will of Mary Baker G. Eddy, 1875), 472–73.
12. Chopra, *Ageless Body, Timeless Mind*, 6.
13. Mary Baker Eddy, *Miscellaneous Writings, 1883–1896*, 21.
14. Chopra, *Ageless Body, Timeless Mind*, 5–6.
15. Napoleon Hill, *Think and Grow Rich*, 49.
16. Chopra, *Ageless Body, Timeless Mind*, 5.
17. Ibid., 7, 10.
18. David Van Biema, "Emperor of the Soul," *Time*, June 14, 1996, 24.
19. Conversations with Marc Abrahams, June 1996.
20. Victor J. Stenger, "Quantum Quackery," *Skeptical Inquirer*, January/February 1997, 37–40.
21. Williamson, *The Healing of America*, 36.
22. Rob Boston, "Florida's Bible Battle," *Church and State*, January 1998, 4.
23. Richard Milner, "Charles Darwin and Associates Ghostbusters," *Scientific American*, October 1996, 96.
24. Martin Gardner, "Thomas Edison, Paranormalist," *Skeptical Inquirer*, July/August 1996, 9–12.

25. Natalie Angier, "Survey of Scientists Finds a Stability of Faith in God," *New York Times*, April 3, 1997, sec. A, 12.

26. Kenneth L. Woodward, "Is God Listening," *Newsweek*, March 31, 1997, 57.

27. George Johnson, "Science and Religion: Bridging the Great Divide," *New York Times*, June 30, 1998, sec. C, 4.

28. "Scientists and Theologians Discuss a Common Ground," *U.S. News & World Report*, July 20, 1998, 52.

29. James, "Sentiment of Rationality," in *The Will to Believe and Other Essays in Popular Philosophy*, 95.

30. George Johnson, "Elusive Particles Continue to Puzzle Theorists of the Sun," *New York Times*, June 9, 1998, sec. F, 1.

31. Ibid.

32. Malcolm Gladwell, "The Breakfast Table," *Slate*, Slate.com, June 9, 1998.

33. Dan Barry, "The N.Y.P.D.'s Psychic Friend," *New York Times*, July 21, 1997, sec. A, 19.

34. See Edward Rothstein, "It's a Battlefield Out There, Culturally Speaking," *New York Times*, December 7, 1998, sec. C, 2.

35. Christopher Wren, "Drugs, Alcohol Linked to 80% of Inmates," *New York Times*, January 9, 1998, sec. A, 14.

36. See, generally, Steven Duke, "Clinton and Crime," *10 Yale Journal on Regulation 575*, 1993, and Mike Gray, *Drug Crazy: How We Got Into This Mess and How We Can Get Out* (New York: Random House, 1998).

37. Giovanna Breu, "Cocaine Claims Its Tiniest Victims: Babies Born Addicted," *People*, September 8, 1986, 123. John Langone, "Crack Comes to the Nursery," *Time*, September 19, 1998, 85.

38. Sandree Blakeslee, "Crack's Toll Among Babies," *New York Times*, September 17, 1989, sec. A, 1. Barbara Kantrowitz, "The Crack Children," *Newsweek*, December 12, 1990, 62.

Charles Krauthamer, "Crack Babies Forming Biological Underclass," *St. Louis Post Dispatch*, July 30, 1998 sec. B, 3.

39. I've relied primarily on Katherine Greider, "Crackpot Ideas," *Mother Jones*, July 1995, 52.
40. Ibid.
41. Ibid.
42. Helen Hamilton Gardner, "Sex in Brain," in Helen Hamilton Gardner, *Facts and Fictions of Life* (Boston: Arena Publishing Company, 1893), 112.
43. Ibid.
44. "The Human Brain Still Puzzles Scientists," *New York Times*, October 9, 1927, sec. 9, 3.
45. Gina Kolata, "Men and Women Use Brain Differently, Study Discovers," *New York Times*, February 16, 1995, sec. A, 1.
46. Gina Kolata, "Men's World, Woman's World? Brain Studies Point to Differences," *New York Times*, February 28, 1995, sec. A, 1.
47. Ibid.
48. See Marjorie Heins, "Indecency: The Ongoing American Debate over Sex, Children, Free Speech, and Dirty Words." The Andy Warhol Foundation for the Visual Arts, Paper Series on the Arts, Culture, and Society, Paper no. 7, 1997; and Marcia Pally, *Sense and Censorship: The Vanity of Bonfires* (Chicago, Ill.: Freedom to Read Foundation, 1991).

6. THE THERAPEUTIC ASSAULT ON REASON AND RIGHTS

1. For an eloquent exposition of this perspective, see Jonathan Rauch, *Kindly Inquisitors: The New Attacks on Free Thought* (Chicago: University of Chicago Press, 1993).
2. Richard Ofshe and Ethan Watters, *Making Monsters: False*

Memories, Psychotherapy, and Sexual Hysteria (New York: Scribners, 1994), 188.

3. A. S. Ross, "Blame It On the Devil," *Redbook*, June 1994, 86.

4. Debbie Nathan and Michael Snedeker, *Satan's Silence: Ritual Abuse and the Making of a Modern American Witch Hunt* (New York: Basic Books, 1995), 1.

5. William J. Broad, "Air Force Details a New Theory in UFO Cases," *New York Times*, June 25, 1997, sec. B, 7.

6. Bruce Handy, "Roswell or Bust," *Time*, June 23, 1997, 62.

7. Sacha Pfeiffer, "Dissecting the Roswell Furor," *Boston Globe*, August 31, 1997, West Weekly, 1.

8. Frederick Crews, "The Revenge of the Repressed," *New York Review of Books*, November 17 and December 1, 1994.

9. Ellen Bass and Laura Davis, *Courage to Heal: A Guide for Women Survivors of Child Sexual Abuse*, 3d ed. (New York: Harper Perennial, 1988).

10. Ibid., 9.

11. Ofshe and Watters, *Making Monsters*, 30.

12. Bass and Davis, *Courage to Heal*, 485.

13. Ofshe and Watters, *Making Monsters*, 87–93.

14. Ibid., 66–67. Bass, Davis, *Courage to Heal*, 39–44.

15. Ofshe and Watters, *Making Monsters*, 59.

16. Lawrence Wright, *Remembering Satan* (New York: Alfred A. Knopf, 1994).

17. Ibid., 21, 108.

18. Bass and Davis, *Courage to Heal*, 523.

19. Ibid., 104, 320.

20. Wendy Kaminer, *It's All the Rage: Crime and Culture* (Reading, Mass.: Addison Wesley, 1995).

21. Ofshe and Watters, *Making Monsters*, 253–73.

22. Joan Acocella, "The Politics of Hysteria," *New Yorker*, April 6, 1998, 64–79.

23. Ofshe and Watters, *Making Monsters*, 7.

24. August Piper, Jr., "Multiple Personality Disorder: Witchcraft Survives in the Twentieth Century," *Skeptical Inquirer*, May/June 1998, 44–49. Ofshe and Watters, *Making Monsters*, 225–51.

25. Ian Hacking, *Rewriting the Soul: Multiple Personality and the Sciences of Memory* (Princeton: Princeton University Press, 1995), 48.

26. See Goldsmith, *Other Powers*.

27. *Jones v. Clinton*, 990 F. Supp. 657 (1998). See also Francis X. Cline, "Testing of a President: The Overview," *New York Times*, April 2, 1998, sec. A, 1.

28. Mari Matsuda, "Legal Storytelling: Public Response to Racist Speech: Considering the Victim's Story," 87 *Michigan Law Review* 2320 (1989).

29. Ibid.

30. Alan Charles Kors and Harvey A. Silverglate, *The Shadow University: The Betrayal of Liberty on America's Campuses* (New York: The Free Press, 1998).

31. Ibid., 9–33.

32. Matsuda, "Legal Storytelling."

33. Catherine MacKinnon, *Feminism Unmodified: Discourses on Life and Law* (Cambridge: Harvard University Press, 1987), 154–55.

34. *Loving v. Virginia*, 388 U.S. 1 (1967).

7. CYBERSPACY

1. David H. Freedman and Sarah Schafer, "Vonnegut and Clancy on Technology," *Inc. Technology*, no. 4, 1995, 063, www.inctechology.com.

2. John Perry Barlow, "A Declaration of the Independence of Cyberspace," February 8, 1996, barlow@eff.org.

3. John Brockman, *Digerati: Encounters with the Cyber Elite* (San Francisco: HardWired, 1996), 159.
4. David S. Bennahum, Brooke Shelby Biggs, Paulina Borsook et al., "Technorealism: get real," *The Nation*, April 6, 1998, 19.
5. Brockman, *Digerati*, xxv. Karen Armstrong, *A History of God*, 221, 226–27.
6. See Donald Meyer, *The Positive Thinkers: Religion as Pop Psychology from Mary Baker Eddy to Oral Roberts* (New York: Pantheon Books, 1980).
7. Brockman, *Digerati*, xxv.
8. Sven Birkerts and Kevin Kelly, "The Electronic Hive: Two Views," *Harper's Magazine*, May 1994, 17.
9. James, *Varieties of Religious Experience*, 115.
10. Meyer, *The Positive Thinkers*, 93.
11. Birkerts and Kelly, "The Electronic Hive: Two Views," *Harper's Magazine*.
12. Ibid.
13. Sherry Turkle, *The Second Self: Computers and the Human Spirit* (New York: Simon & Schuster, 1984), 58, 161.
14. Barlow, "A Declaration of the Independence of Cyberspace."
15. James, "Is Life Worth Living," in *The Will to Believe and Other Essays in Popular Philosophy*, 51.
16. Russell Shorto, "Belief by the Numbers," *New York Times Magazine*, December 7, 1997, 60–61.
17. Chip Berlet, "Apocalypse Soon," *Boston Globe*, July 19, 1998, sec. E, 1.
18. Joshua Cooper Ramo, "Finding God on the Web," *Time*, December 16, 1996, 60.
19. Jennifer Cobb, *Cybergrace: The Search for God in the Digital World* (New York: Crown, 1998), 15, 23, 45, 43.
20. Ibid., 33, 40.

21. See Laura Miller, "Bookend: www.claptrap.com," *New York Times Book Review*, March 15, 1998, 43.

22. Birkerts and Kelly, "The Electronic Hive," *Harper's Magazine.*

23. Brockman, *Digerati*, 40.

24. Jon Katz, *Media Rants: Post Politics in the Digital Nation* (San Francisco: HardWired, 1997), 84.

25. Quoted in Jon Katz, "Mrs. and Mr. Roberts' Neighborhood," www.hotwired.com/netizen, April 16, 1997.

26. Ibid.

27. "White Power, by Plebescite," *Financial Times* (London), May 23, 1998, 9. And see Peter Schrag, *Paradise Lost: California's Experience, America's Future* (New York: New Press, 1998).

28. William Saletan, "The Drudge Retort," *Slate*, slate.com, June 12, 1998.

29. Katz, *Media Rants*, 46.

30. Hannah Arendt, *The Origins of Totalitarianism* (Orlando, Fla.: Harcourt Brace Jovanovich: 1973), 382.

31. Brockman, *Digerati*, 76.

32. John McChesney, "James Fallows: The New Is Good for Media," www.hotwired.com/synapse/archive, September 10, 1997.

33. Brooke Shelby Biggs, "The Cyberscare Phenomenon," www.hotwired.com/synapse/archive, July 7, 1997.

34. See Sean Flynn, "Unbelievably Barnicle," *Boston Magazine*, August, 1998, 280; and Dan Kennedy, "Hanging Barnicle," *The New Republic*, September 7, 1998, 18.

35. See Robin Pogrebin, "Rechecking a Writer's Facts, A Magazine Uncovers Fiction," *New York Times*, June 12, 1998, sec. A, 1.

36. Sherry Turkle, *Life on the Screen: Identity in the Age of the Internet* (New York: Simon & Schuster, 1995), 14, 180.

37. Ibid., 105–14.
38. Ibid., 133.
39. Ibid., 85.

8. THE STRENUOUS LIFE

1. H. L. Mencken, "The Beloved Turnkey," in *A Second Mencken Chrestomathy* (New York: Alfred A. Knopf, 1994), 67.
2. "Excerpt from Remarks to House After Re-election as Speaker," *New York Times*, January 8, 1997, sec. B, 9.
3. Pat Robertson, Speech Delivered to William and Mary Law School, February 23, 1995, in *Christian American*, April 1995.
4. Williamson, *The Healing of America*, 196, 251.
5. H. L. Mencken, *Treatise on the Gods*, 4.
6. Antonio Damasio, *Descartes' Error: Emotion, Reason, and the Human Brain* (New York: Putnam, 1994), 125.
7. John Dewey, *A Common Faith* (New Haven: Yale University Press, 1934), 79.
8. Bertrand Russell, "What Is an Agnostic," *The Basic Writings of Bertrand Russell*, 583.
9. Remarks by Charles Colson at the Presbyterian Pro-Life Caucus, during General Assembly, Presbyterian Church (USA), Albuquerque, New Mexico, July 1996.
10. William James, "The Dilemma of Determinism," in *The Will to Believe and Other Essays in Popular Philosophy*, 169.
11. John Dewey, *Human Nature and Conduct* (New York: Random House, 1957), 316, 327, 330.
12. Dewey, *A Common Faith*, 21–22.
13. Eadie, *Embraced by the Light*, 67.
14. Dewey, *A Common Faith*, 21, 43.

15. See Glenn Tinder, "Can We Be Good Without God," *The Atlantic Monthly,* December, 1989, 68.
16. Speech by James Alcock, delivered at the New York Academy of Sciences Conference "The Flight from Science and Reason," New York, New York, May 31, 1995.

ACKNOWLEDGMENTS

I've had the privilege of spending the past twelve years at Radcliffe College, during which time I've published five books. For this I am deeply grateful and, I hope, loyal to people at Radcliffe who have sheltered and supported me.

Thanks, once again, to former Radcliffe president Linda Wilson, for my appointment as a Public Policy Fellow and for her tolerance, good humor, and good sense. (Whenever she received an irate letter asking how Radcliffe could house someone as terrible as I, she responded respectfully and firmly, explaining Radcliffe's commitment to free speech.) Thanks as well to Sue Shefte for sagely looking after me and to my smart, reliable research assistant, Jennifer Couzin.

I'm grateful, as always, to my agent Esther Newberg and to my editors, Linda Healey and Dan Frank, for their sound advice. Thanks to Jack Beatty, a gifted writer, editor, and talker for encouraging me to take on religion.

My father taught me to be skeptical and quite wary of religious belief. My mother tried to teach me to be nice about my disbelief. I hope that both perspectives are reflected in this book. My parents showed me how to be good without God. My partner, Woody Kaplan, shows me how to be fearless, and keeps me entertained.